IMAGES
of America

SOUTH FORK CEMETERIES

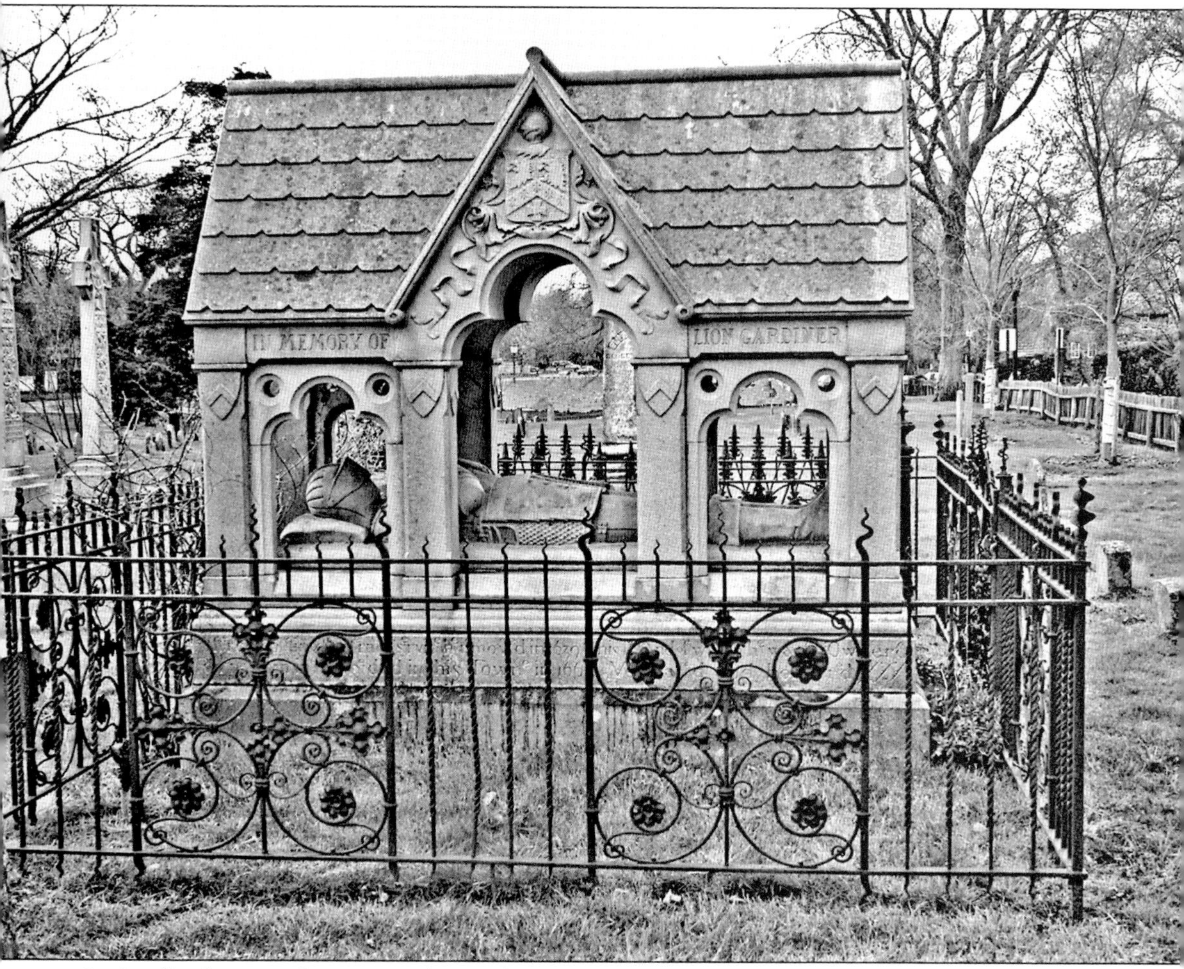

Let's talk of graves of worms, and epitaphs;
Make dust our paper, and with rainy eyes
Write sorrow on the bosom of the earth.
Let's choose executioners, and talk of wills:
And yet not so, —for what can we bequeath,
Save our deposed bodies to the ground?
Our lands, our lives, and all are Bolingbrook's,
And nothing we can call our own but death,
And that small model of the barren earth
Which serves as paste and cover to our bones,
For God's sake let us sit upon the ground,
And tell sad stories of the death of kings;
How some have been depos'd; some slain
in war;
Some haunted by the ghosts they have depos'd;
Some poisoned by their wives; some
sleeping kill'd;
All murder'd; —for within the hollow crown
That rounds the mortal temples of a king
Keeps death his court; and there the antic sits,
Scoffing his state, and grinning at his pomp;
Allowing him a breath, a little scene,
To monarchize, be feared, and kill with looks;
Infusing him with self and vain conceit,
As if his flesh which wall about our life,
Were brass impregnable; and humour'd thus,
Comes the last, and with a little pin
Bores through his castle-wall, and—farewell,
King!

—William Shakespeare
King Richard II, Act III, Scene II

On the cover: Shown is the South Cemetery in East Hampton. (Author's collection.)

IMAGES
of America

SOUTH FORK CEMETERIES

Clement M. Healy

ARCADIA PUBLISHING

ISBN 978-0-7385-4508-0

Published by Arcadia Publishing
Charleston, South Carolina

Printed in the United States of America

Library of Congress Catalog Card Number: 2006921064

For all general information contact Arcadia Publishing at:
Telephone 843-853-2070
Fax 843-853-0044
E-mail sales@arcadiapublishing.com
For customer service and orders:
Toll-Free 1-888-313-2665

Visit us on the Internet at www.arcadiapublishing.com

Welcome to our world, Ruby Sue.

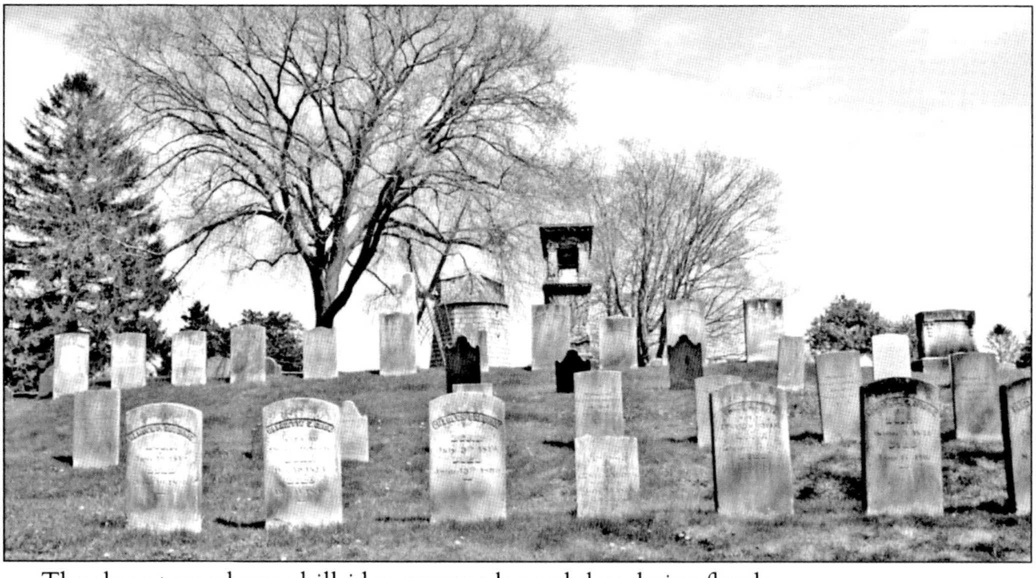

They haunt your breezy hillsides, green vales and thundering floods,
they linger by your gliding streams and mid your moss-draped woods,
they sit beside your green old graves in shadow and in sheen, and
move among your household gods though voiceless and unseen. Then
ye who make your happy homes where once their homes have been,
deem also this your heritage, to keep their memories green,
to shield within your heart of hearts, the glorious trust ye hold, and bear
unstained the names they bore, those brave proud men of old."

—Cornelia Huntington

CONTENTS

ACKNOWLEDGMENTS

I wish to thank the following women and men for all the support they so freely gave to me, as I would otherwise have been unable to write this book: Tara D'Amato, director, and Marci Vail, historian, East Hampton Library and the Pennypacker Collection; Richard Barons, director, and Sharon Dykeman and Laurie Collins, librarians, Southampton Historical Museum, as well as the Collins children Patrick and Tara for information on Jack Dempsey and Ferdinand Downs; Cliff Benfield, for information, help, and patience; Redge Bennett, president, Westhampton Beach Historical Society; Wallace Broege, director, Kathy Then and David Kerkhof, librarians, and the staff, Suffolk County Historical Society; Ralph Downs; Geoffrey Fleming, director, Southold Historical Society; Bill Hulse, who continues to amaze with his knowledge of East End history; Maryann Horan and Suzanne McGrattan for information and a photograph of Jack Dempsey; Hugh King, East Hampton Town Crier; Lawrence and Josephine Pearlstein; Barbara Moeller, director, and the staff, Hampton Bays Historical Society; Charles Peck; Bob Penny; the nurses at Seafield Center; Dewey M. and Clarice A. Rose, for sharing the story of their son Dennis Rose; Joan Scannlan, director, Quogue Historical Society; Rev. Michael Smith, pastor, Shinnecock Reservation; Robin Strong, archivist, Montauk Library, for help far beyond the call of duty; F. Jason Torre, university archivist, Special Collections Department and University Archives Frank Melville Jr. Memorial Library; Kathleen Tucker, director, Eastville Historical Society; Michael Slade and Jennifer Belt, Artes; Michael Lapides, New Bedford Whaling Museum; Jonathan Wells, Picture History; Carrie and Jonathan Ballone for assistance in preparing the text; and Joseph Ballone for assistance in preparing the images.

INTRODUCTION

The earliest visitors to North America were the Vikings, Norse warriors who settled the northern regions sometime during the first and second centuries. Upon hearing of Columbus's voyage to the Indies, the Italian explorer John Cabot, sailing under the English flag, while looking for Asia, landed somewhere between Nova Scotia and Maine in 1497. Giovanni da Verrazano, an Italian sailing for France, became the first to explore the northern Atlantic coast in 1524. He sailed along the shores of what is now South Carolina, northward to the bay of New York harbor. He then continued along the south shore of Long Island, assuming it to be a peninsular extension of the mainland.

A lapse in exploration of almost 100 years occurred until stimulated by the trading companies of the English and the Dutch. The search for the true nature of the area was revived in 1607 with Henry Hudson's search for a northwest passage to the Orient. Hudson sailed his ship, the *Half Moon*, along the east coast of North America. He traveled 150 miles up the Hudson River before abandoning the search. This led the Dutch to claim the area as a colony they called New Amsterdam. Hudson failed, however, to discover the true nature of the island as he then continued his search northward. On a later journey in 1611, Henry and his son met an ignominious end when they were set adrift in a small boat in Hudson Bay by a mutinous crew and were never heard from again.

Hudson's explorations stimulated interest among the Dutch merchants. In 1611, Adrian Block (1567–1627), visited the area and returned to the Netherlands with not only pelts, but two Native Americans as well. As a result of this voyage a statement was issued by offering incentives to stimulate further exploration. With this offer in mind, Block made another voyage in 1614, aboard the *Tyger*. He received a setback when the ship caught fire while moored in the bay in lower Manhattan and was destroyed. Undaunted by the accident, Block and his men spent the winter building a second ship, which they named the *Restless*. This small ship, only 42 feet long and weighting in at a mere 16 tons, allowed Block to continue his journey. With it he was able to navigate the sometimes violent straight connecting the East River to the sound. He called this narrow channel Hellegat, "bright passage," after a tributary of a river in Flanders. Whether or not the name was also intended to reflect the waters he sailed through is problematical. Depending on the stage of the tide, the conditions range from halcyon to dangerously turbulent, as many a captain has found out too late to save his ship. Block continued his journey eastward, and one of his crew may well have been the first European to step ashore at Montauk. He returned home after hitching a ride aboard another vessel. Block's map was the first to show that the presumed peninsula was, in fact, a long island. Other maps of the period, such as Visscher's in 1683, were based on Block's exploration.

And, coming late to the party were two puritan groups. Both Southold and Southampton arrived at the eastern end of Long Island in 1640. The South Fork was settled by a group from

Lynn, Massachusetts, who had been evicted from the site of their first landing at Oyster Bay. The English settlers were seeking religious freedom. Initially they were largely their own masters politically as well.

All that changed in the year 1664, when Charles II, King of England, gave to his brother, the Duke of York, a patent in the New World. Overnight, the duke became the proud possessor of Long Island, Westchester, and Staten Island, as well as upstate New York and the western portion of Connecticut. Early Long Island was now under the rule of the Duke of York, and life for the puritan colonists "out East" was never the same.

The stories of the East Enders who made the history of these and later times may be found in many of the cemeteries of the South Fork. In the pages that follow, a few (too few) of these courageous men and women are recalled. The book is organized as a tour, from West to East. The reader may, of course, join the tour at any point. The only regret the author has is that there are far more cemeteries that will be found here. The readers are encouraged to institute their own searches. They will find the results most rewarding.

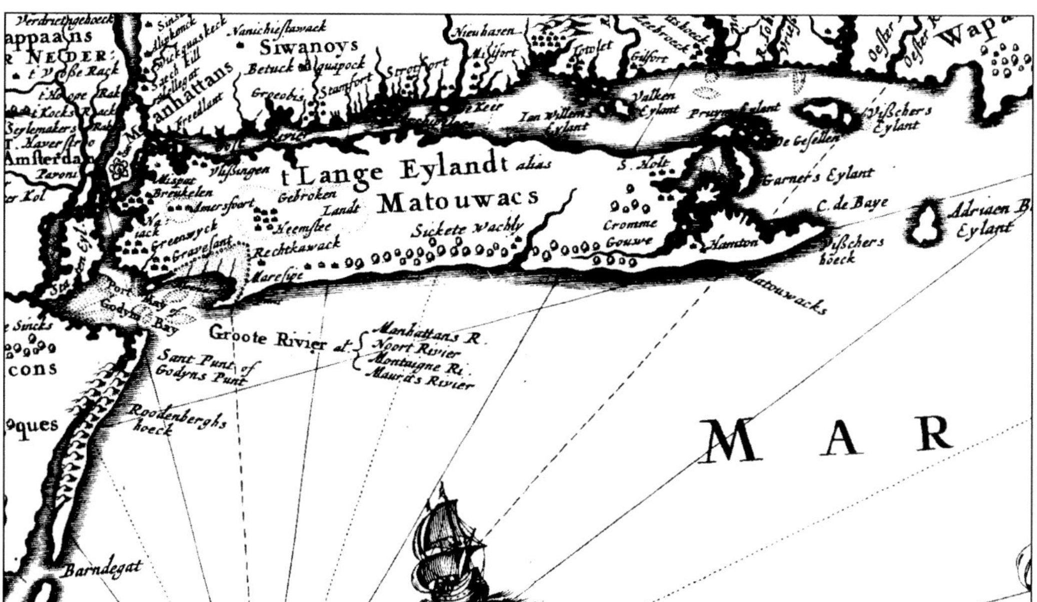

This detail from a facsimile of Nicholaes Visscher's "New Belgium and New England," 1656, shows Long Island. (Courtesy Stony Brook University, Special Map Collection.)

One

Eastport to Westhampton Beach

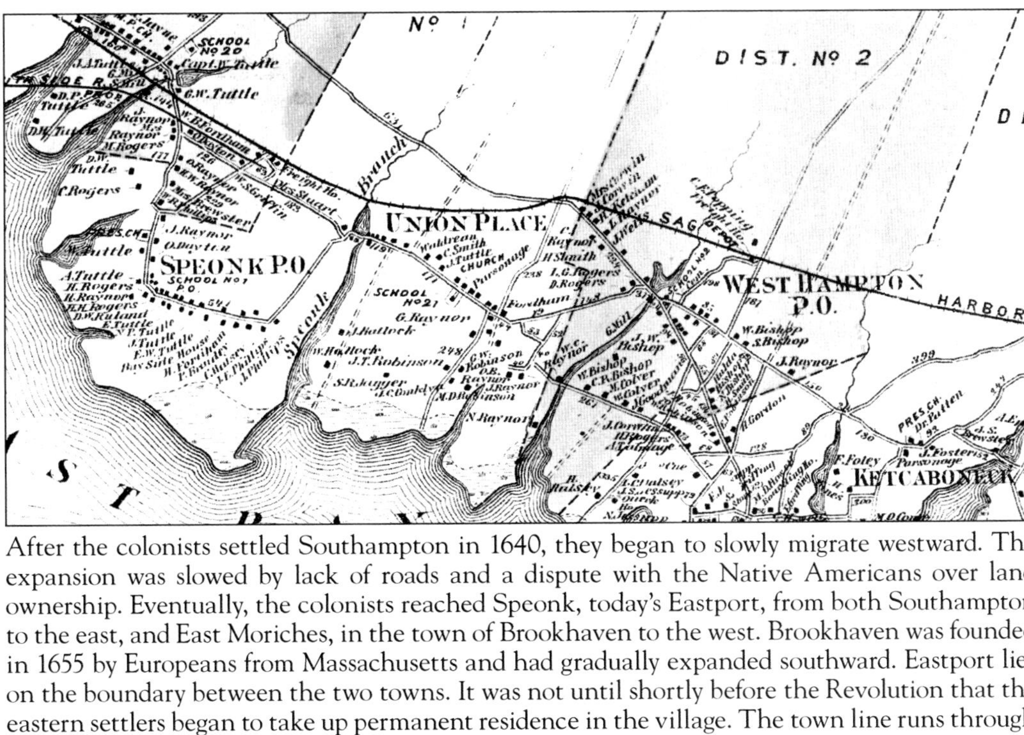

After the colonists settled Southampton in 1640, they began to slowly migrate westward. The expansion was slowed by lack of roads and a dispute with the Native Americans over land ownership. Eventually, the colonists reached Speonk, today's Eastport, from both Southampton to the east, and East Moriches, in the town of Brookhaven to the west. Brookhaven was founded in 1655 by Europeans from Massachusetts and had gradually expanded southward. Eastport lies on the boundary between the two towns. It was not until shortly before the Revolution that the eastern settlers began to take up permanent residence in the village. The town line runs through the Speonk River, on which, in the late 1700s, Col. Joshua Smith of East Moriches built a dam. A gristmill and a sawmill were then built on West Pond, upstream of the dam. Eastport was, for a while, the center of the Long Island duck industry. To the east are the hamlets of Speonk, Remsenburg, and Westhampton. The latter, especially, is the first of the summer playgrounds for the "city dwellers" to the west. (Courtesy Stony Brook University, Special Map Collection.)

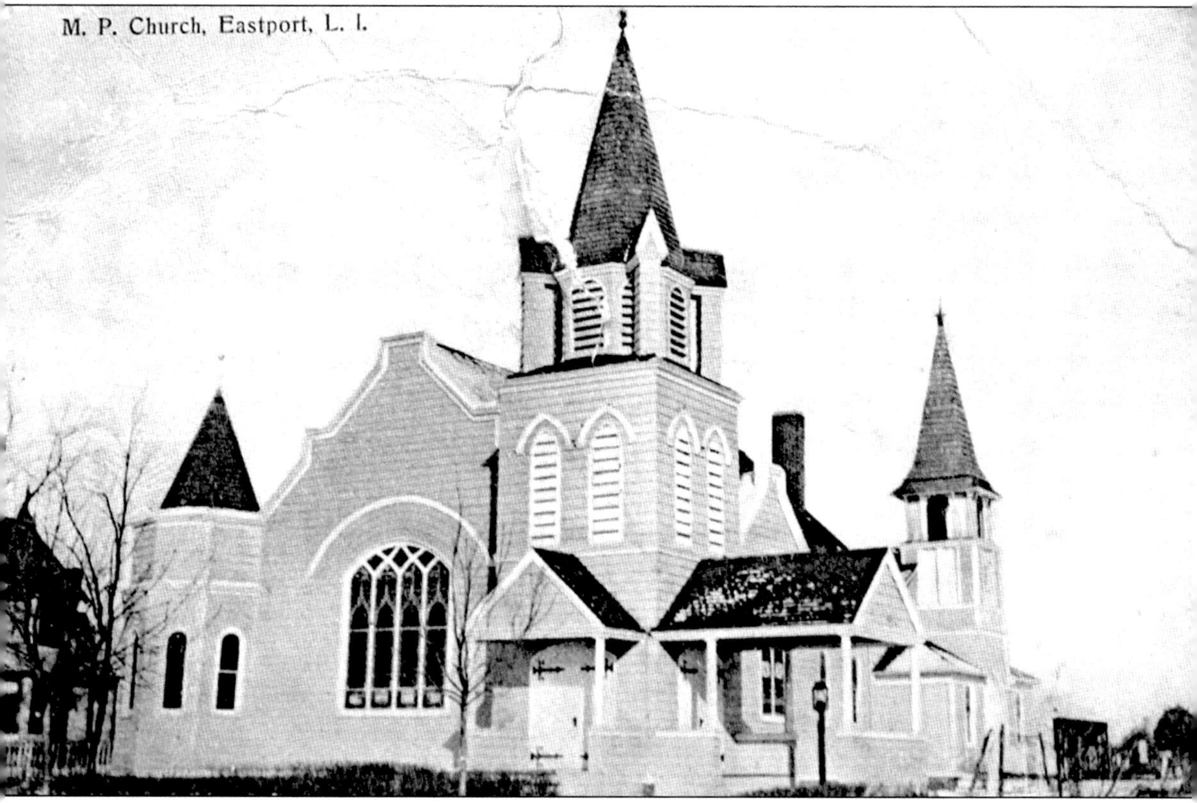

Methodism came late to Long Island. The early settlers were initially free of any religious establishments. Eventually, the Presbyterian and Congregational churches began to flourish. It was not until 1764, when the Rev. John Whitfield preached in the Hamptons, that the voice of a Methodist was heard on the East End. The first Methodist church was built in New York City in 1768, and the first on Long Island was built 17 years later. After the Revolution ended in 1783, Methodist circuit riders began to visit the East End. Although the larger part of the village is in Brookhaven, a cemetery lies just east of the boundary, behind the Methodist Protestant Church, which was built in 1845. (Courtesy Suffolk County Historical Society.)

Dennis Dewey Rose was born on October 31, 1946. He was a 1964 graduate of Eastport High School. In 1968, he graduated New York Maritime College at Fort Schuyler as an Ensign in the Naval Reserve and third officer in the Maritime Service. By 1983, he had advanced his license to master and was a lieutenant commander and in the Naval Reserve. He was then also the first officer of the SS *American Trader*, the largest container ship afloat at that time. (Courtesy Dewey and Clarice Rose.)

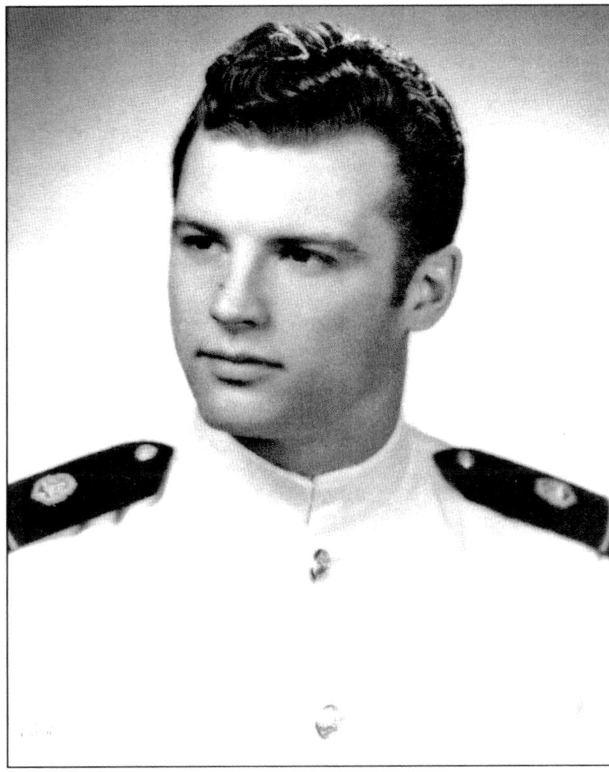

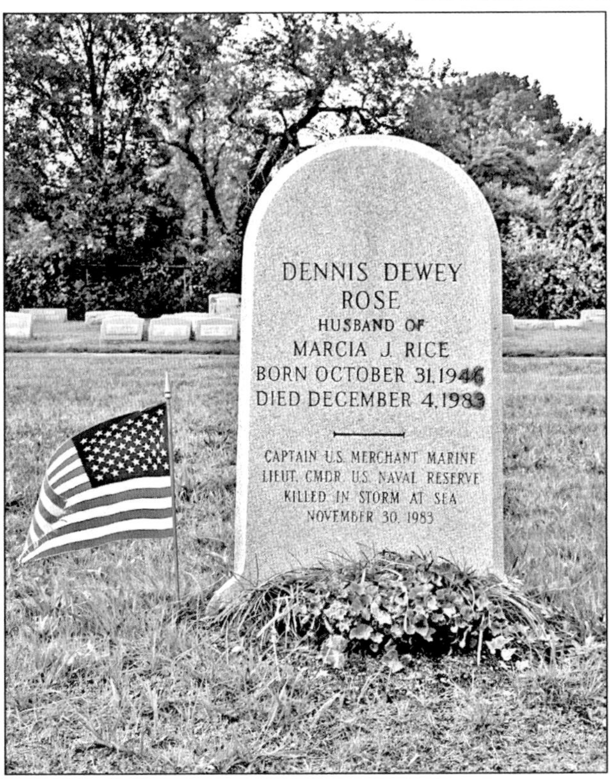

Dennis Dewey Rose was killed in a tragic accident when a massive wave struck his ship, off the coast of California. He foreshadowed, perhaps, the impending tragedy while visiting a cemetery in Remsenberg. Accompanied by his wife, he turned to her and said, while looking at a particular stone, that that was the type he wanted for his own marker. His wife, Marcia Rice Rose; two sons, Dewey D. and Ryan R.; as well as his parents, Dewey and Clarice Tuthill Rose, survive Dennis.

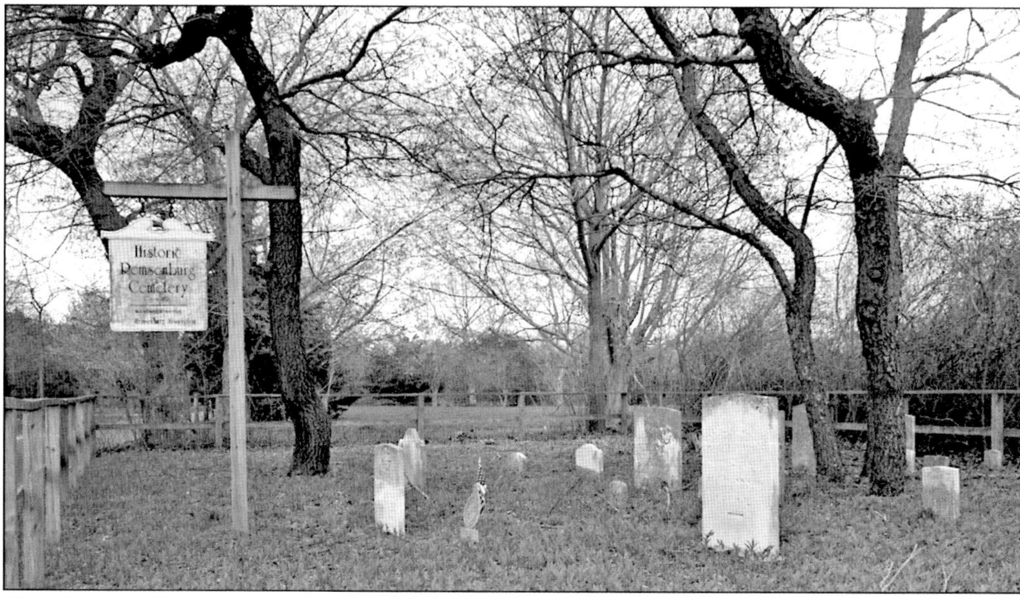

The Historic Remsenburg Cemetery is located on a quiet lane and is well maintained by the Remsenburg Association. There are about 11 to 15 graves in this Tuthill family cemetery, including John Tuthill (1728–1805). He came to Speonk with his four sons and built a blacksmith shop on the main road. Shown is the first example of a historical marker placed by the Daughters of the American Revolution. The inscription reads "James Tuthill / 1758–1826 / Erected by / Col. Josiah Smith Chapter."

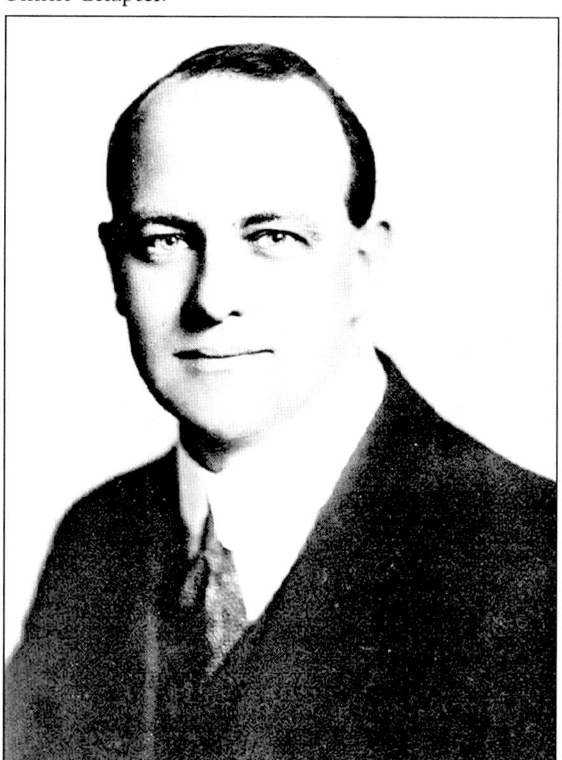

Buried in this cemetery behind the church is Sir Pelham Grenville Wodehouse (1881–1975). The son of a civil servant, he was born in England in Guildford, Surry. After graduating from Dulwich College, he worked for two years at a bank prior to taking up writing as his profession. Upon moving to Hollywood, he became a highly successful screenwriter. He eventually became a prolific novelist, writing well over 100 novels and other stories under various pseudonyms as well as his own name.

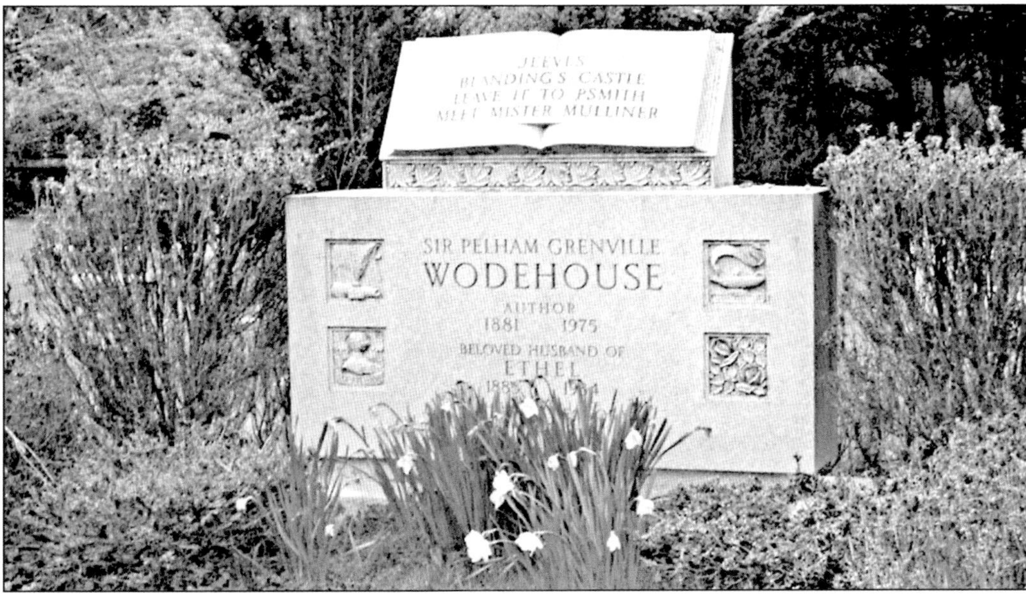

P. G. Wodehouse's best-known characters are the valet Jeeves and Berti Wooster. His best-known novels are *Jeeves* and *Blandings Castle*. Wodehouse was also an accomplished lyricist and collaborated with Cole Porter on the musical *Anything Goes*. He wrote the lyrics for the song "Bill" in *Showboat*. In 1955, he became an American citizen and lived out his years in Remsenburg, which he called Bensonburg in the novel *French Leave*. He died on Valentine's Day in 1975.

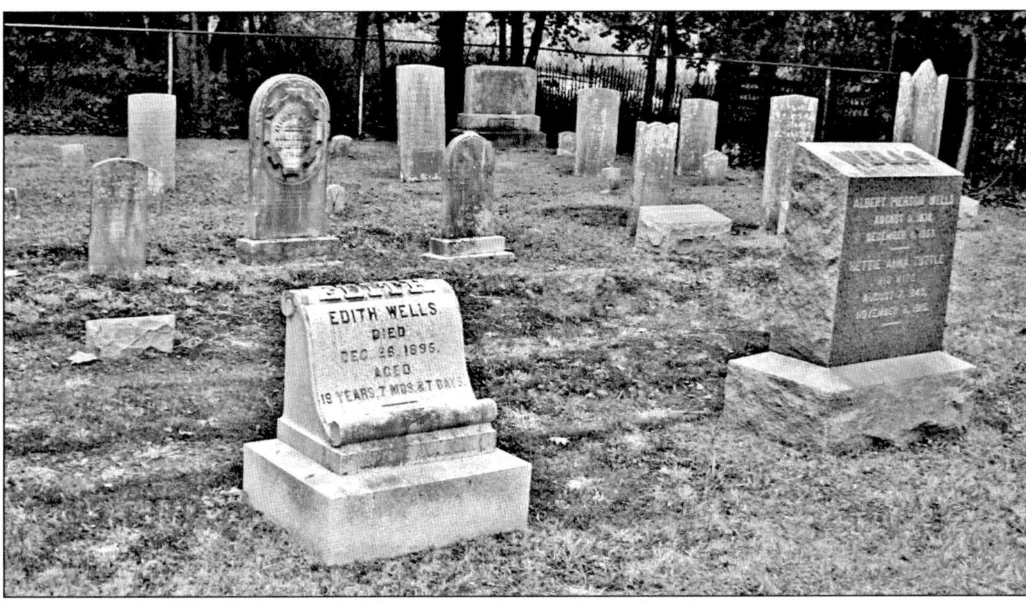

The Jagger-Waldo family cemetery is one of the many small family burial grounds found on the South Fork. Located on the south side of Montauk Highway, it is well maintained and still in use. In defiance of the duke's laws of 1665, which forbade burials on private property, East Enders continued to bury family members on farms and private land. Among the many Jaggers found here is Albert P. Wells (1838–1903), a cotton broker who lived on the opposite side of the highway.

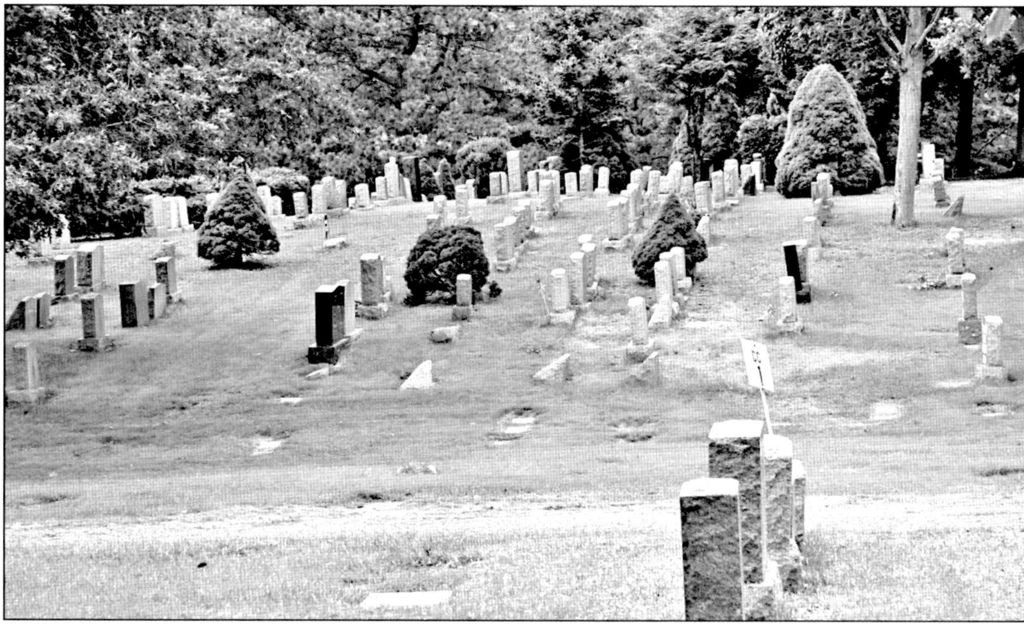

Every year, Bide-A-Wee (stay awhile) takes in thousands of unwanted animals from both public and local animal control agencies. The animals are given shelter, food, and medical care. Most animals are successfully placed with carefully screened adopters. Only the incurably ill are put to sleep. A fully equipped clinic is also open to the public. At the Westhampton Beach facility, a retirement home and bereavement counseling are also offered to the pet owners.

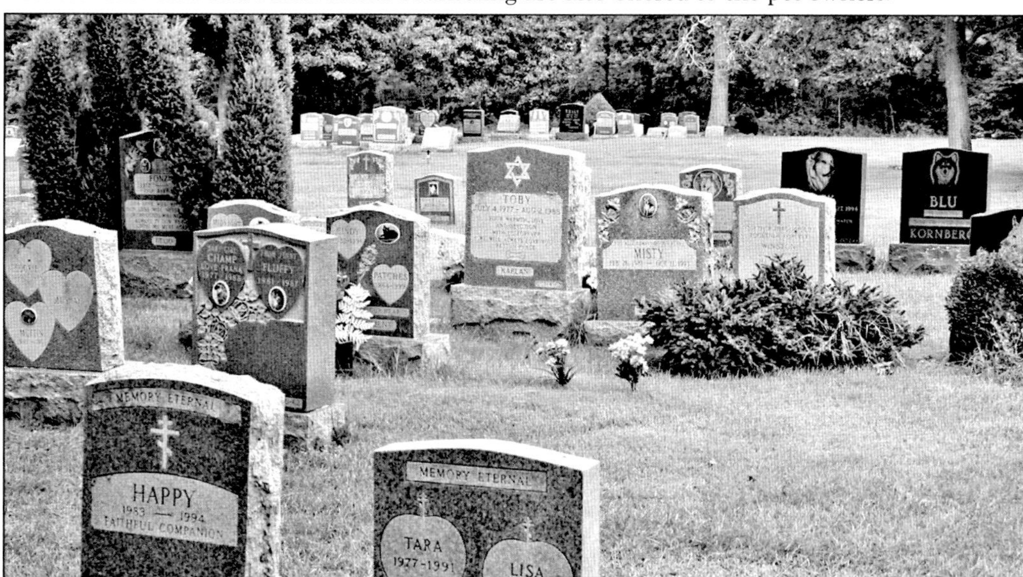

At Wantagh and Westhampton, there is also a Memorial Park that offers a final resting place for deceased animals. The love between the owners and their pets may be seen throughout the cemetery. Religious symbols are commonly inscribed on the tombstones. Expressions of love are everywhere. Some of the more famous animals found in the parks include Richard Nixon's Checkers, New York City Fire Department Dalmatians, New York City Police Department horses, and World War II K-9 Corps mascot Sarg.

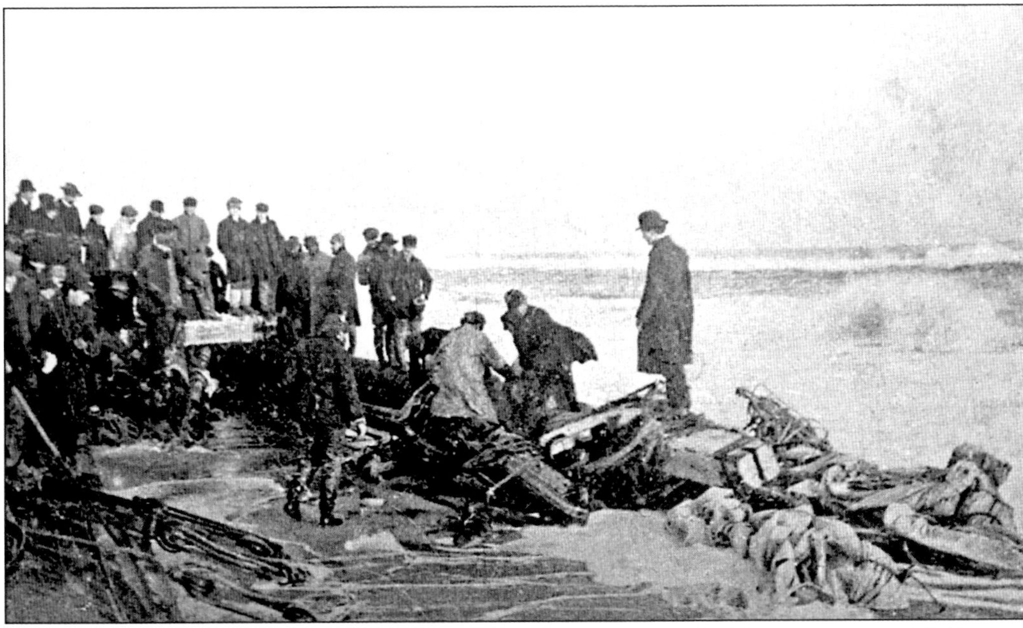

The most prominent feature in the Westhampton Cemetery is the Veterans memorial. There is a much smaller monument in memory of the *Augustus Hunt* and two other vessels that wrecked off the nearby beaches. The *Hunt* was a four-masted schooner with a cargo of soft coal, which sailed into a southerly gale on the night of January 22, 1904. It mistook the Shinnecock Light for a steamer and ran aground on the bar off Westhampton Beach.

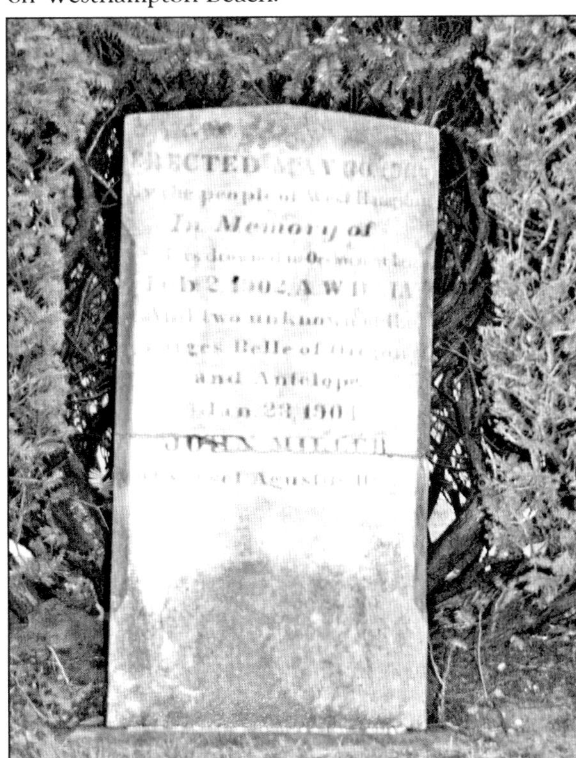

Despite heroic efforts of a lifesaving crew, eight of the *Hunt*'s 10 crewmen were lost in the frigid waters when the ship was torn into pieces by the waves of the raging sea. The two other vessels, the coal barges *Belle of Oregon* and *Antelope*, ran aground on the night of February 2, 1902, with the loss of six lives.

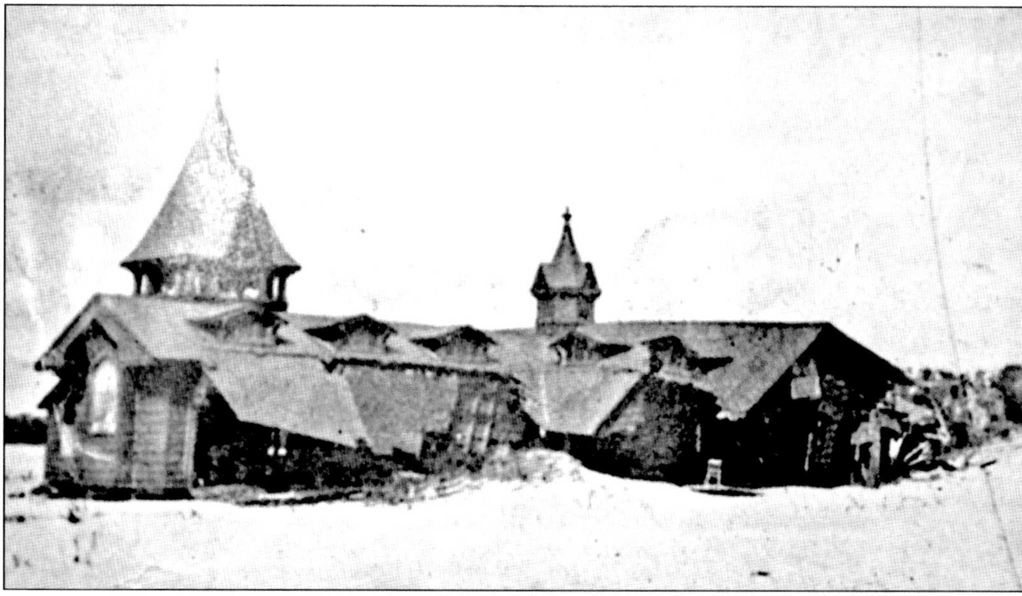

On September 21, 1938, without warning, Long Island was struck by a fierce, nameless, hurricane. The center of the hurricane passed over Westhampton Beach at 3:00 p.m. and wrought death and havoc for the next two hours. Damage was estimated to be over 40 percent of the assessed property value of that waterfront community. Those living near the dunes were unaware that death was at their doorstep. The first inkling of the pending carnage came 20 minutes earlier when the lights went out. (Courtesy Suffolk County Historical Society.)

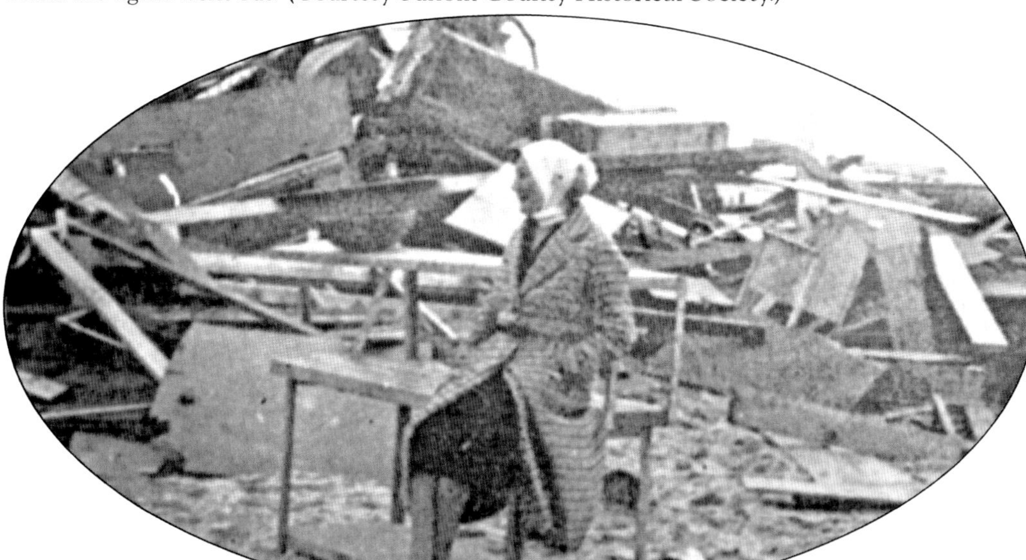

The winds shifted from the east to the southwest, drawing a bead on the vulnerable ocean beach. Had the storm attacked a few weeks earlier, it would have caught hundreds more in its sights. This was no consolation to the many summer residents whose decision to stretch the season a little longer cost them their lives. They were not the only victims. The storm cut a wide swath of destruction across the South Shore, from Fire Island east to Southampton and up into New England. (Courtesy Suffolk County Historical Society.)

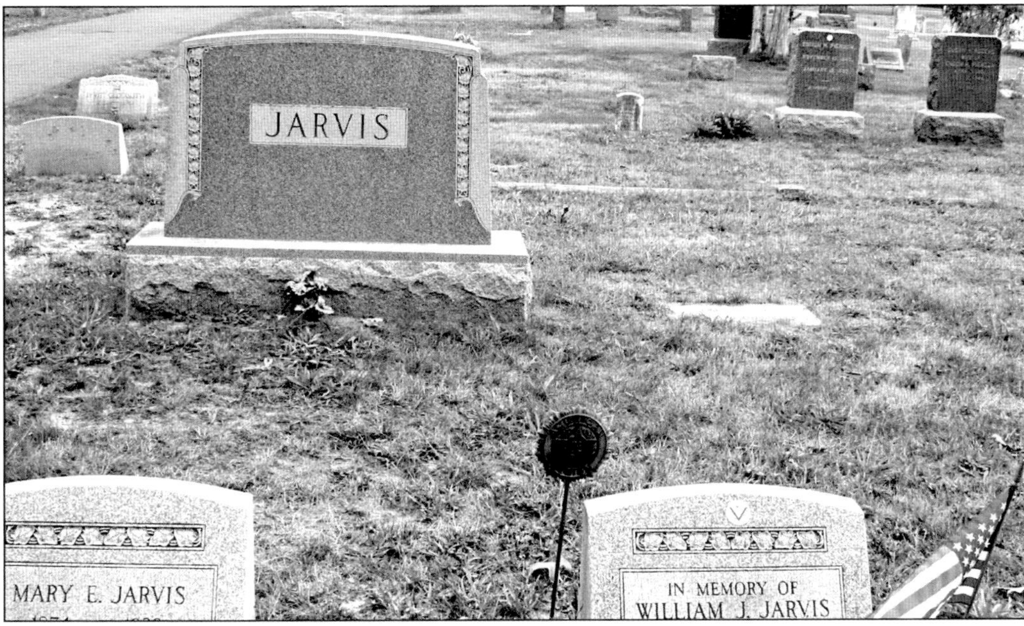

The statistics for the hurricane were tragically impressive: winds steady at 126 knots, gusting to 186 miles per hour; over 700 dead; 6,300 homeless; 8,900 buildings destroyed; and 3,300 boats lost. Several of the 28 persons who died in Westhampton Beach are buried in the Westhampton Cemetery. Among them are Mrs. William Jarvis, aged 63, and Mr. and Mrs. Warren G. Lewis, the proprietors of the Surf and Dune Club.

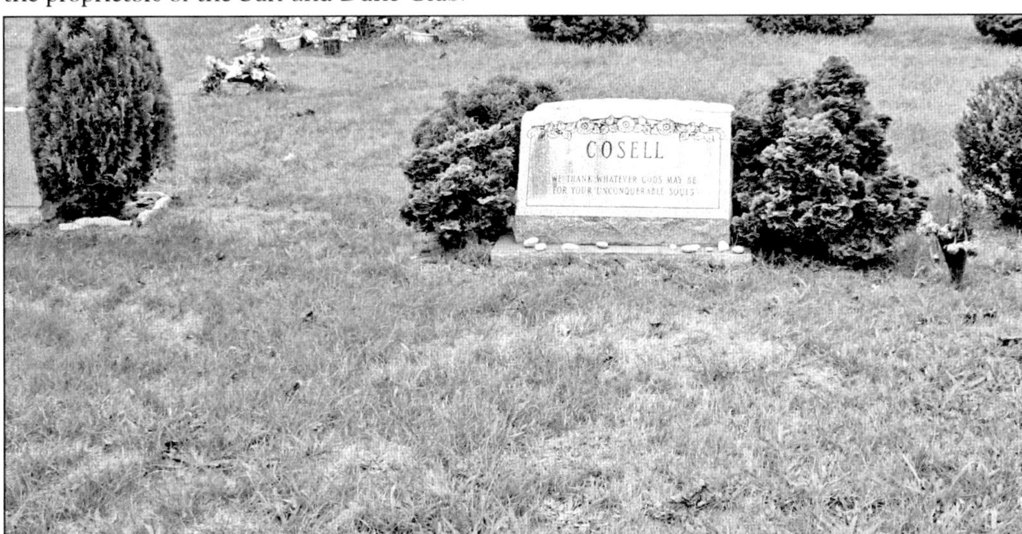

Roone Arledge and ABC brought NFL professional football into prime time in the fall of 1970. Together with Howard Cosell, whom Arlege hired as the announcer, they changed the landscape of sports broadcasting. No one would dispute that Cosell was opinionated and abrasive in his technique. And yet, *Monday Night Football* (September 21, 1970–December 26, 2005) became an instant success. Cosell had first become popular as a boxing announcer covering Muhammad Ali. He later hosted several television shows, including *Battle of the Network Stars*. He died in 1995, at age 77.

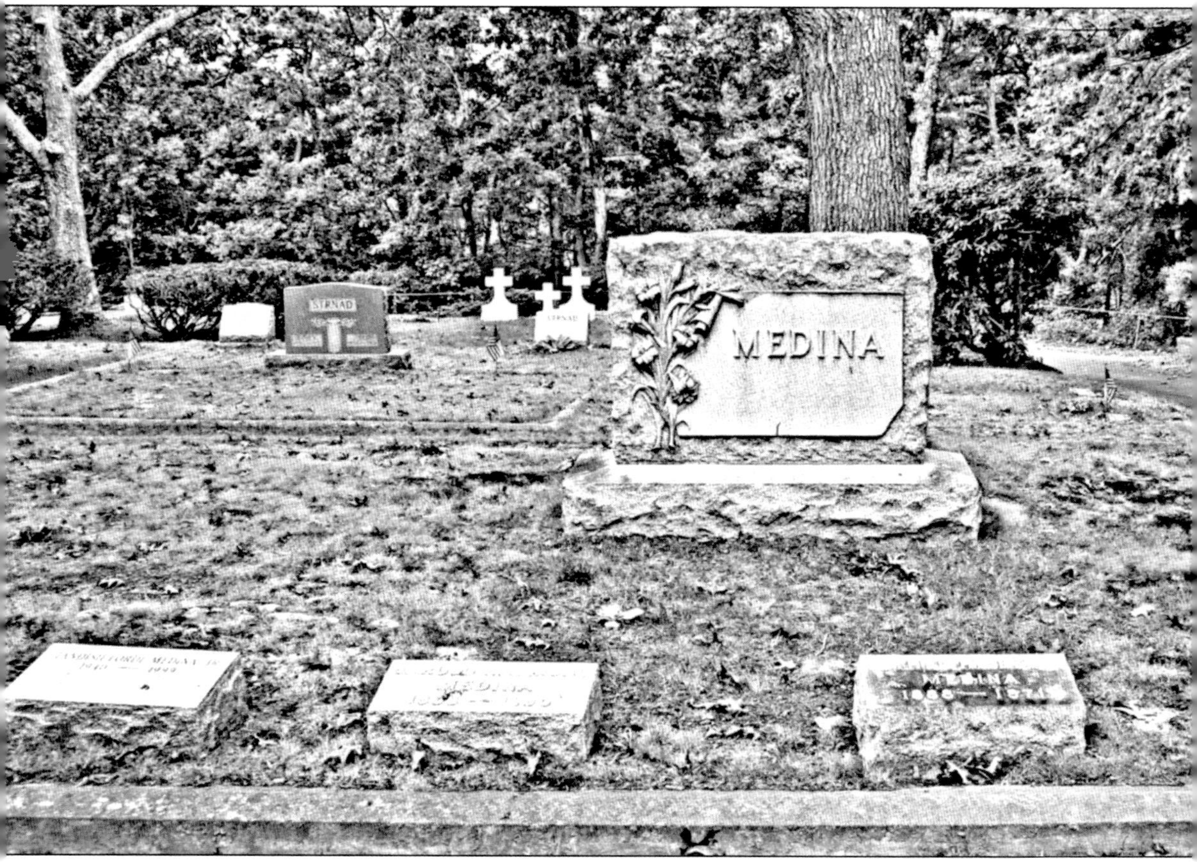

In 1940, Congress passed the Smith Act, which made it illegal to advocate overthrowing state or national governments. It was not until 1949, as the cold war heated up, that the law was invoked against the Communist party. On July 20, 1948, Eugene Dennis, general secretary of the American Communist party, was arrested with 11 other party leaders and charged with conspiring to advocate the violent overthrow of the American government. The trial was presided over by Judge Harold Medina, who ruled for the prosecution. The defendant appealed to the Supreme Court, claiming the conviction was a violation of their rights under the First Amendment. On June 4, 1951, the Court, in a six-to-two vote, ruled in favor of upholding Judge Medina's ruling. Justice Vincent, writing the plurality opinion, concluded that the First Amendment did not apply. In writing a dissenting opinion, Justice Black wrote "there is hope, however, that in calmer times . . . this or some later court will restore the First Amendment liberties to the . . . place where they belong in a free society."

The Presbyterian Church of Ketchaponack had its beginnings in 1742, when the town of Southampton granted land for a Presbyterian gospel ministry. The Rev. William B. Reeve (1812–1888) was appointed pastor of the congregation in 1869, a position in which he served for 16 years. The church, which serves the Westhampton Beach area, is actually located in the hamlet of Quogue.

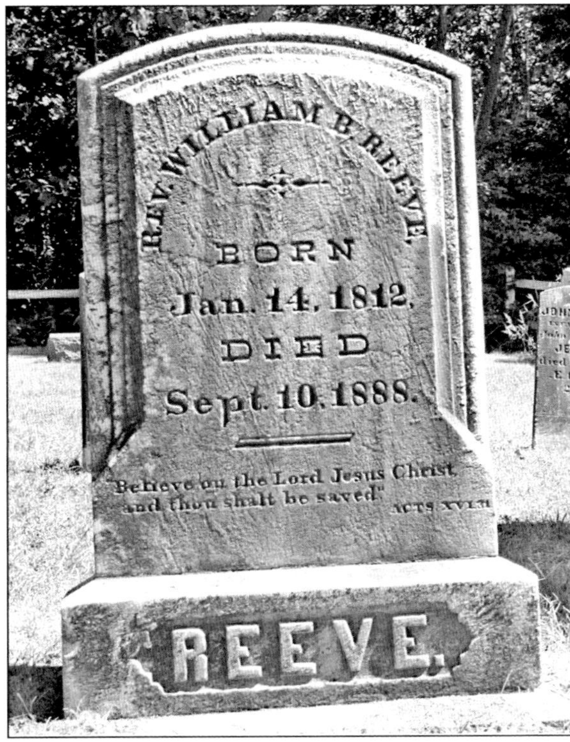

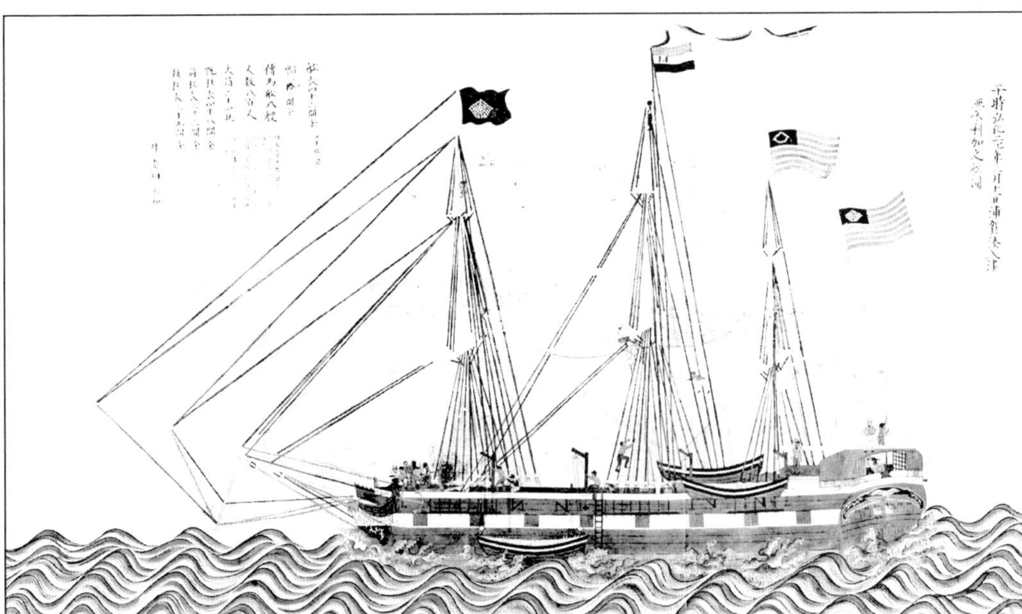

This small cemetery is located behind the Presbyterian Church of Ketchaponack and is designated as a historic cemetery. In this quiet spot are many members of the Jessup family who were among the early settlers in the village. Of particular interest is Capt. Franklin C. Jessup. In 1841, at age 18, Jessup first ventured to sea on the whaler *Huron*, commanded by Capt. Henry Green. He next shipped out aboard the *Manhattan*, under Capt. Mercator Cooper, on what became a historic journey to Japan. (*The Manhattan*, Courtesy New Bedford Whaling Museum.)

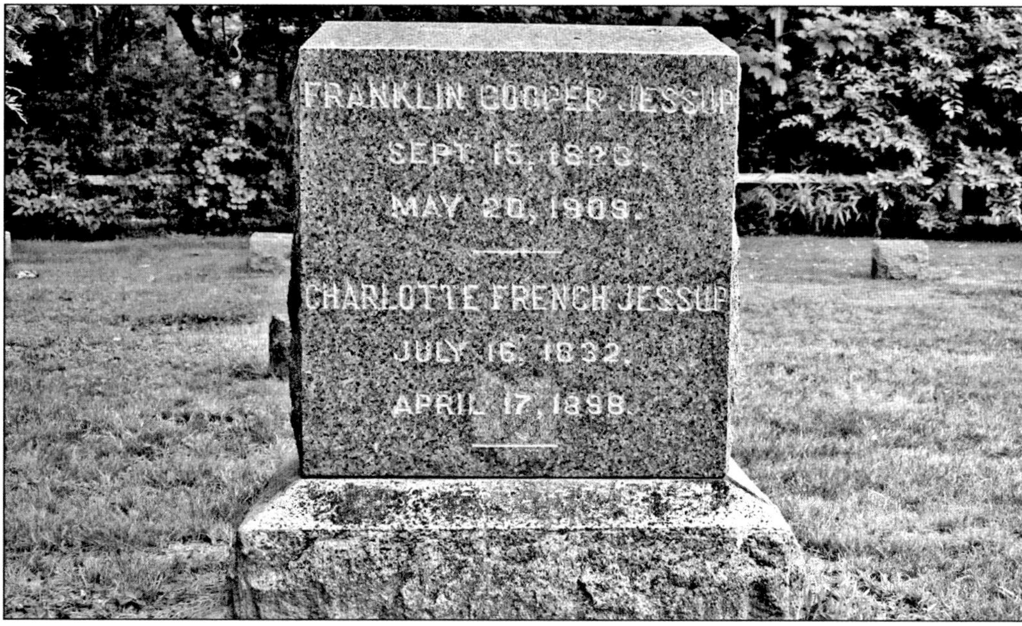

The *Manhattan* returned from that trip with many artifacts. Upon his return, Franklin C. Jessup again joined Capt. Henry Green, this time aboard the *Sabina* in search of California gold in 1849. Jessup eventually spent 30 years as keeper of the Potunk Life Saving Station. He died in 1909, at age 86.

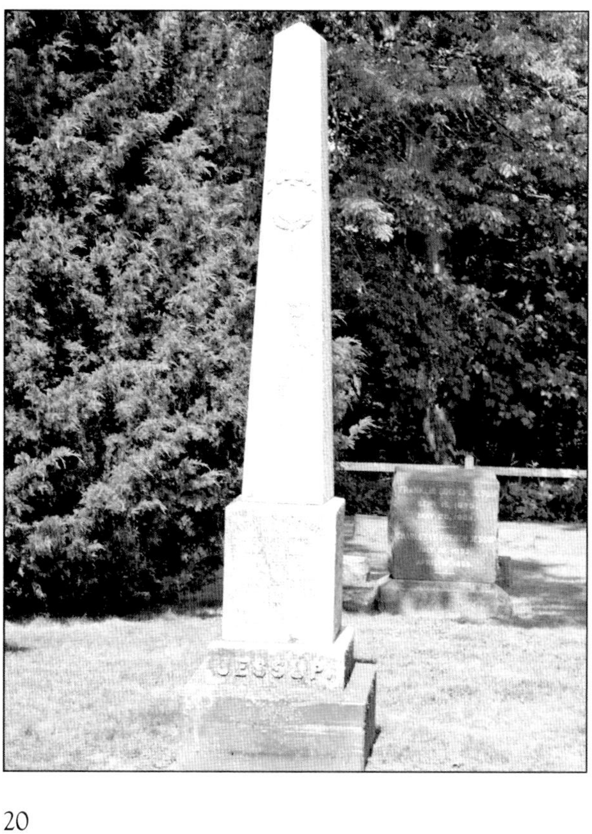

Also in the Jessup family plot is a memorial that reads, "Mortally wounded at a battle at Davis Neck, SC, Dec 6, 1864, and died Dec. 7th, John Henry Jessup of the 127th Reg., N.Y. State Vol. Aged 21 yrs., 10 mo. and 15 ds." The 127th Volunteer Regiment, the Monitors, was composed of men from the East End.

Two

QUOGUE TO FLANDERS

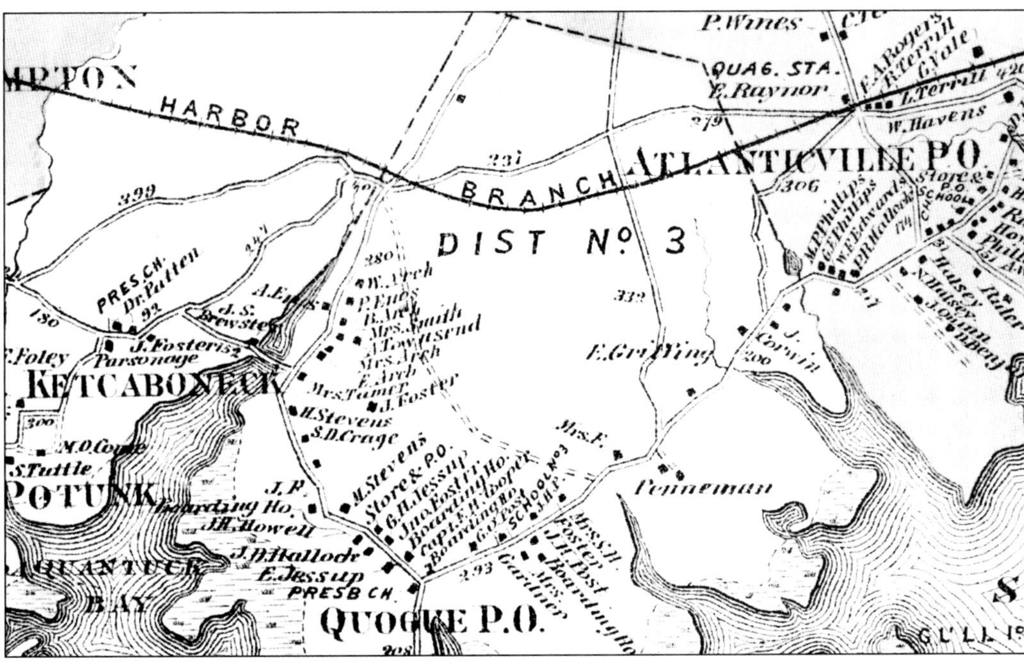

The first colonists arrived in Quaquanatuck (today's Quogue) from Southampton around 1659. They came in pursuit of the whales that the Shinnecocks had, long before them, hunted from the beach. The land was also used for raising sheep and woodcutting. They did not live here year round, but rather built shacks near the beach, or in the meadows, as temporary shelter. Two miles to the east is the hamlet of East Quogue. When the railroad came to Quogue in 1870, it brought with it the first wave of the "summer people." The next village to the east and north is Flanders, so called by the Dutch who settled there in the late 1700s. (Courtesy Stony Brook University, Special Map Collection.)

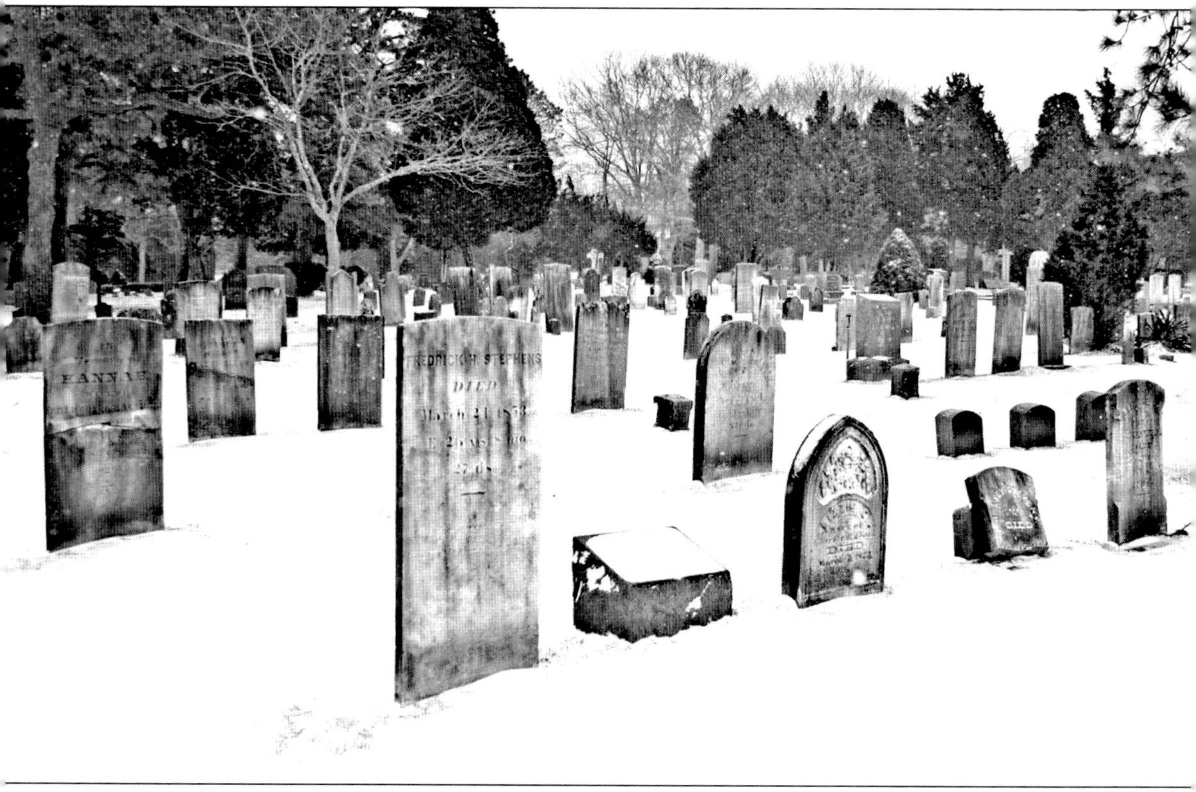

By 1740, the settlement had grown into a quiet fishing village. And so it remained until the coming of the railroad in the late 1800s. The new, fast transportation transformed the village into a major summer resort for the city dwellers. Quogue became a village of boardinghouses, and the summer migration has never since abated. The cemetery was founded in 1879. However, the oldest part of the cemetery contains much earlier graves. In the mid-1800s, when historian Richard M. Bayles visited the area, Bayles noted that "the village cemetery lies in back of the settlement, in the fields." Today, it is in the middle of Quogue. The cemetery is well maintained and is still active.

It was not until Cap. John Post moved from Southampton to Quogue around 1734 that permanent dwellings were built. Post bought the title to his land from Hezekiah Howell for 44 pounds. He also inherited other land from his father-in-law, Joshua Halsey. Descendants of the captain have lived in the village ever since.

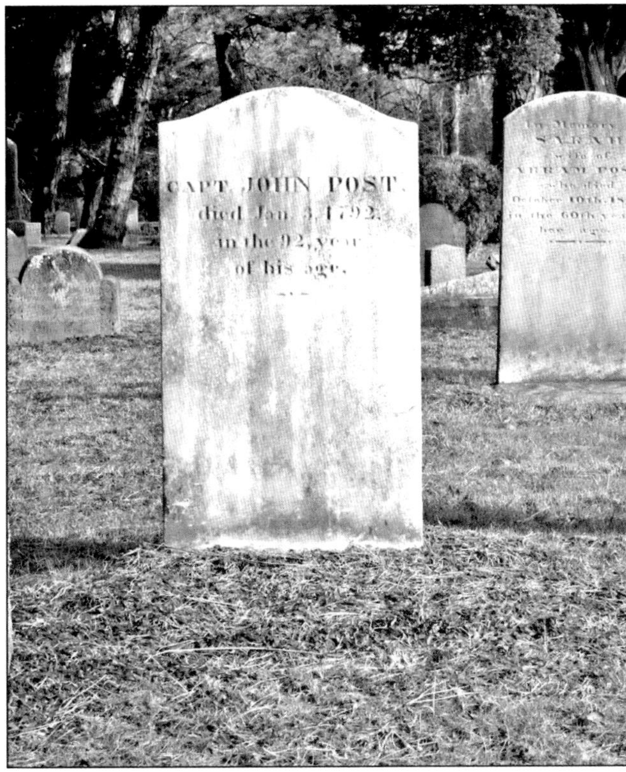

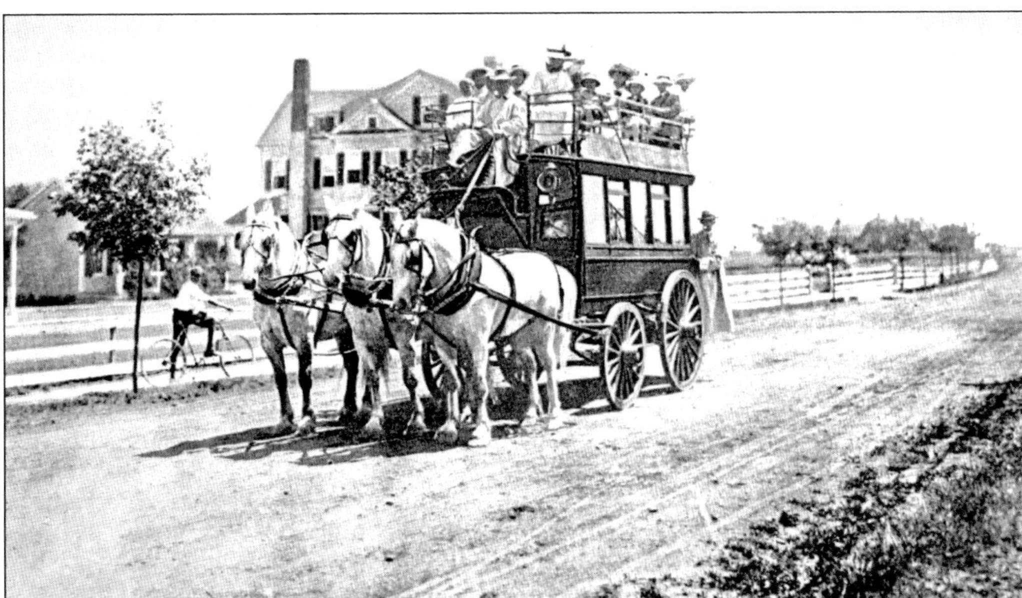

The stagecoach served as local taxi in Quogue, meeting the train and delivering the city dwellers to the myriad of boardinghouses in town. In 1902, there were over 500 registered guests in the village. The Hallock House register listed the names of Adm. Alfred Thayer Mahan and his wife as frequent guests before they moved to Quogue after the admiral retired. (Courtesy Suffolk County Historical Society.)

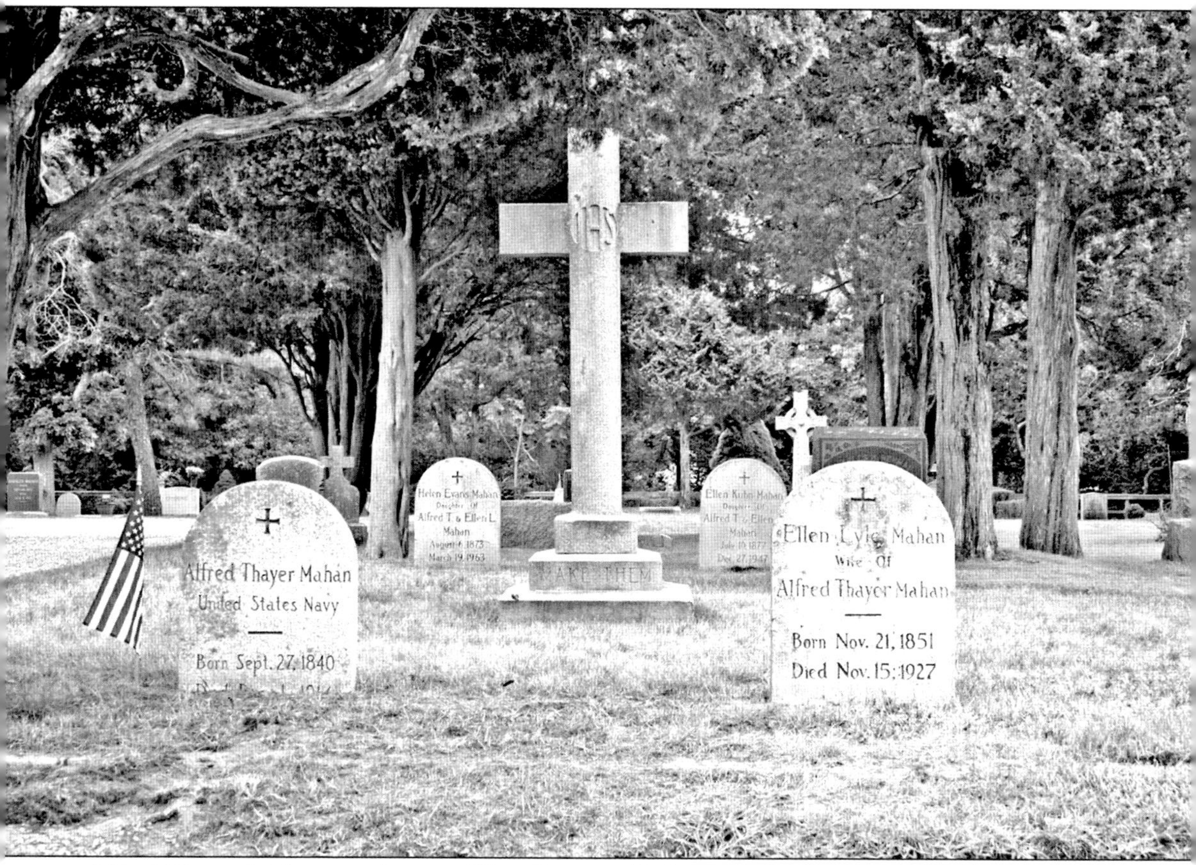

Alfred Thayer Mahan was born at West Point in 1840, where his father taught at the Military Academy. Against his parents' wishes, he attended the Naval Academy, graduating second in his class in 1859. He then served the Union cause during the Civil War aboard several vessels, including the USS *Pocahontas*. Despite his lack of skill aboard ship, he was promoted to commander. Eventually, he turned to education, becoming commander at the Naval War College in 1856. Mahan was a prolific writer, publishing 12 books on naval strategy. His most influential title, *The Influence of Sea Power upon History, 1660–1783*, was published in 1890. The book promoted his passionate belief in the need to dominate the sea, an idea unique at that time. The books were well received and influenced the shape of military forces in future wars. Mahan was promoted to rear admiral in 1906, and he died at the U.S. Naval Hospital on December 1, 1914. In 1996, the navy commissioned the USS *Mahan*, a guided missile Aegis destroyer, in Mahan's honor.

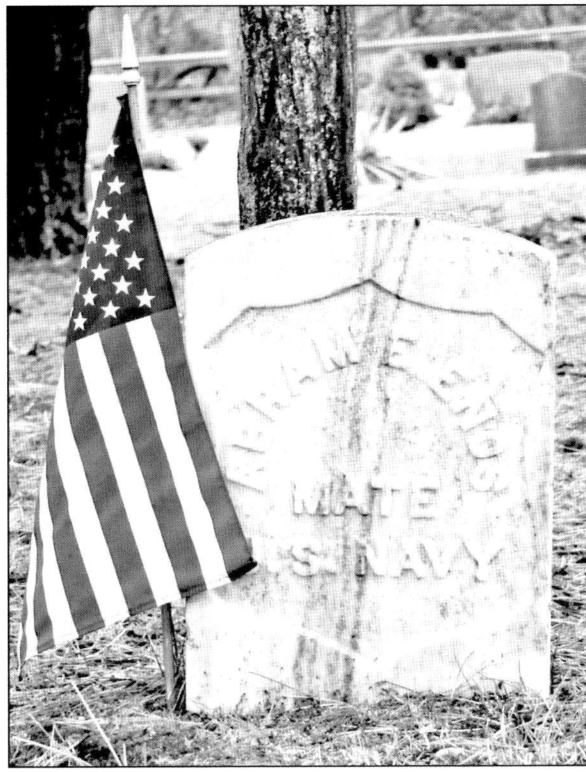

Abram E. Enos, an African American sailor, served aboard the steamer *Aroostook* during the Civil War. The ship was a 507-ton, six-cannon gunboat. While engaged in the blockade of the West Gulf, the ship captured several British vessels bringing supplies to the South. In one encounter, it stopped the schooner *Marion* by firing a Howitzer. After taking the prize crew and captain aboard, the *Aroostook* sent a carpenter aboard to cut a hole through the deck of the *Marion*. It then fired a 24-pounder from its Dahlgren and sunk the schooner.

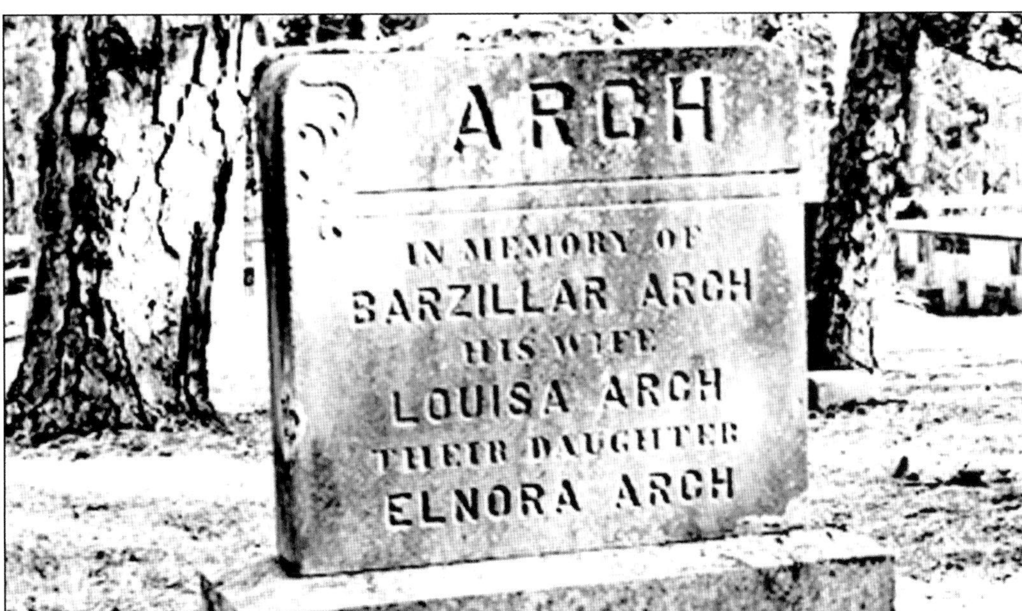

Few blacks lived in Quogue, the first of whom were slaves. There were four slaves in the hamlet in the 1790 census. Among the earliest African Americans here were members of the Arch, Enos, and Hawkins families. It is said that the first Arch came to Quogue as the sole survivor of an otherwise unrecorded shipwreck. He lived out his life as a free man in Quogue. Many members of these families are buried in the Quogue Cemetery.

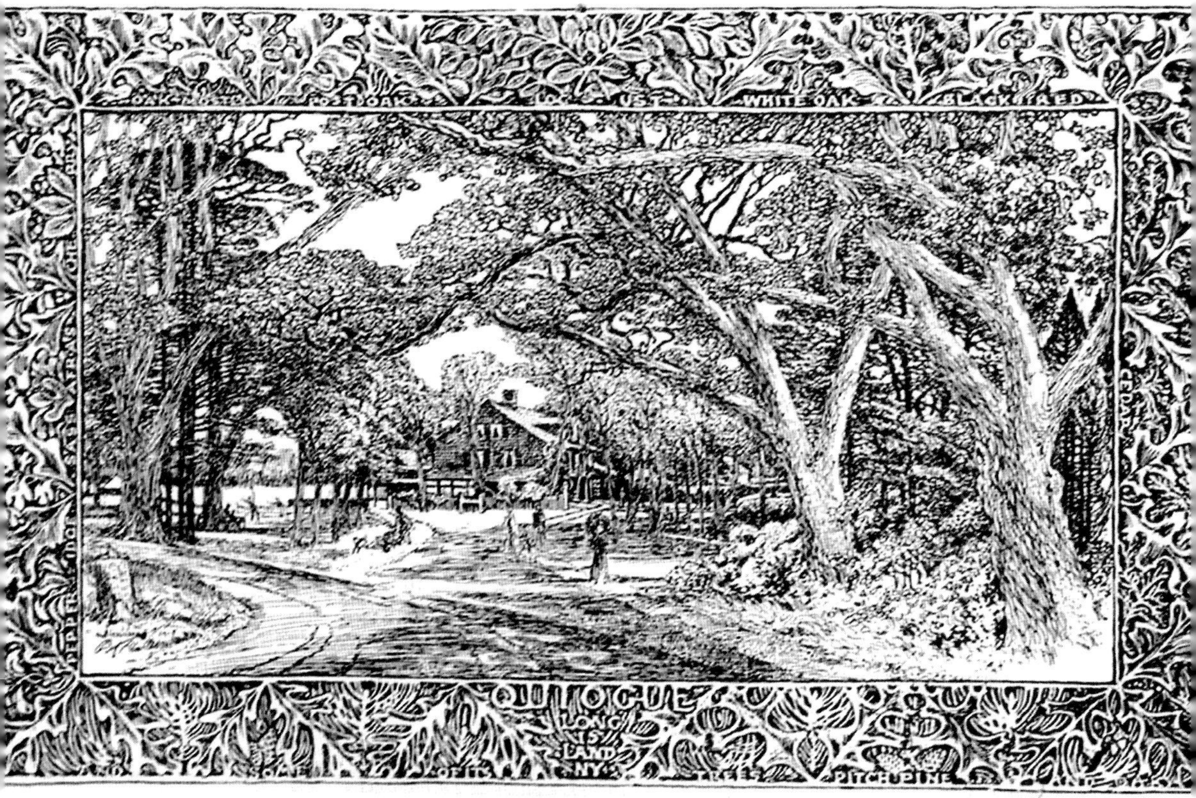

In the late 1800s, a strange phenomenon occurred on the beaches of Quogue. Almost overnight, the sands turned black. None other than inventor Thomas Edison recognized the "black gold" as iron and set up a "mining" corporation. As part of his operation, Edison built a small processing plant on the beach. No sooner had the factory begun operations, however, than Edison learned a lesson known to East Enders long ago. He may have been able to tame electrons to light his lamps, but neither he nor anyone of purely human origin was a match for the sea. A fierce storm arose and washed his dreams away. (Courtesy Suffolk County Historical Society.)

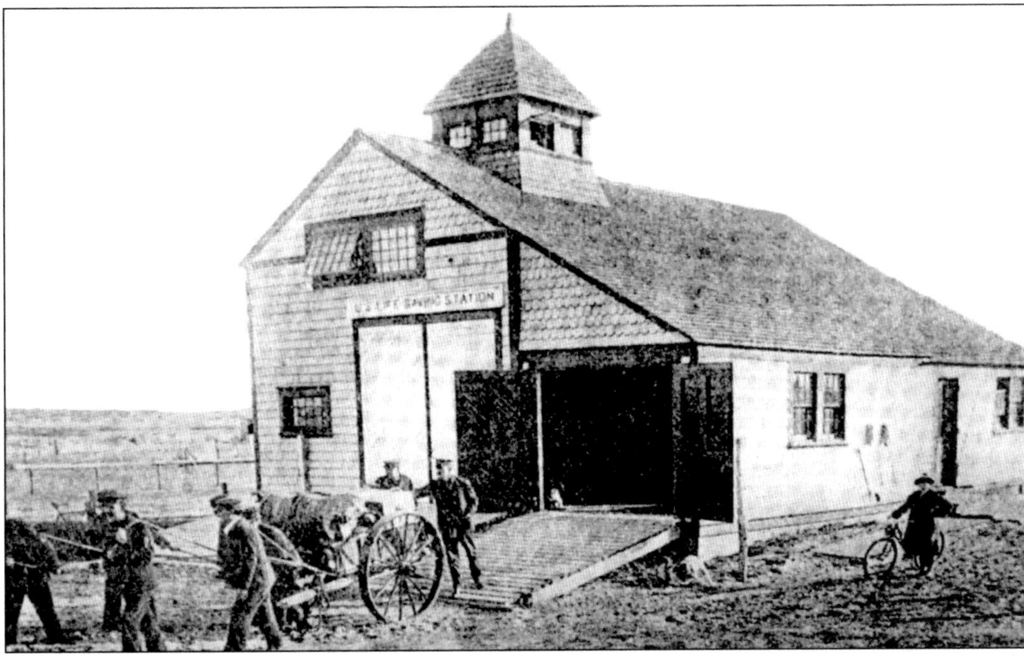

The loss of "black gold" was among the more trivial losses on the South Shore beaches. From the earliest times, the loss of many ships and crew was an almost everyday occurrence. To deal with these ever recurring disasters, the South Shore beaches were dotted with lifesaving stations. (Courtesy Quogue Historical Society.)

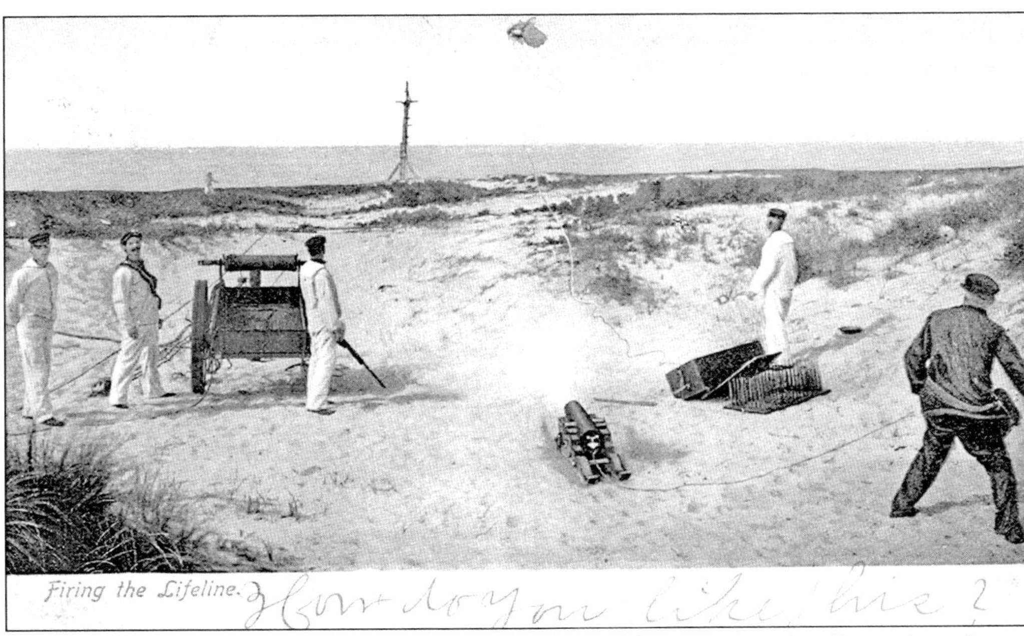

Every few miles, a station, equipped to respond quickly to news of still another ship in distress, was manned around the clock. Breaches buoys, boats, cannon to send a line, and of course, the dedicated crews of the station were always at the ready. (Courtesy Suffolk County Historical Society.)

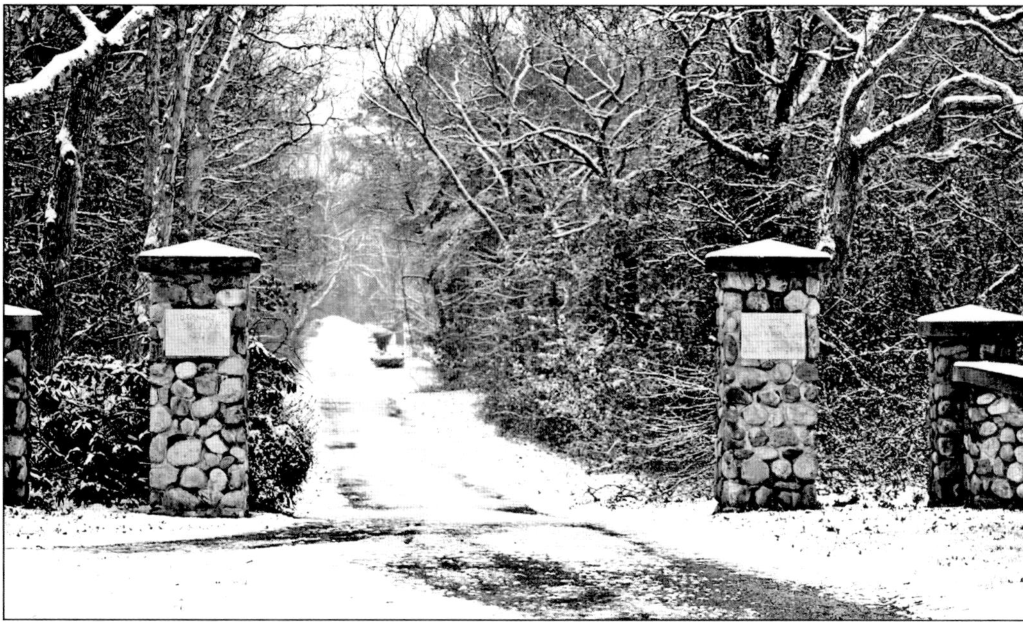

On May 20, 1924, a funeral was held for Ferdinand J. Downs at the Eastport Gospel Church. Downs, a retired New York City policeman, was murdered in cold blood by rumrunners four days earlier. On the night of May 16, Downs, working with federal agents, had staked out a road in Manorville. They were on the lookout for a large shipment of illegal liquor. A sedan was seen approaching with its headlights out. The officers began to pursue the bootleggers.

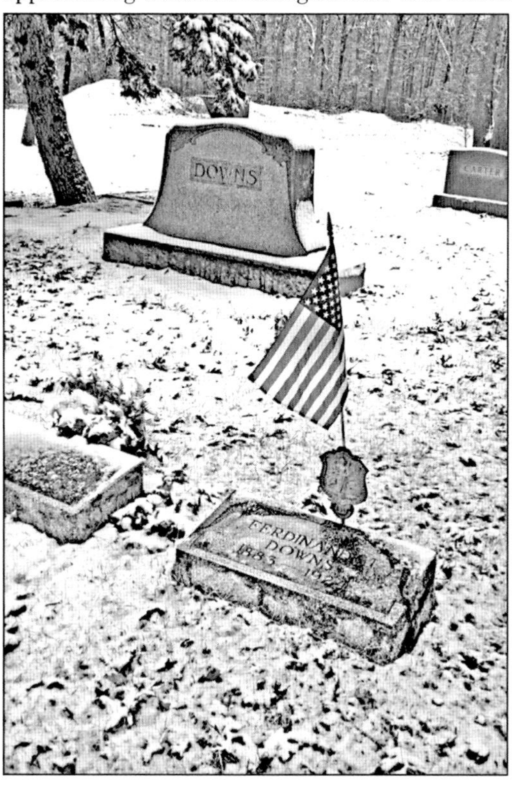

Ferdinand J. Downs aimed a searchlight on the fugitives, who immediately opened fire in the direction of the light. Downs was struck in the head and was instantly killed. His funeral began with a procession from the church to the Oakwood Cemetery in East Quogue. Some 2,000 Ku Klux Klan members, ministers, family, and friends joined in the march. Howard Powell, aged 18 years, joined the march out of curiosity. At age 96, he told his great-granddaughter that speeches were made and crosses were burned. Patrick Ryan was put on trial for the murder but is said to have gotten off.

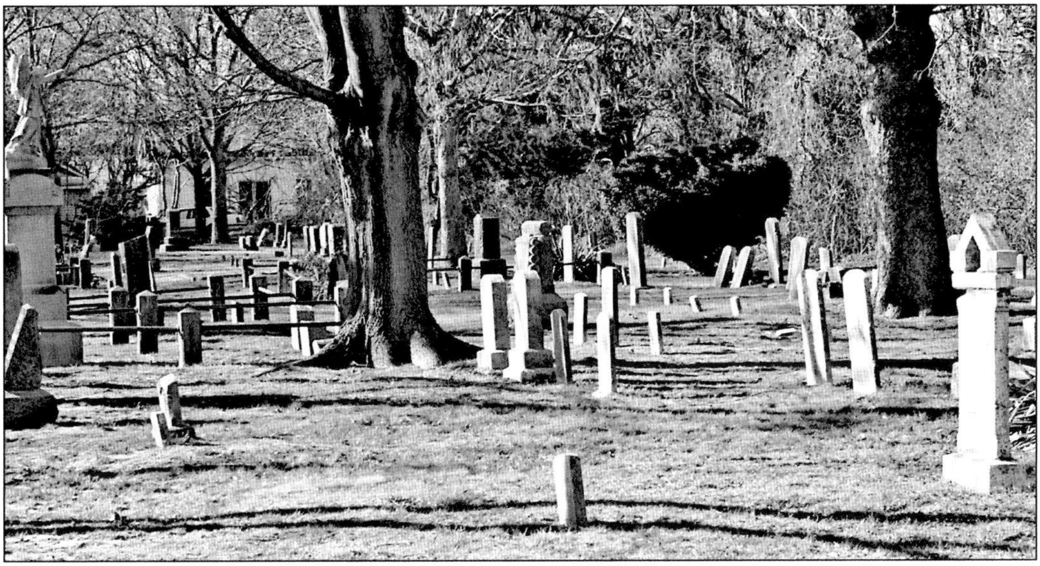

Many of the early residents of East Quogue are buried in the cemetery behind the Methodist church. Originally called Atlanticville, it was renamed East Quogue in 1891. Although the church was built in 1852, there are many older stones in the graveyard. The earliest is that of two-year-old John A. Rider. The cemetery is now under the care of Southampton Town. There are, however, many tipped-over and broken tombstones. Whether the destruction is due to natural causes or vandalism is not clear.

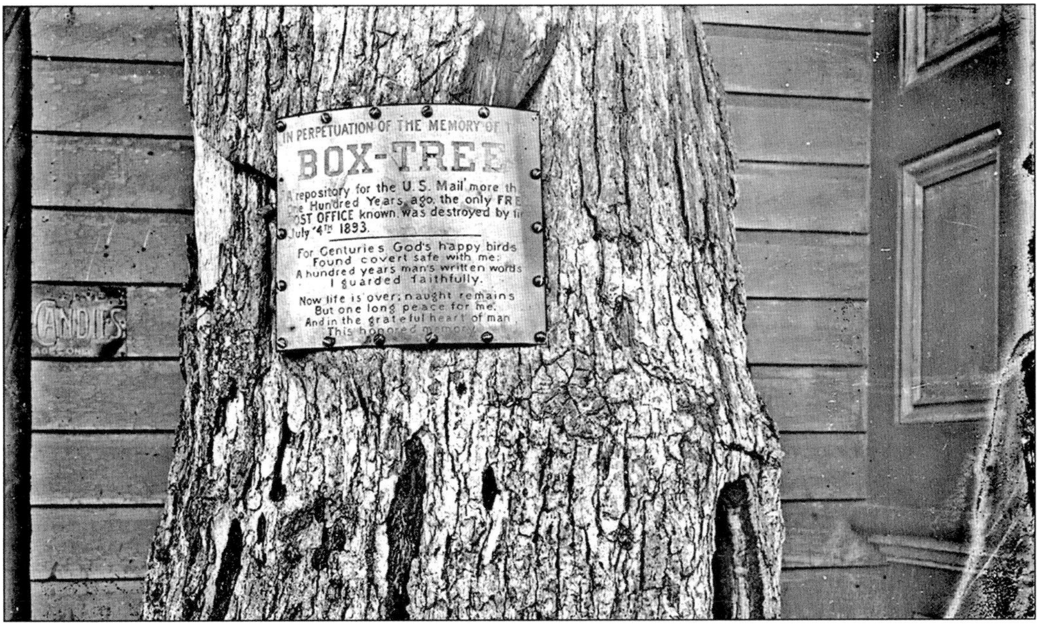

Before there were post offices, a post rider would drop off mail at a certain stone or bush. In the Quogue Museum there are the remnants of a tree in which a box had been placed for mail in 1765. The location of the original box-tree is marked by a monument to the first known letter box. William H. Foster (1830–1910) was the first appointed postmaster when a post office was established in 1858. Foster and his wife are buried in the church graveyard. (Courtesy Suffolk County Historical Society.)

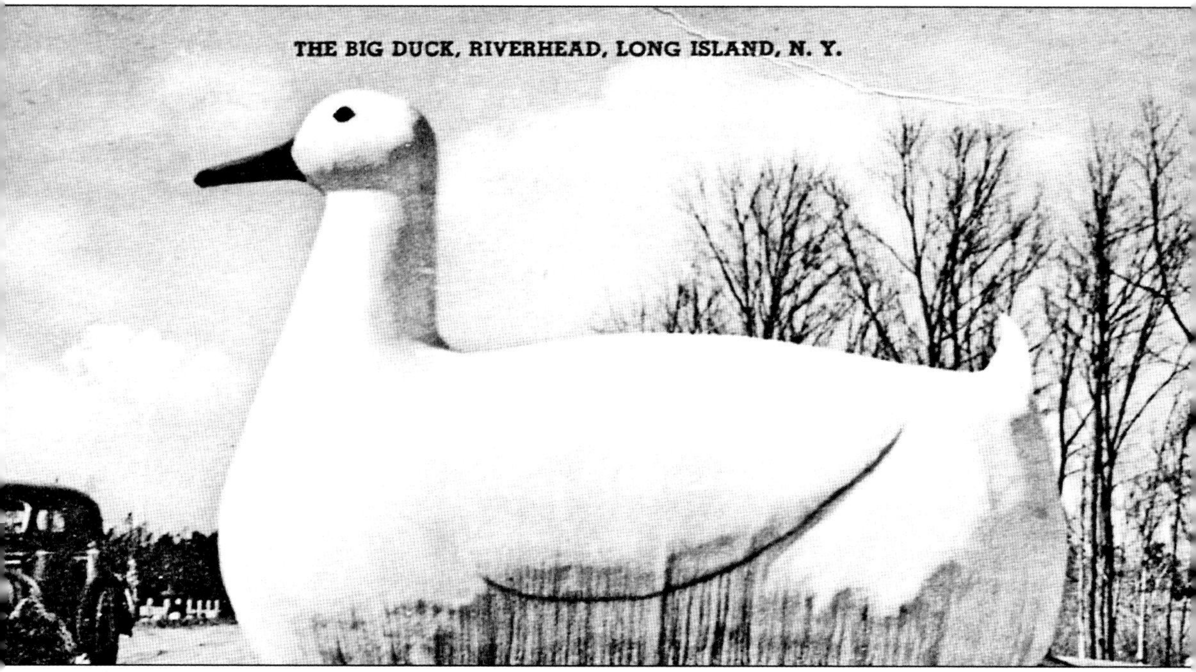

The Big Duck was originally built by Martin Mauer and his wife to promote the sales of his fresh Peking ducks and duck eggs. It is said to have been inspired by a coffee shop they had seen on a visit to California. Built during the Great Depression of 1930–1931, it stands 20 feet tall. Two show set designers created its design. Made of cement on wire mesh, the taillights of a Model T Ford glow red after dark. It is one of a myriad of "Big Critters," including the "Booming Prairie Chicken" in Minnesota, several giant roosters, and a host of others along America's highways. The duck's original roost was in Riverhead, but it has been moved several times. It now resides at the entrance to Sears Bellows County. Each year shortly after Thanksgiving, a duck-lighting ceremony kicks off the holiday season. Although Peking ducks are no longer available, shirts and other "duck-belia" are offered to immortalize the visit. The Big Duck is listed on the National Register of Historical Places. (Courtesy Suffolk County Historical Society.)

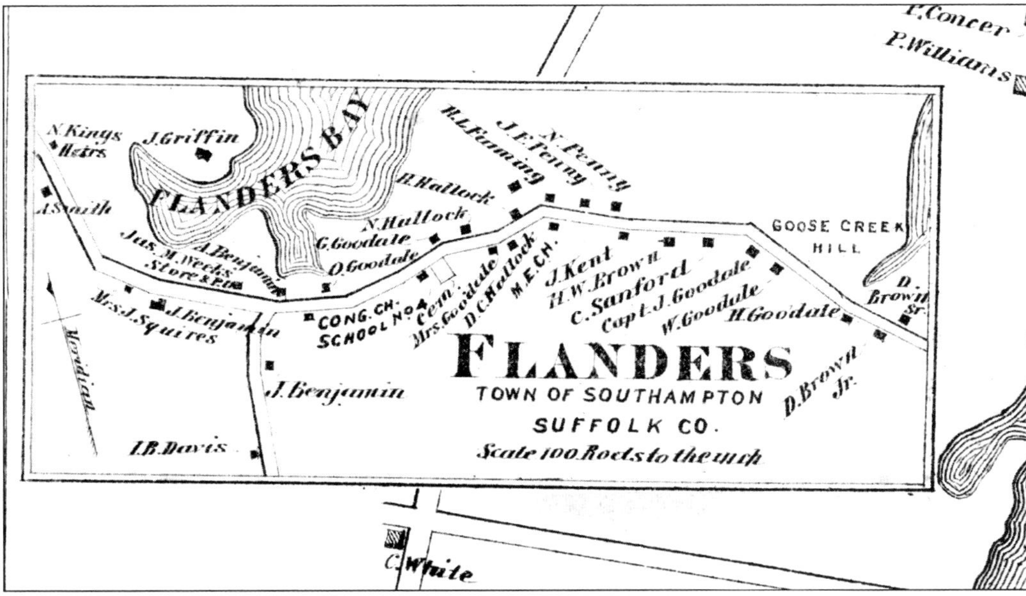

In his visit to Flanders in 1871, historian Richard M. Bayles described it "as a village of fisherman lying on an indentation from Picnic Bay." At the time, there were about 30 houses, a school, a store, and two churches. It is said that the hamlet was named after a region in the Netherlands. The Congregational church was built in about 1840. The major income-producing ventures were woodcutting and, later, raising ducks. The area was also a prime hunting ground for deer and wild birds. (Courtesy Stony Brook University, Special Map Collection.)

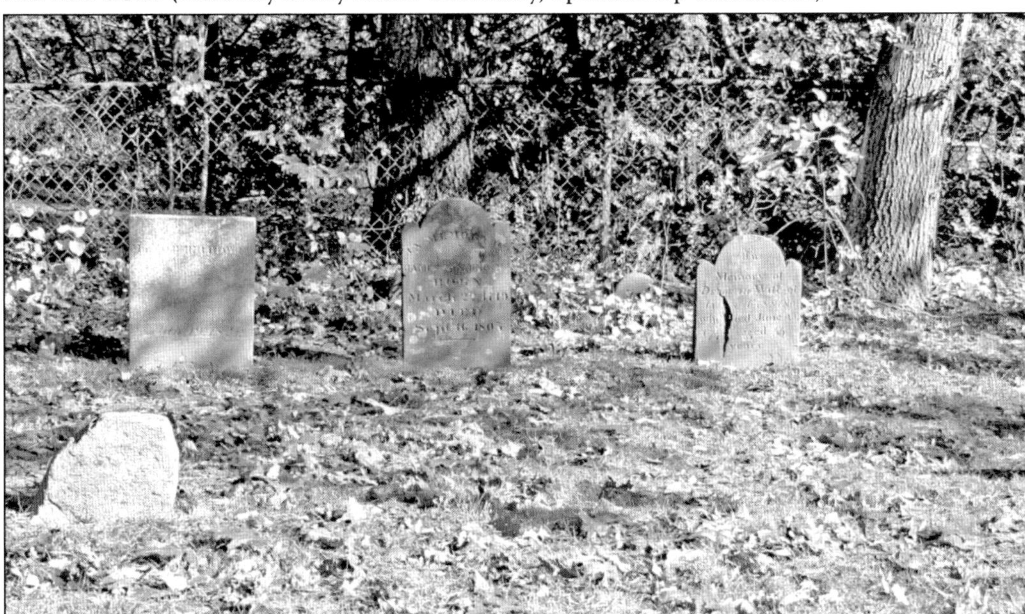

Although the cemetery in Flanders was opened in the late 1800s, there are several much older graves. Tucked away in a dark corner are the remains of James Fanning and family. Fanning (1719–1780) was the eldest son of Capt. James Fanning, whose tall monument stands in the Riverhead town burial ground. The son and his three wives were buried on his farm, now the site of the Flanders Cemetery. Of his three wives, only Deborah Fanning has a marked tombstone.

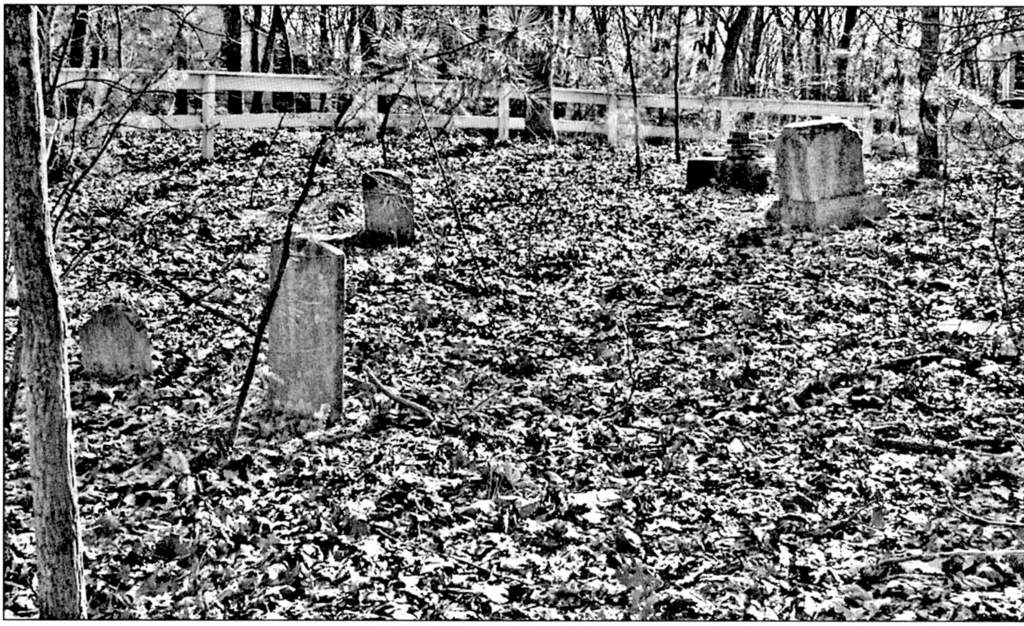

One concern addressed by the duke's laws was that of someone dispatching a not-so-loved one and burying the evidence in the backyard. On the East End, the edict was largely ignored. It was common practice to bury family members on the farm. This graveyard is virtually in a current resident's backyard, behind the Flanders firehouse. Among several members of the Haven family found here is Walter, who died in October 1840.

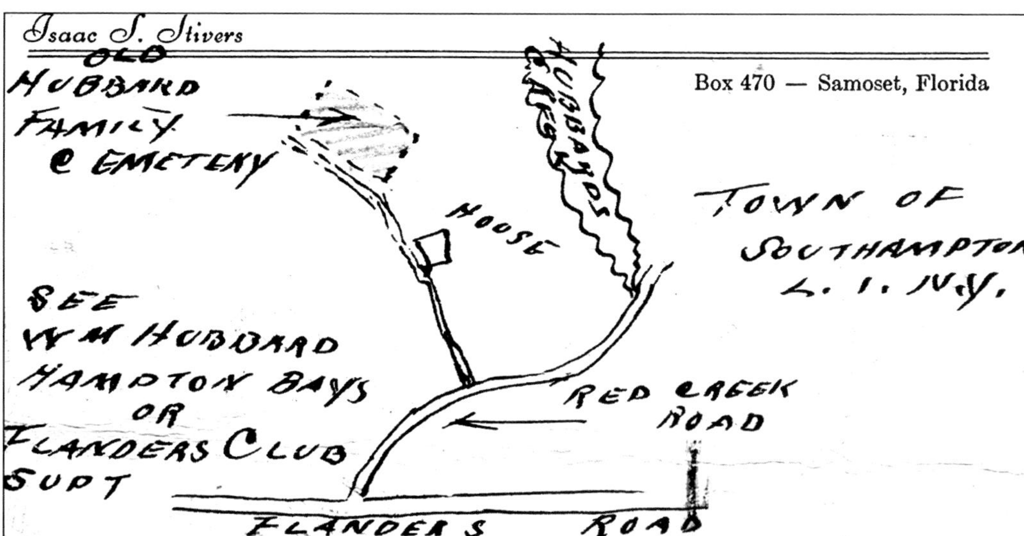

There are many other small family burial grounds on the South Fork. In Flanders, along with the Haven graveyard, is one in nearby Saul Bellows Park. A third is said to be on the property of the former Flanders Gun Club. This map, drawn on the back of a postcard some years ago, shows the site of the cemetery. The adventuresome reader is invited to find it—something this writer was unable to do. (Courtesy Suffolk County Historical Society.)

Three

Hampton Bays to the Shinnecock Reservation

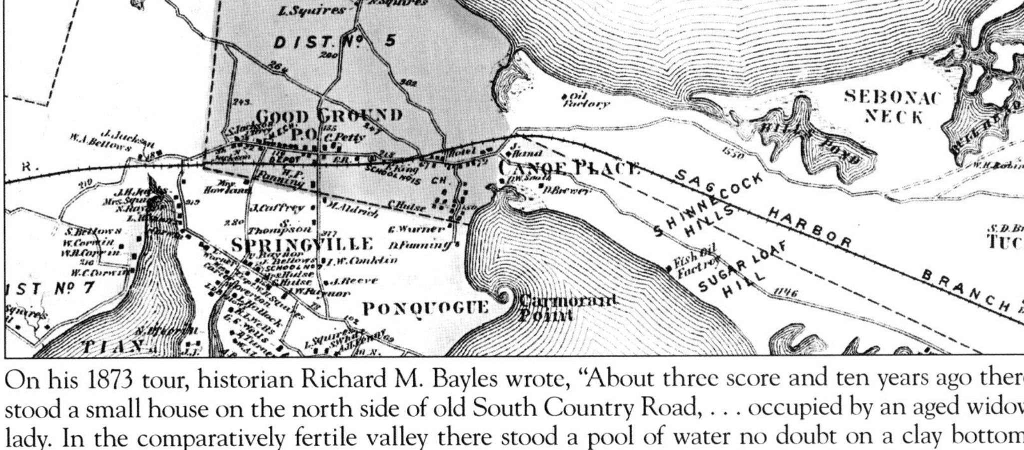

On his 1873 tour, historian Richard M. Bayles wrote, "About three score and ten years ago there stood a small house on the north side of old South Country Road, . . . occupied by an aged widow lady. In the comparatively fertile valley there stood a pool of water no doubt on a clay bottom. Walking by it one day, she stooped down and picked up a lump of soil and made the chance remark 'this is good ground.' From this important incident the village of Good Ground got its name. Such is the tradition handed down among the natives of this place." (There is, however, at least one earlier reference to the name.) In any event, in 1922, the name was changed to Hampton Bays, to be more closely identified with the Hamptons. To the north are two small communities: Squiretown, settled in 1773, and Red Creek, founded by the Fourniers. To the east of Good Ground is the Shinnecock Canal, located at the original boundary of Southampton when the town was founded in 1640. (Courtesy Stony Brook University, Special Map Collection.)

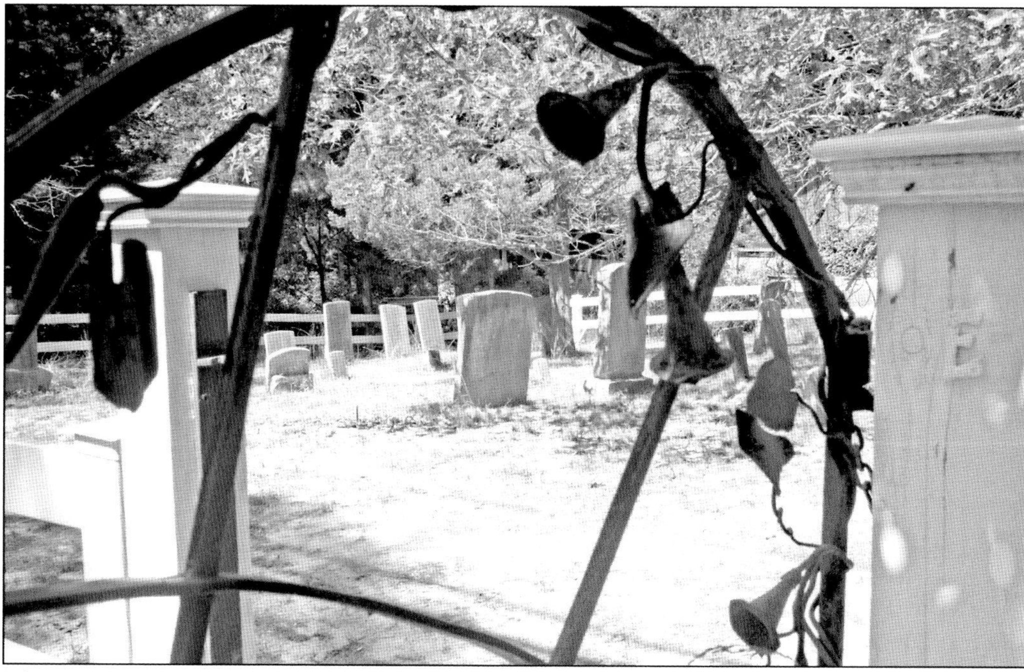

The Fournier Cemetery is located in Red Creek. Francois Fournier (1730–1807) was a native of France. The family came to Squiretown from Southold. Both Fournier and his son John fought in the Revolutionary War. They both were captured by the British and imprisoned on the hulk *Jersey* on the East River. Similar floating prisons were anchored in Wallabout Bay and were notorious for the inhuman treatment given to the prisoners aboard.

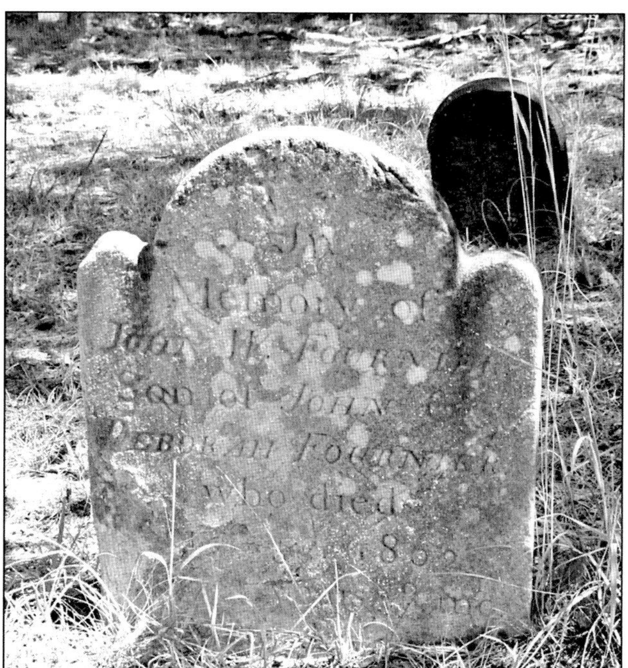

The *Jersey* was a 64-gun ship of the line no longer fit for service. Along with the rest of the fleet, the *Jersey* was a stripped-down, decrepit, aging hulk. In an account given by a prisoner who had somehow survived, diseases such as smallpox and yellow fever were rampant. It has been estimated that over 11,000 prisoners died in the hellholes.

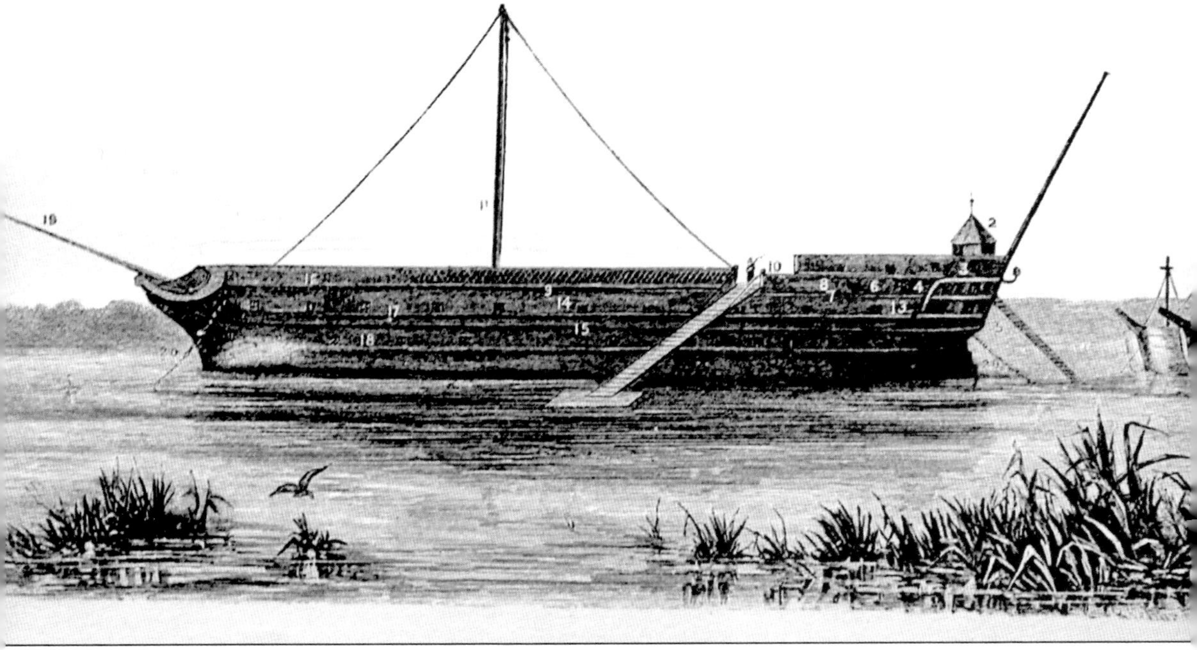

At first, patriot prisoners were held in local buildings such as churches, public facilities, even Columbia College. Despite overcrowding, they soon became totally inadequate. And so, ships that were no longer seaworthy were pressed into service. Ordinarily, a provost is charged with the safekeeping of prisoners. Such was not the case with New York Provost Marshal Capt. William Cunningham. Under his watch, over 11,600 prisoners died. After the war, Cunningham was arrested in London and brought to trial. He told the court: "I, William Cunningham . . . was appointed provost marshall to the Royal Army, which placed me in a situation to wreak my vengeance on the Americans. I shudder to think of the murders I have been accessory to . . . " Although he repented, Cunningham was executed on August 10, 1791. (Courtesy Suffolk County Historical Society.)

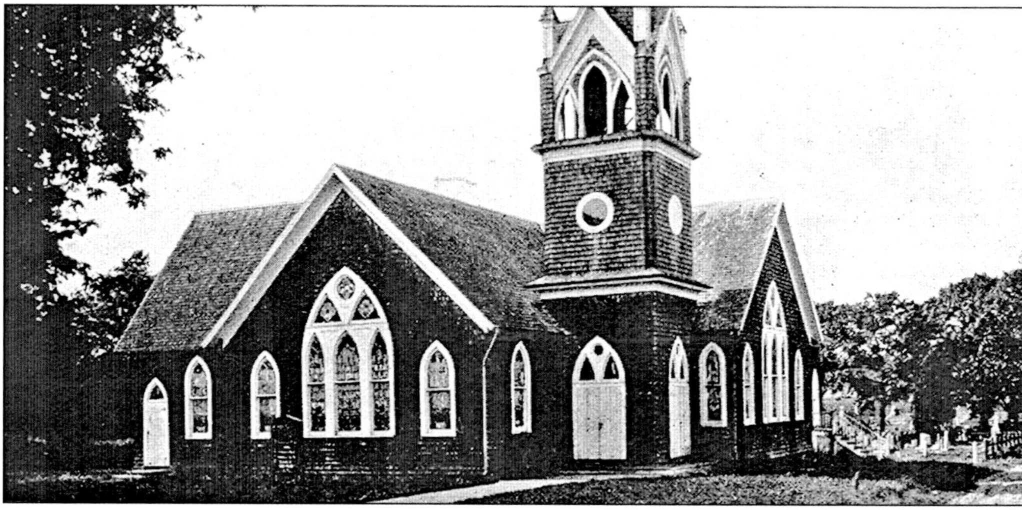

The Methodist Society was established in Good Ground in 1836. A meetinghouse was completed in 1840, and a new church was built in 1863. The nondenominational cemetery behind the church was opened in 1882 on land donated by Sylvanus R. Jackson (1812–1879). Many stones much older than that, which have been relocated from their original site, may be found here. (Courtesy Suffolk County Historical Society.)

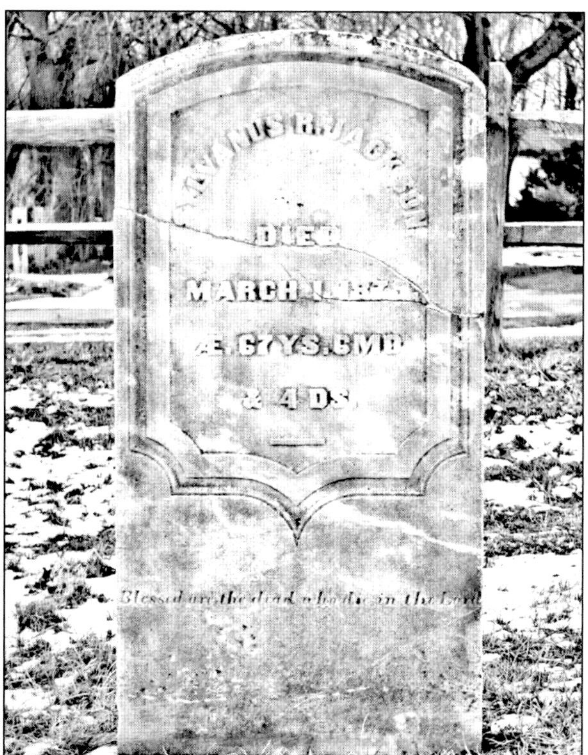

An interesting story concerns a small family cemetery located just a few yards west of the church. A Judge Lazansky and his wife owned the property. After his death, she tried to sell the house. No one was interested, however, in becoming the proud owner of a graveyard. So one night the tombstones simply disappeared. Today, the site is in back of a local restaurant.

A victim of a January gale, the *Louis V. Place* came aground at Sayville. The ship was within sight of the Fire Island lifesaving station, but fierce winds and crashing breakers prevented the lifesaving crews on the shore from launching a rescue boat. The *Place*'s captain and his men froze to death in the rigging, while those on shore stood by helpless. Only Claus Stuvens survived long enough to tell of the *Place*'s terrible ordeal. (Courtesy Suffolk County Historical Society.)

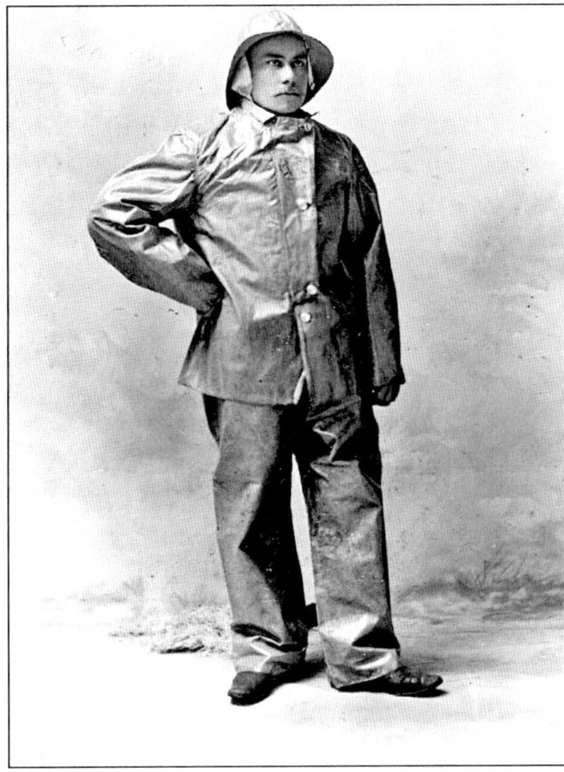

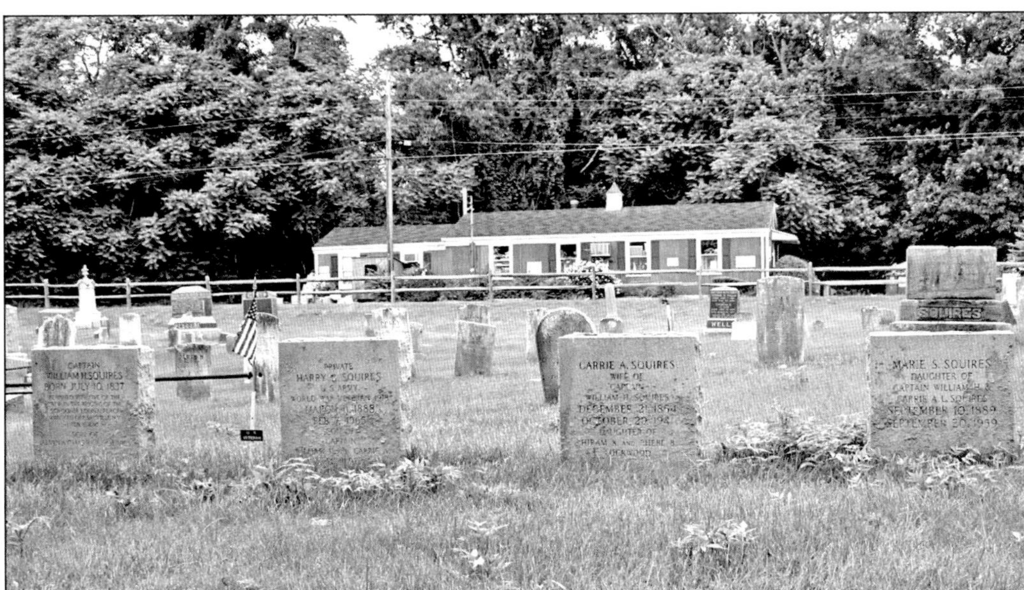

The Squires family is buried in Captain Squires's hometown at the Good Ground Cemetery. In an ironic twist of fate, his body came ashore two weeks after he had fallen, frozen, into the sea, on the shores of Good Ground. It is said that his body was found only yards from his house. The captain had come home.

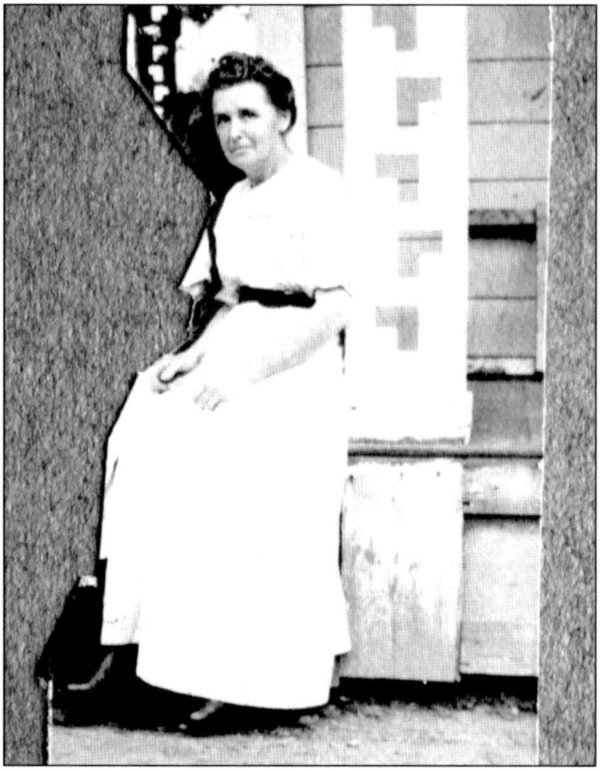

The captain left behind a widow, Carrie, and a son, Harry, only eight years old at the time of his father's death. The tragedy made an indelible imprint on the son's life. He literally immersed himself in shipwrecks. He researched them in obsessive detail. Handwritten logbooks, photographs, and newspaper clippings fill several boxes at the Suffolk County Historical Society. A researcher cannot help but come away with a sense of the loss the boy felt for his father, whom the sea had snatched way. (Courtesy Suffolk County Historical Society.)

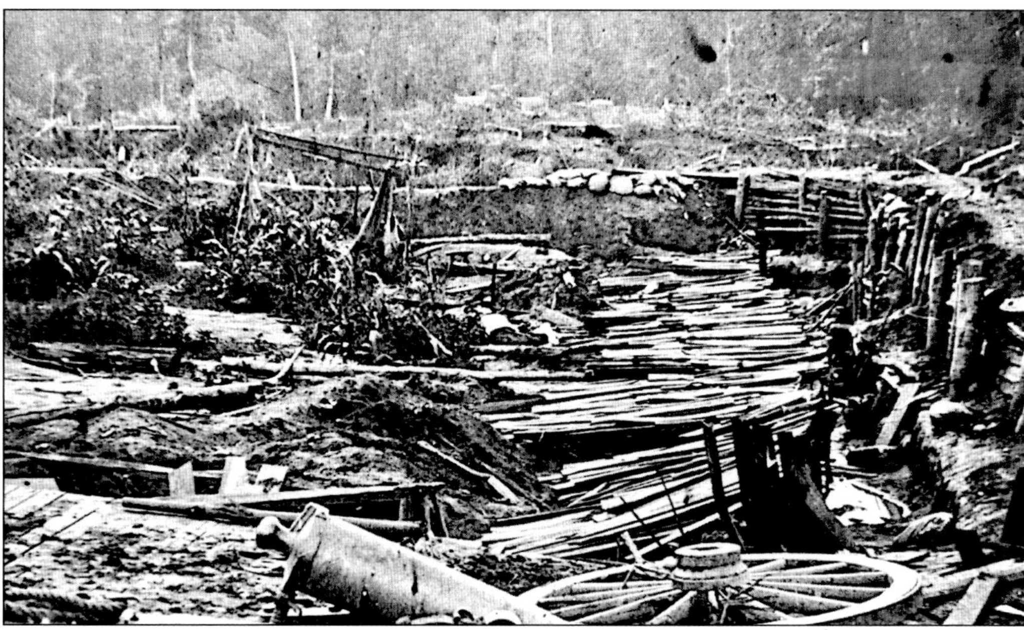

The Mississippi River was the major supply route for the Confederate army. Port Hudson was a primary target of the Union forces in the drive to take control of the mighty Mississippi. Troops held off a Union force of 30,000 until surrendering on July 9, 1863. It was the longest siege in American military history. Now a state historical site, the cemetery holds the remains of more than 3,000 mostly unidentified Union soldiers. (Courtesy Picture History.)

Enthusiasm for the war was initially high, forcing New York regiments to compete for recruits by offering incentives. The Senatorial Regiment poster reads, in part, "$225 Bounty . . . Rally 'round the flag, boys! Come one! Come all!" Perhaps this lured John R. Brooker to join up in Manhattan rather than with the 127th New York Volunteers, the Monitors, who recruited the majority of the East End soldiers. "'Tis sweet, O 'tis sweet, for one's country to live or die!" And, sadly, die Brooker did. (ac03178 C Senatorial Poster, Collection of the New York Historical Society.)

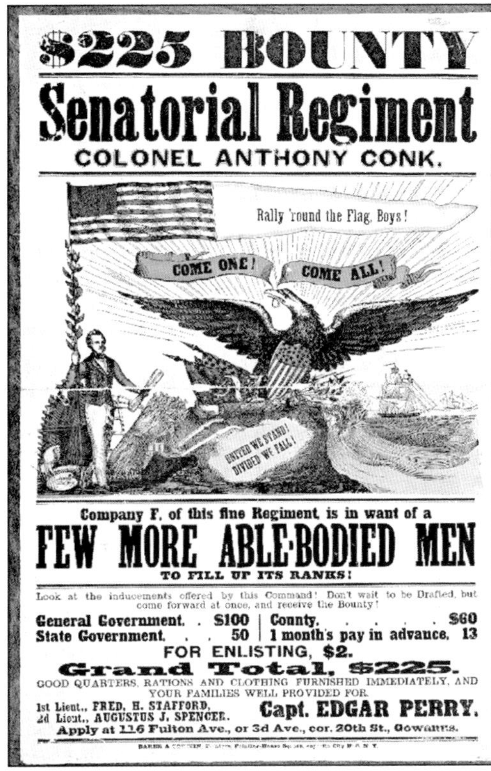

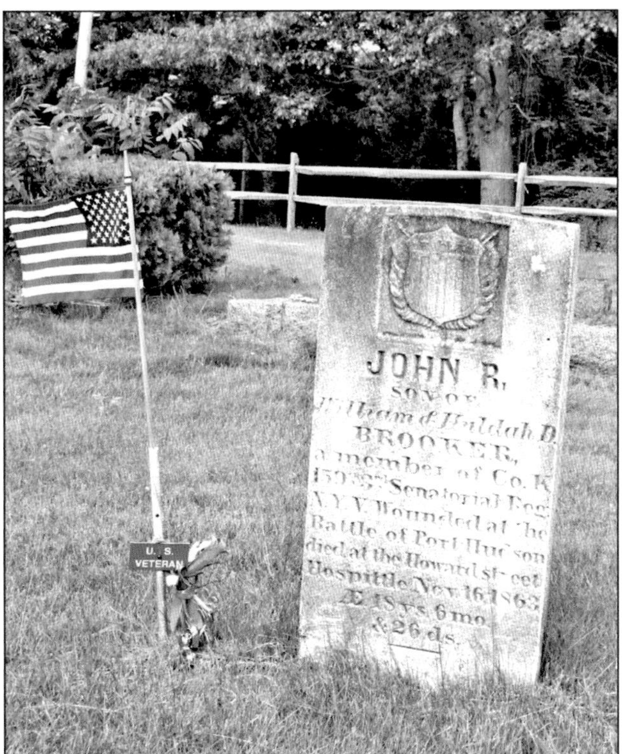

Brooker's tombstone reads, "John R., son of William & Huldah D. Brooker, a member of Company K 159th, 3rd Senatorial Reg. N.Y.V. Wounded at the Battle of Port Hudson, died at the Howard street hospital Nov. 16, 1863 AE 18 ys. 6 mo. & 26 ds."

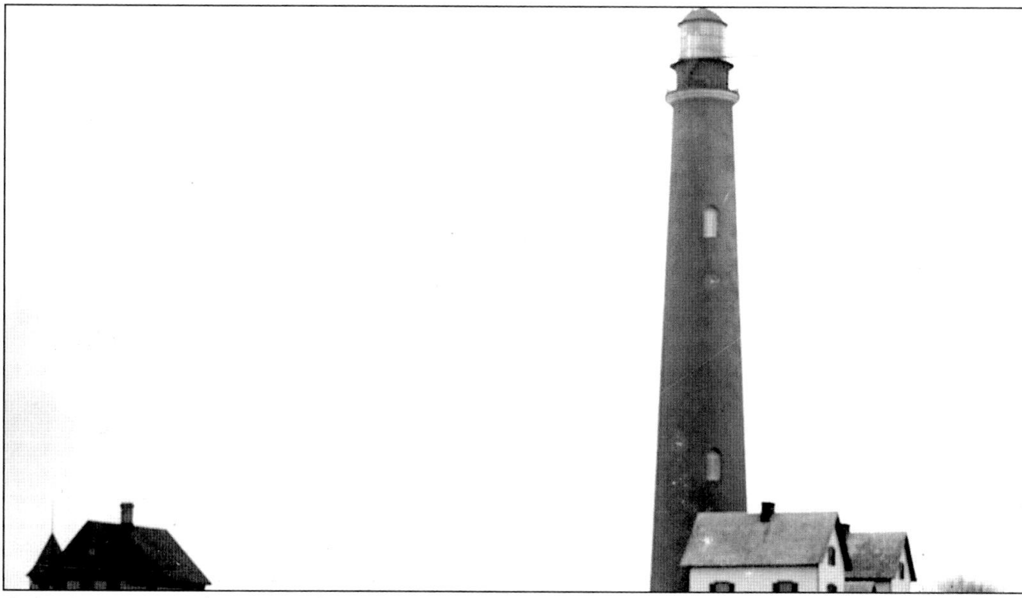

Col. George Washington identified the need for lighthouses on the East End when he recommended a light be established at Horton's Point in 1756. Montauk Point Lighthouse was built in 1791, and the Fire Island Lighthouse in 1827. These lights helped the many coastwise ships avoid the treacherous beaches of the South Shore. The two beacons were almost 70 miles apart, however, leaving a gap of at least 30 miles—on a clear night, when they were least needed. (Courtesy Suffolk County Historical Society.)

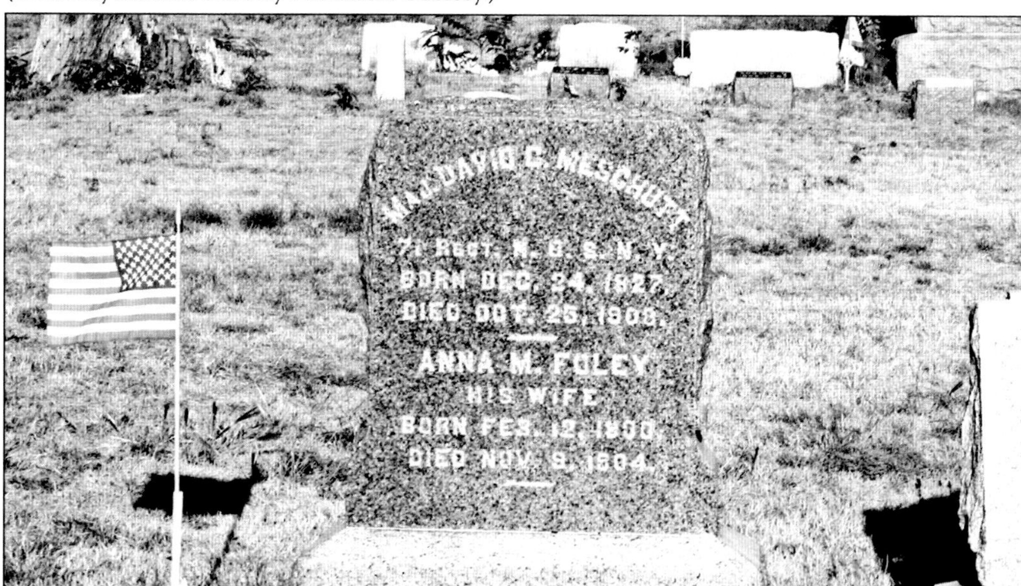

The two beacons were too similar at first, leading to at least one shipwreck. This problem was finally addressed by Congress in 1854, and the Shinnecock light greeted the New Year on January 1, 1858. The area near the light was teeming with wildlife, a natural attraction for hunters and fishermen. Maj. David C. Meschutt ran an inn to cater to these sportsmen. Civil War veterans often served as lighthouse keepers. Alonzo Foster held the position for three years. Both are buried in Good Ground.

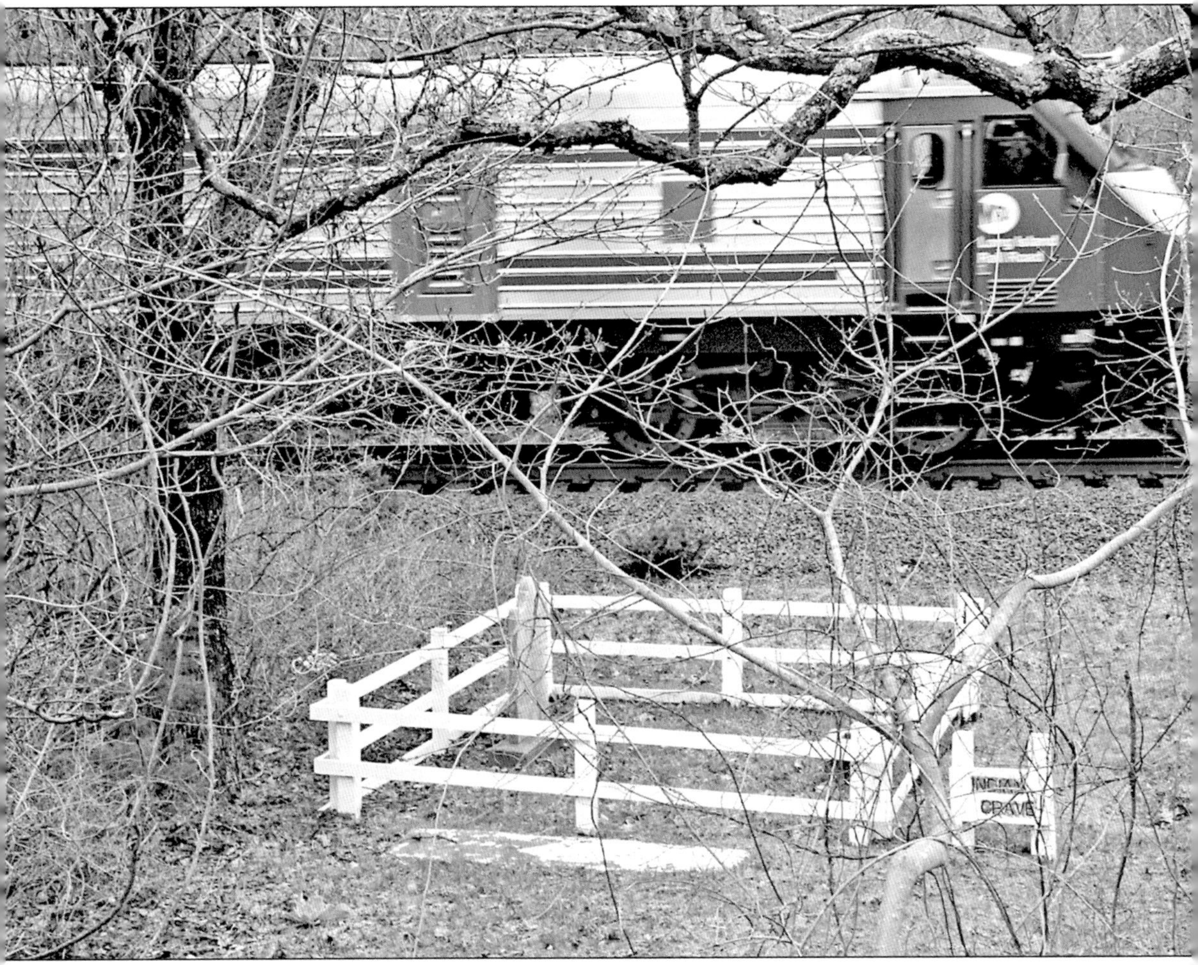

Paul Cuffee, a Shinnecock, was born a slave and early in life had been "addicted to the pleasures of the revel and the midnight dance." During the religious awakening in 1778–1779, he told his followers he "surrendered his heart" to the Lord Jesus. In Hampton Bays, alongside the railroad tracks that were forced to change their course, stands a single grave. A plain headstone is inscribed in part with the words: "In Memory of / The Rev. Paul Cuffee / An Indian of the Shinnecock Tribe / He labored with fidelity and success / Humble, pious, and indefatigable / He finished his course with joy / On the 7th of March, 1812 / Aged 55 years and three days." As historian Richard M. Bayles noted in 1871, the grave site may be seen from a car window as the train speeds by. However, today, there is no longer any evidence of the church he spoke of or of the other graves that were once a part of the original American Indian cemetery.

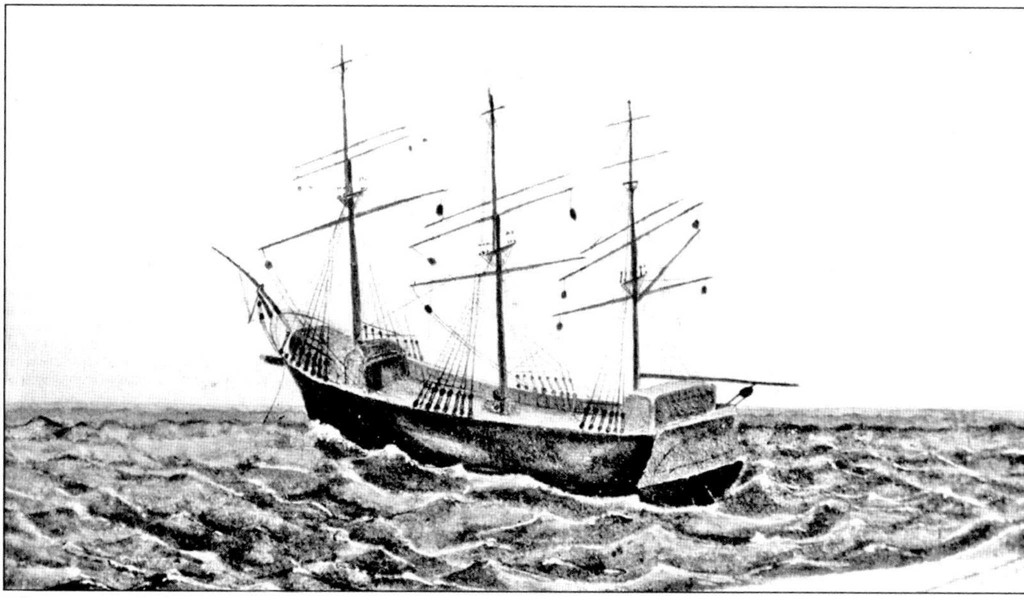

The story of the *Circassian* began, in a sense, on an optimistic note. The ship itself was a full-rigged iron ship, 280 feet long. A blockade runner, it had been captured by the United States during the Civil War. On December 11, 1876, it was sailing along the coast of Long Island, toward New York's harbor from Liverpool. It never made port. At 10:45 that night, it went aground off Bridgehampton. (Courtesy Suffolk County Historical Society.)

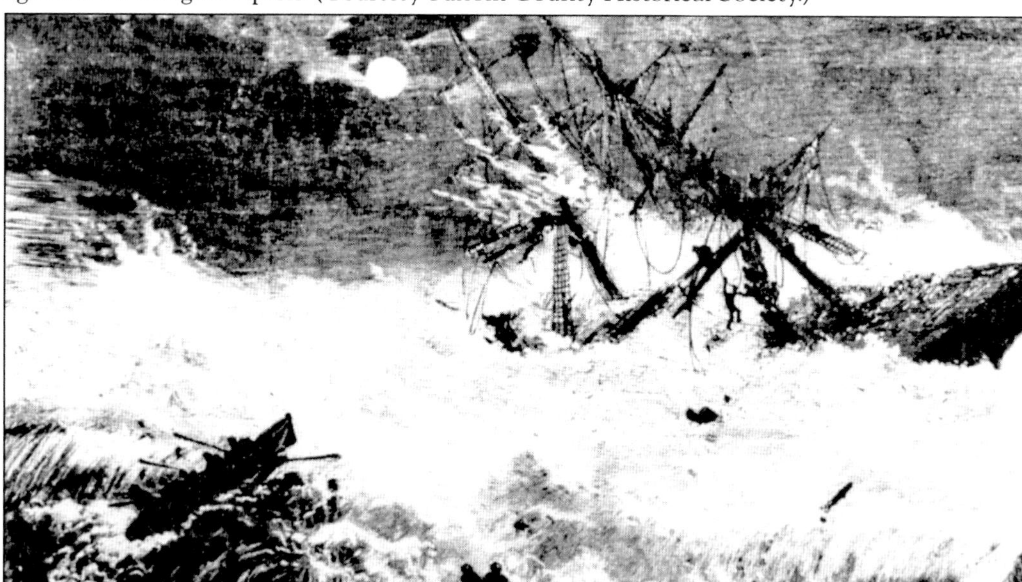

The captain of the *Circassian*, Richard Williams, blamed a faulty compass for the accident. The crew of the nearby Mecox lifesaving station rescued all aboard. The men had challenged the sea and won, or so they thought. The Coast Wrecking Company was hired to salvage the *Circassian* and its cargo. With Capt. John Lewis in charge, the salvagers stayed aboard the ship during the operation. On December 29, a storm arose, but Lewis refused to allow the men to leave the ship. The seas grew violent, attempts at rescue failed, and the sea won after all. (Courtesy Westhampton Beach Historical Society.)

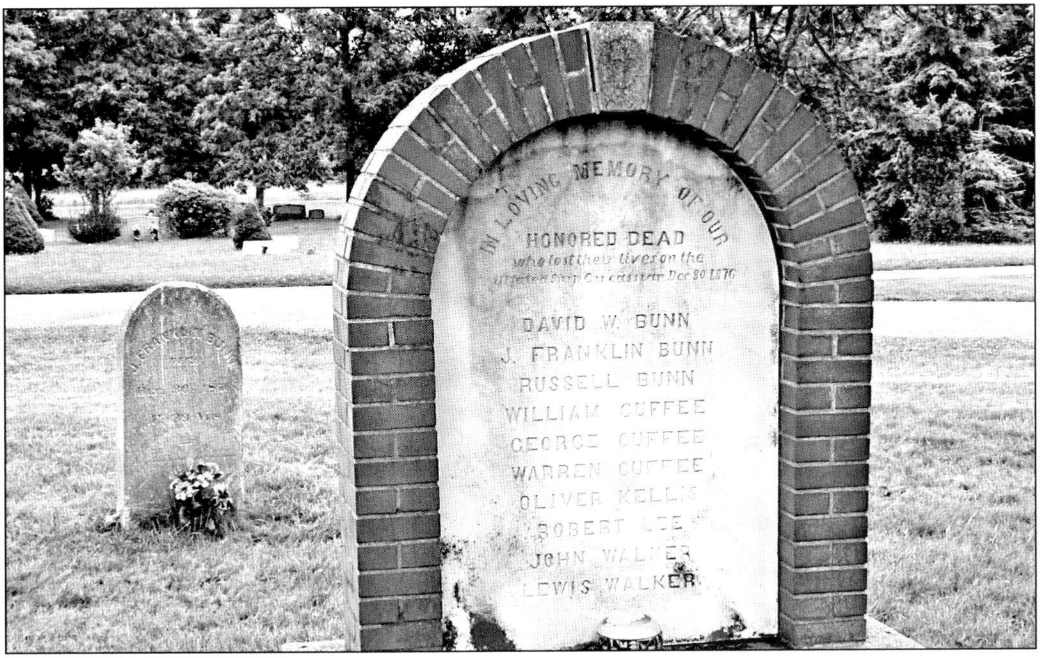

All 28 men aboard the *Circassian* drowned. This monument is located on the Shinnecock Reservation. Ten local Shinnecocks were hired to assist 16 of the regular crew. The captain and the regular crew are said to be buried in East Hampton's South Cemetery, west of the monument to the ill-fated crew of the *John Milton*.

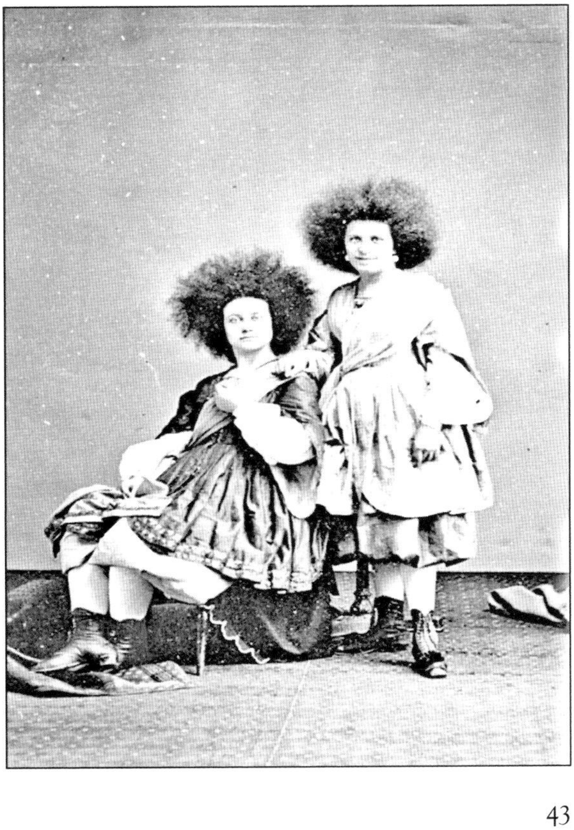

The fate of the ship was foreshadowed by the tragic fate of its namesake. In 1829, Turkey was forced to cede the region of Circassia to Russia. Many of the women, reputed to have exceptional beauty, were sold into slavery. In America, showman P. T. Barnum sought to capitalize on this reputation. He exhibited several of the women in the American Museum in 1865. By the 1870s, the Circassian women had become popular attractions at traveling medicine shows. (Courtesy Picture History.)

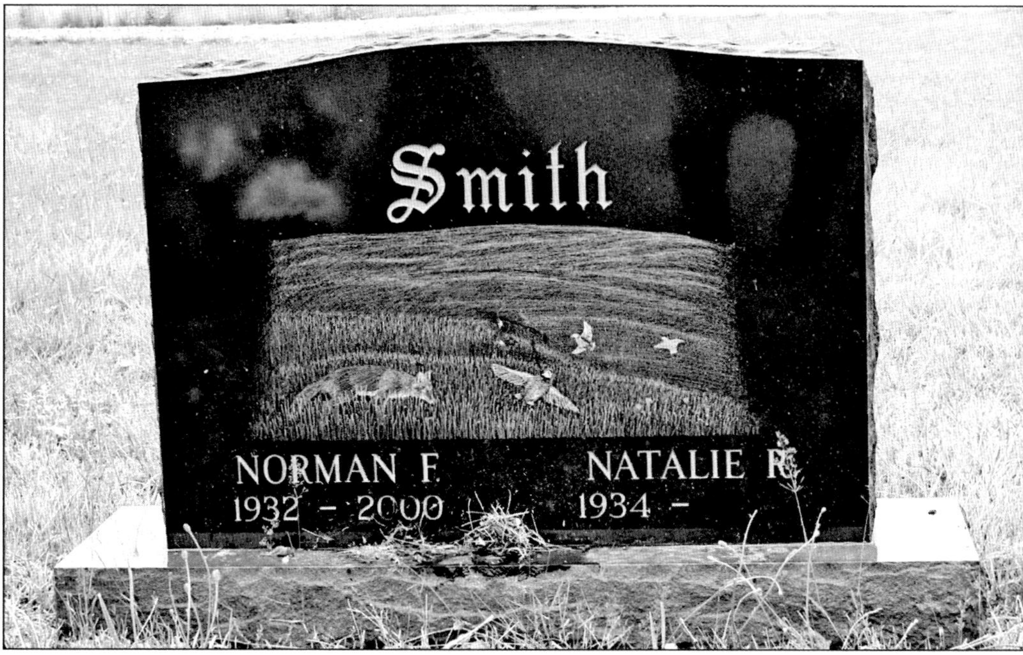

Many Shinnecocks have worked for the Shinnecock Hills Golf Club. One in particular was Norman F. Smith (1932–2000). Smith was an artist whose painting graces a wall in the clubhouse. When he died in 2000, the monument placed over his grave was inscribed with a likeness of that painting.

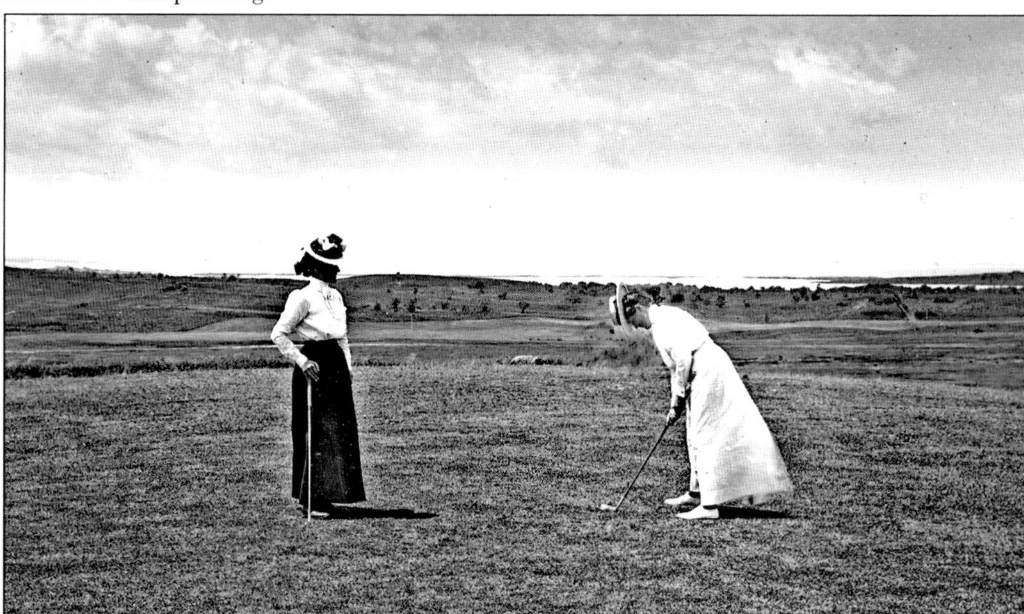

The Shinnecock Hills Golf Club has an old and storied history. It is one of the original founders of the U.S. Golf Association. Founded in 1891, the club was the first to allow women as members and has hosted eight U.S. Opens. Lucie Barns and Beatrix Hoyt, who were members of the club, won the first two U.S. women's amateur championships. (Courtesy Suffolk County Historical Society.)

Four

Southampton Village

The town of Southampton was established in 1664 by the Duke of York. Under Richard Nicolls, the fist English governor of New York, the island was divided into three ridings. The division was modeled after the three trithings in Yorkshire, the duke's hometown. Thus was born East Riding, which included Southampton. The East Enders, saddled with the oppressive duke's laws, reluctantly became a part of New York. When the new governor, Col. Thomas Dongan, allowed the settlers to assemble in October 1683, they quickly repealed some of the more heinous of the laws and adopted a bill of rights. They met twice more, in 1684 and 1685, and then never met again until 1691, after James II had abdicated the throne. One enduring act of the assembly occurred during the first meeting. The ridings were replaced by shires and counties. Thus, on November 2, 1683, Southampton Town became a part of Suffolk County. (Courtesy Stony Brook University, Special Map Collection.)

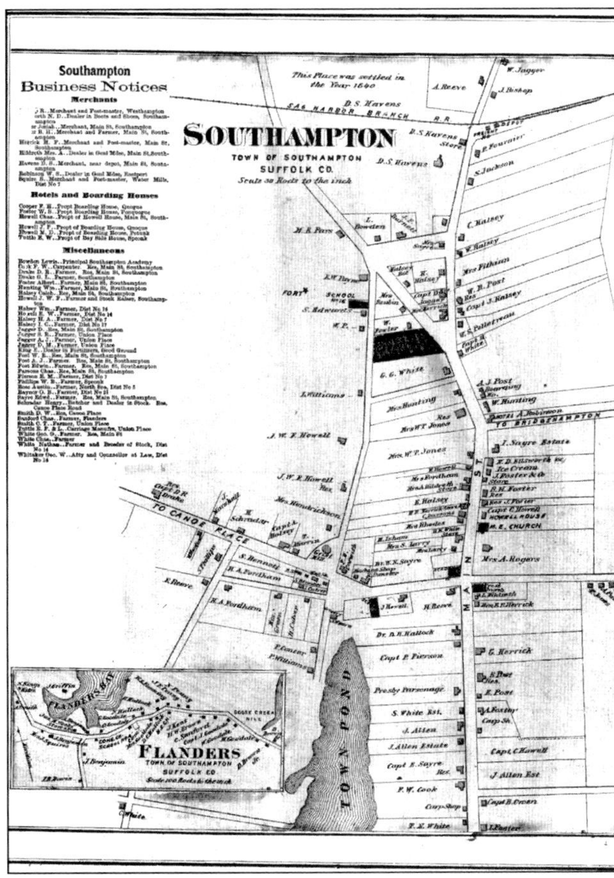

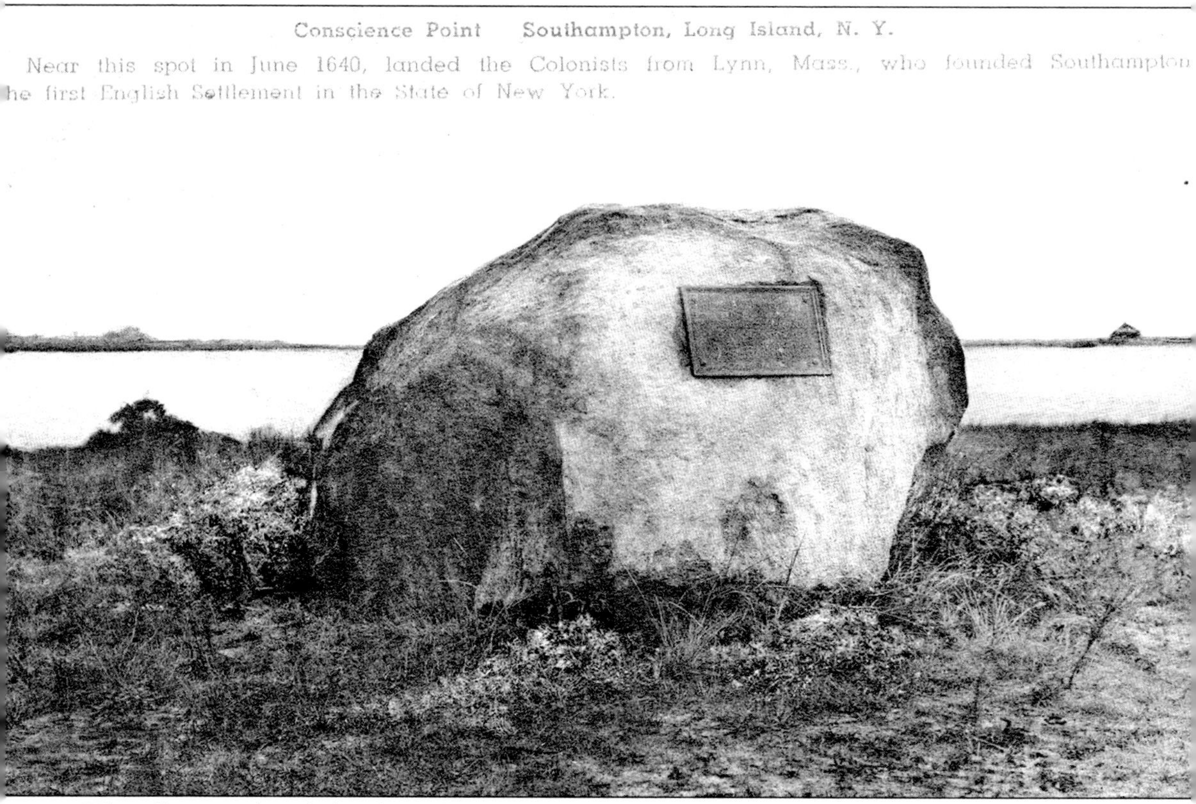

The village was founded in the early part of 1640, when a band of 80 men left Lynn, Massachusetts, aboard a small sloop under the command of Capt. Daniel Howe. They first attempted to establish a settlement at Cow Bay. Upon hearing of their arrival, the Dutch governor of New Amsterdam, William Kieft, sent a squad of soldiers to evict the trespassers. They placed six of the English colonists under arrest until they agreed to abandon the settlement and never darken the door of Dutch property again. The colonists then sailed east along the sound. After rounding Orient Point, they came ashore at North Sea, on the South Fork of Long Island. It is said that a female passenger, upon setting foot on land, exclaimed "For conscience sake, I'm on dry land once more!" A monument at Conscience Point commemorates the founding of Southampton. (Courtesy Suffolk County Historical Society.)

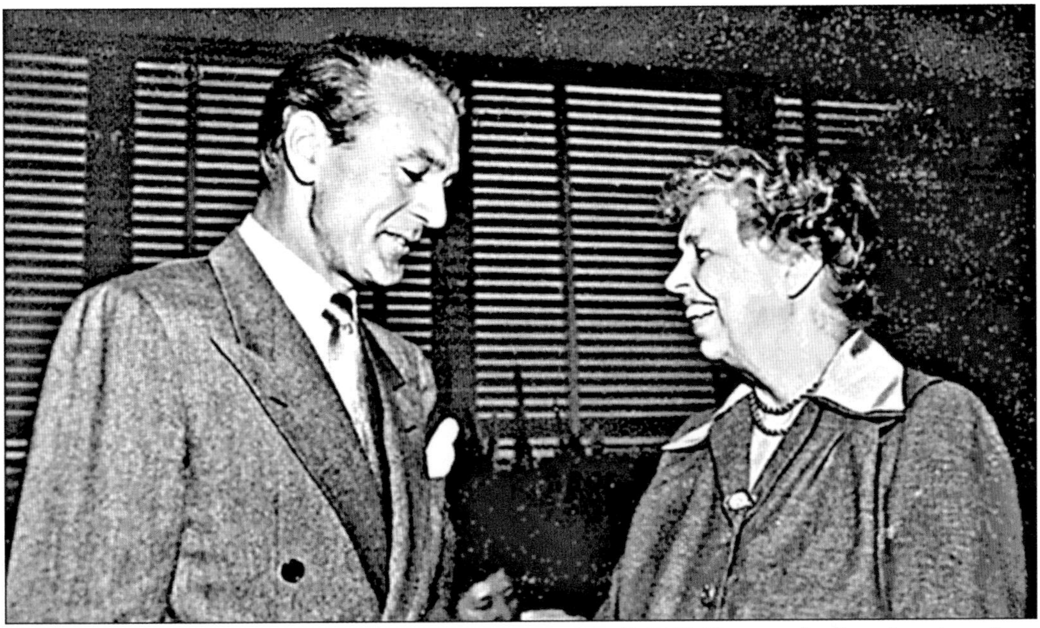

Frank James Cooper was born in Helena, Montana, on May 7, 1901. He moved to Los Angeles, where he began his acting career in 1924. As Gary Cooper, he appeared in over 100 films over a time span of 36 years. He was one of the best-known and well-liked Hollywood actors of the 1950s. Cooper is shown in this 1950 photograph with Eleanor Roosevelt, wife of Pres. Franklin D. Roosevelt.

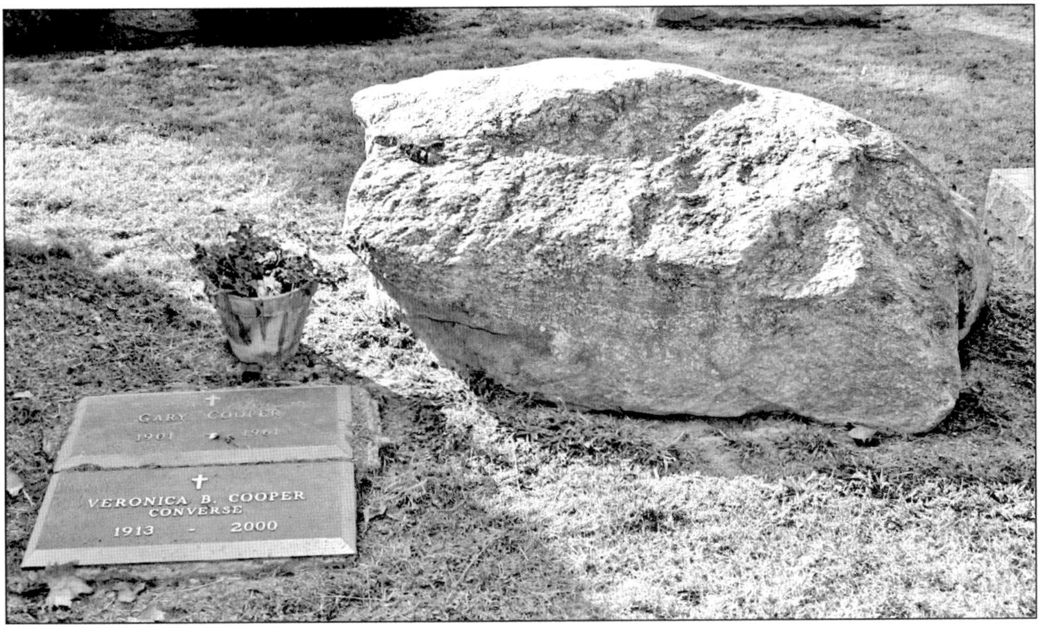

Gary Cooper won two Academy Awards, one of which was for his memorable performance in *High Noon*, in 1952. He died of lung cancer on May 13, 1961. The actor's wife, Veronica Converse Cooper (May 27, 1913–February 16, 2000), an actress and an athlete, is buried next to him. Cooper is one of several well-known names in the Sacred Hearts of Jesus and Mary Cemetery. Another is Roone Arledge, original producer of *Monday Night Football*.

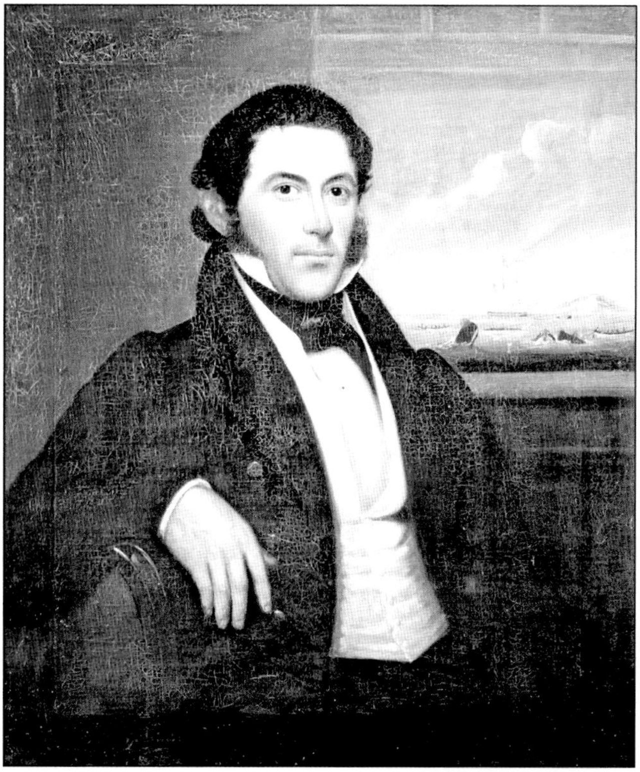

The Southampton Cemetery is the final resting place of many Cooper family members. Mercator Cooper, the captain of the whaler *Manhattan*, gave the following account to Dr. F. C. Winslow of Oaho, Hawaii. About the first of April (1845), Cooper passed a supposedly uninhabited island in the waters near Japan. He went ashore in search of turtles when he came upon 11 shipwrecked Japanese sailors. He recognized the opportunity to perform both a humanitarian, as well as diplomatic, service by returning them to their homeland. (1983.45.1 Mercator Cooper, Courtesy New Bedford Whaling Museum.)

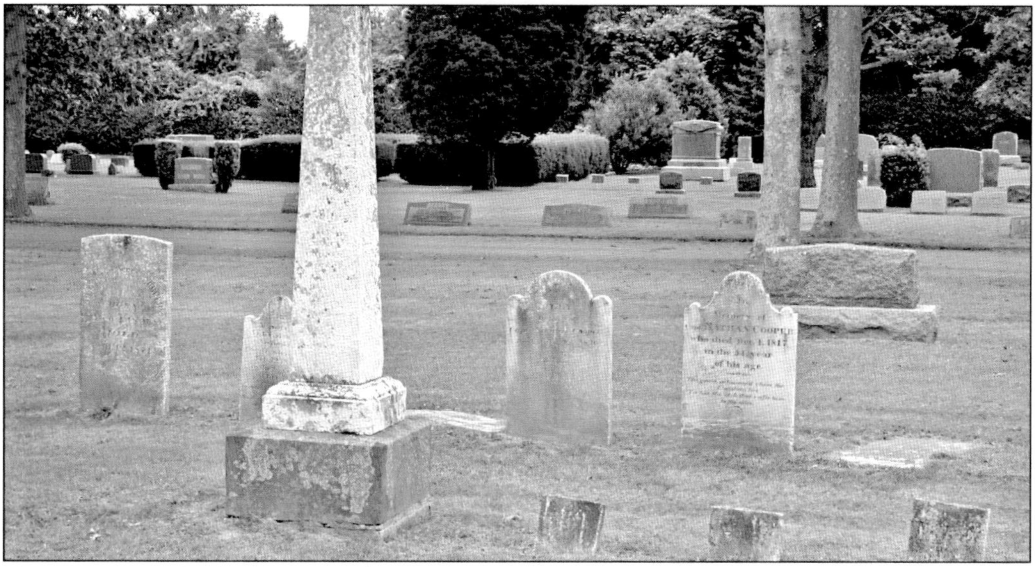

Upon entering the harbor at Jeddo, the *Manhattan* was encircled by nearly a thousand boats, many of which had deployed long lances glistening in the sun. Capt. Mercator Cooper was told, in no uncertain terms, that to attempt to go ashore would guarantee an untimely death. They were otherwise treated with the utmost civility and were showered with gifts and supplies. The *Manhattan* remained at anchor for four days. The day before it sailed away, the Japanese emperor warned Cooper never to return. The visit predated Commodore Perry's historic visit by eight years.

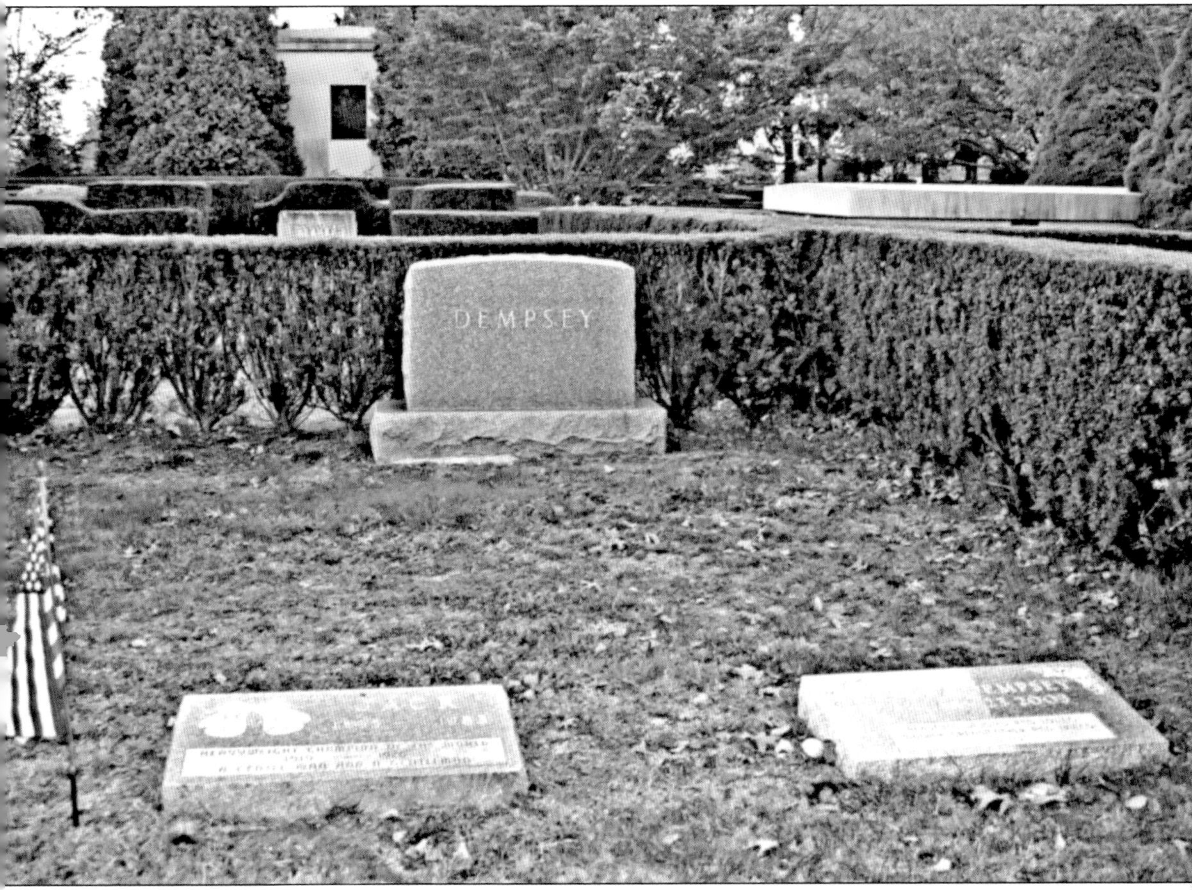

Jack Dempsey was born William Harrison Dempsey on June 24, 1895, in Manassa, Colorado. He ran away from home at age 16 and assumed the name Jack after a former fighter by that name. He won six of his first seven fights by knockouts. He eventually took the boxing title from Jess Willard, who was forced to quit after a brutal beating. Dempsey enjoyed fame as one of the world's top athletes, retaining his title until 1926. That year he faced a former marine named Gene Tunney, losing by points in 10 rounds. The rematch took place exactly one year later. Dempsey was behind on points when he sent Tunney to the canvas with a brutal left-right in the seventh round. Tunney would have been down for the count, except Dempsey, for some reason, failed to go to a neutral corner for at least five seconds before the referee started the count. Tunney got up as the referee said "nine." Given this reprieve, Tunney went on to successfully defend his boxing title.

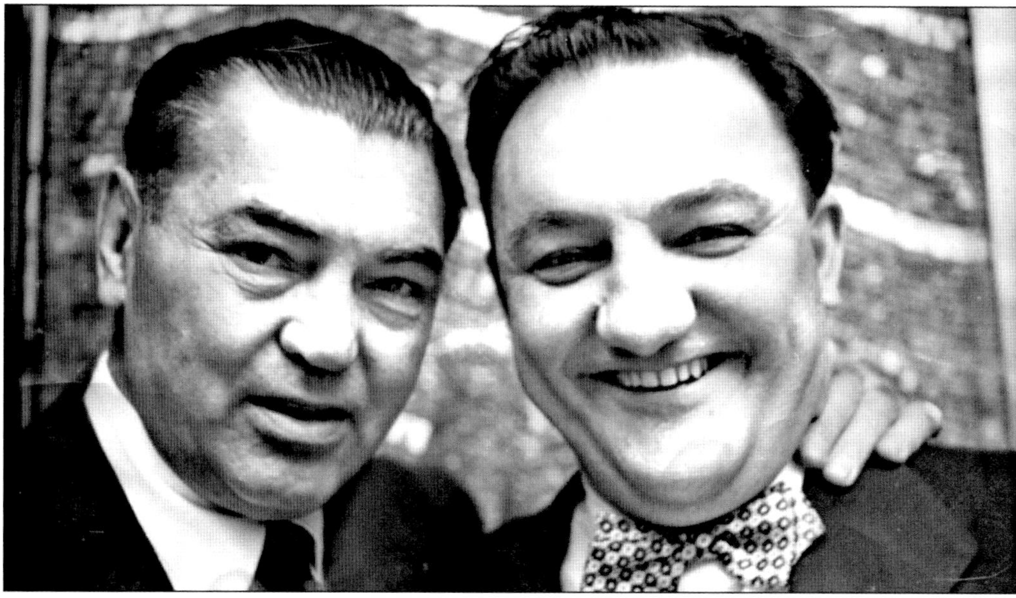

After retiring from boxing with a record of 50 knockouts, 80 wins, and 6 losses, Jack Dempsey (left) opened a sports restaurant in Times Square. The restaurant, called Jack Dempsey's, was popular with both tourists and local celebrities. Dr. Victor T. McGrattan (right), who had turned to professional boxing as a means of financing his education at Fordham University and Flower Fifth Medical School, had this photograph taken many years later, in the early 1930s. Dempsey died on May 31, 1983. He is buried in the Southampton Cemetery. (Courtesy Maryann Horan and Suzanne McGrattan.)

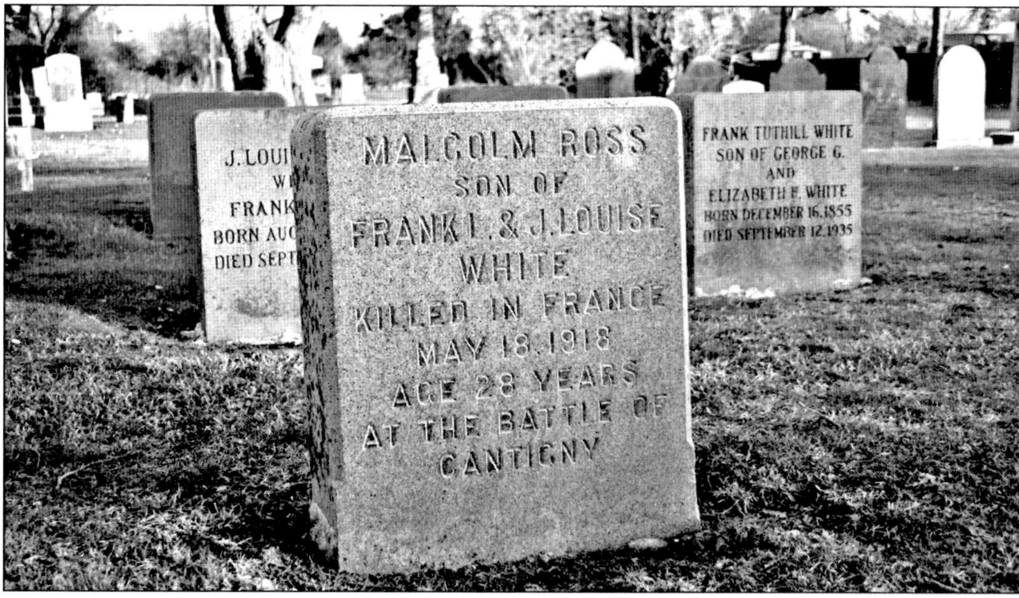

Malcolm Ross White was a first lieutenant of a machine-gun company in World War I. In one of the first engagements of U.S. forces at Cantigny, he received a citation that noted he had "Displayed meritorious conduct" and was awarded the Silver Citation for his bravery. He died in May 1918, before the famous Battle at Cantigny, which was the first engagement involving American forces. Although not of great military significance, the battle was seen as a morale booster.

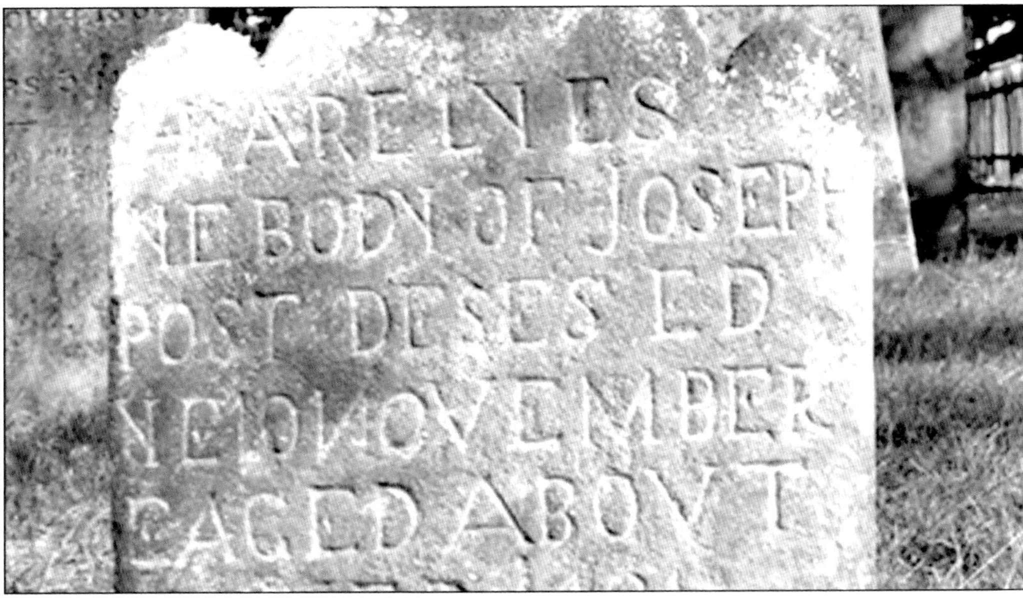

The first burial in the North End Burying Ground was in 1721. The inscription on the old stone reads, "Here lyes ye body of Joseph Post. Deceased 10 November, aged about 72. Died 1721." The footstone (now resting behind the headstone) reads, "Post Joseph, the first entared in this place." There are many soldiers of the Revolution buried here, and the grounds are well maintained by the village of Southampton. Small markers identify graves of patriots, as well as veterans of succeeding wars.

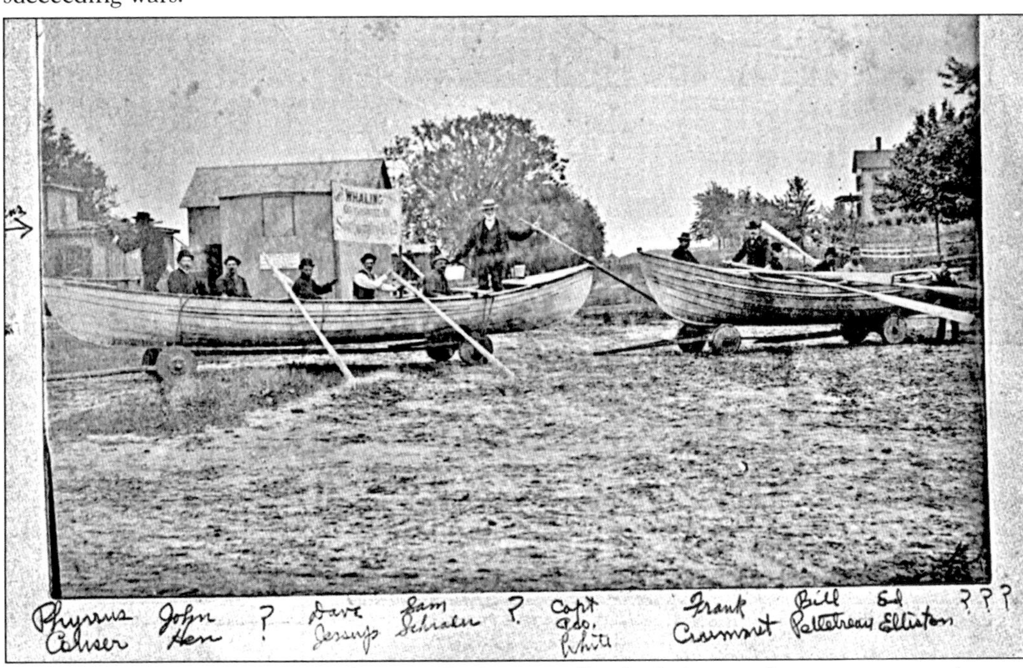

To talk of the early times on the East End is to talk of whaling and its captains and crews. Captured in this picture, taken during a parade in the village, are a number of these early mariners. The sailors manning the whaleboats include Dave Jessup, Bill Peletreau, Capt. A. White, Sid Elliston, and Pyrrhus Concer. (Courtesy Southampton Historical Museum.)

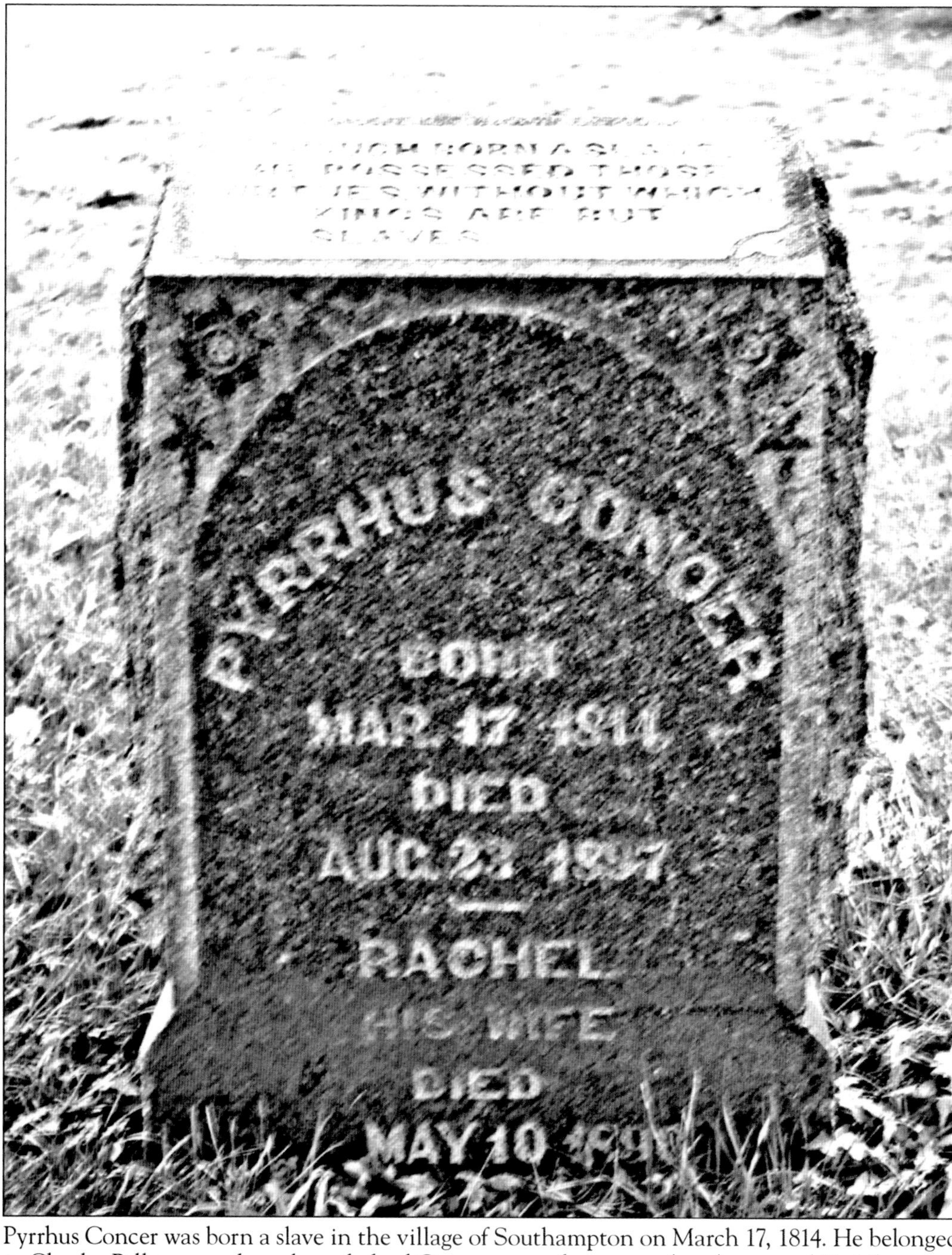

Pyrrhus Concer was born a slave in the village of Southampton on March 17, 1814. He belonged to Charles Pelletreau, who acknowledged Concer was a free man when he turned 21. Like many of his race, Concer lived the life of a mariner. In 1843, he was a member of Capt. Mercator Cooper's crew on the *Manhattan*, which entered the waters of Japan—becoming perhaps the first black man to make such a visit. In 1849, he sailed on the *Sabina* when it carried many whalers in search of California gold. Upon his return he operated a ferry service on Agawam Lake. He died on August 23, 1897. Inscribed on his tombstone are the following words: "Though born a slave, he possessed those virtues without which kings are but slaves."

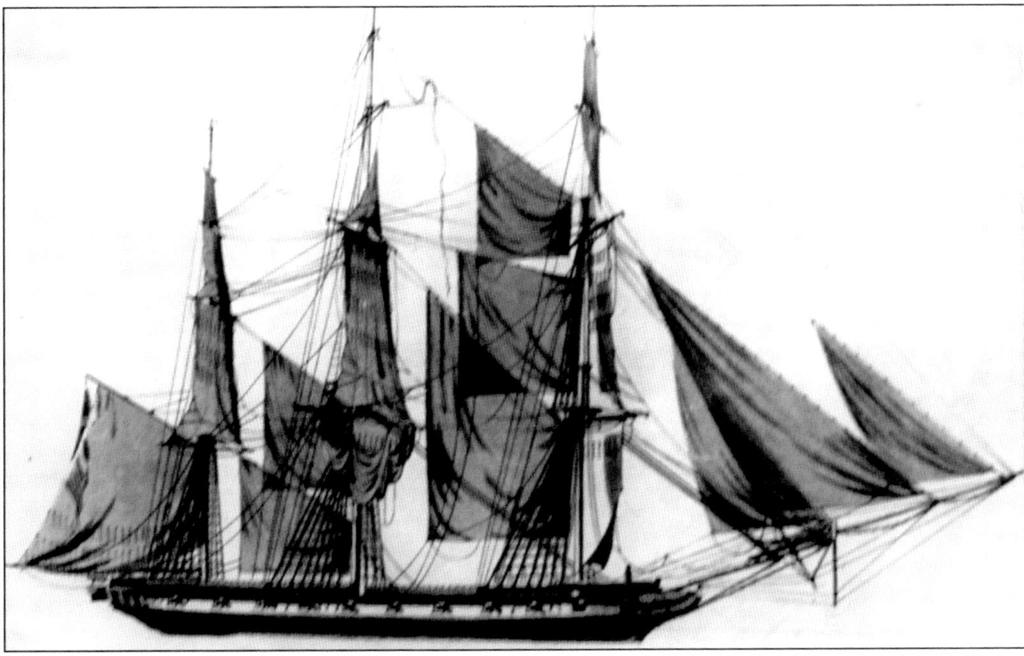

The *Sylph*, a 22-gun British sloop of war, patrolled the East End during the War of 1812. It had one encounter with the local militia on the North Fork that lasted three days. Years later, on the night of January 16, 1815, it became lost in a snowstorm and ran aground off Shinnecock Point. (Courtesy Suffolk County Historical Society.)

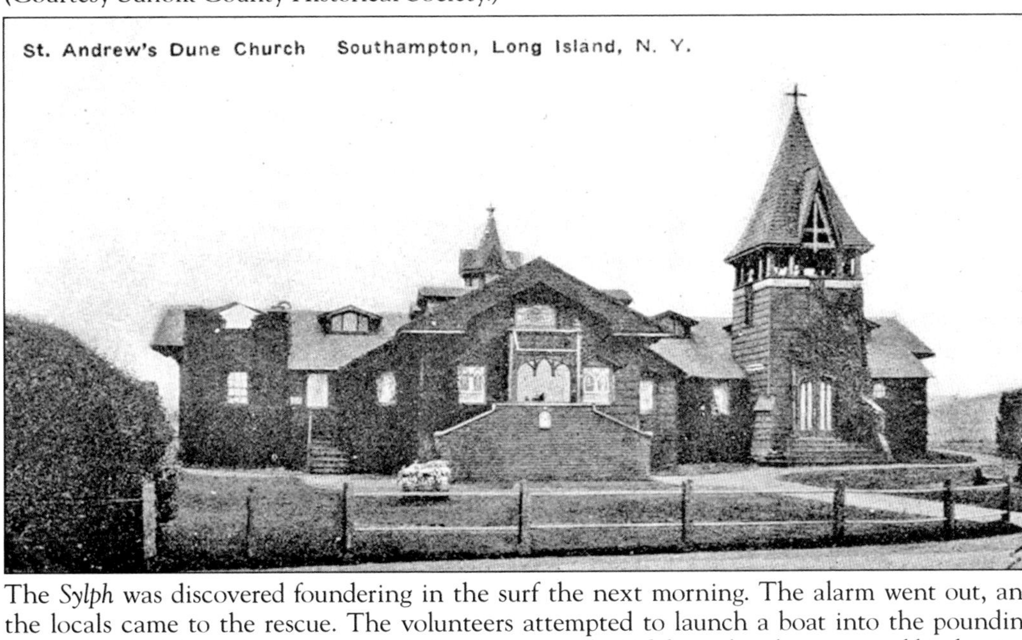

The *Sylph* was discovered foundering in the surf the next morning. The alarm went out, and the locals came to the rescue. The volunteers attempted to launch a boat into the pounding waves, but their initial attempts failed. By afternoon, the *Sylph* was breaking up, and by the time a lifeboat finally reached the vessel, the survivors among 134 officers and crew numbered only six. A spar came ashore through the surf with men lashed to it and six pair of frozen legs sticking up in the air. A plaque in St. Andrew's church commemorates the tragedy. (Courtesy Suffolk County Historical Society.)

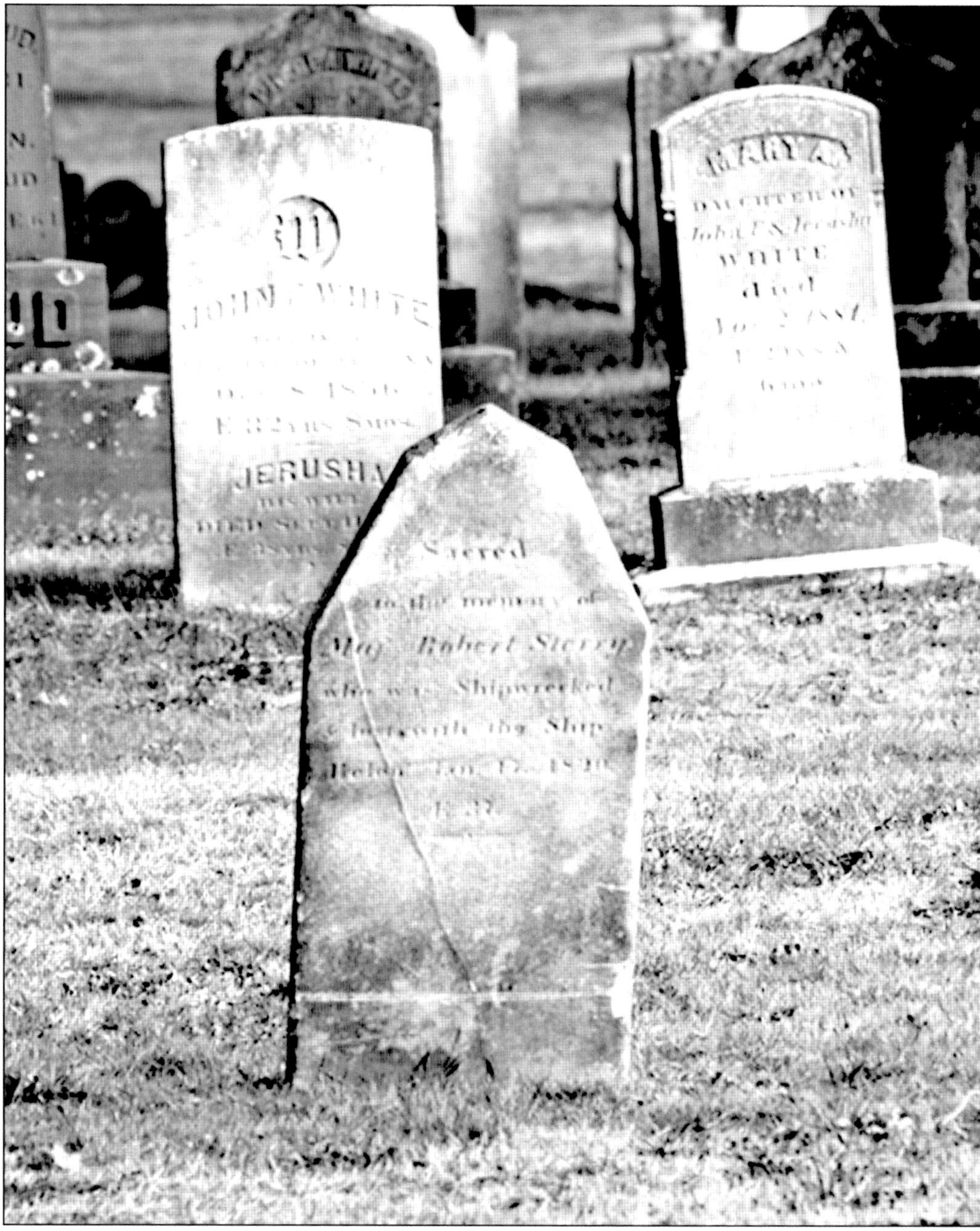

In January 1820, the *Helen*, a merchant ship bound for New York from France, ran into a fierce gale and was driven ashore and wrecked 100 miles east of its destination. All on board were lost: the captain, officers, and passengers including a Frenchman transporting a package of books for the library at West Point. Sometime later, a young woman from Sag Harbor found a package that had washed ashore. She recognized a name on the package as that of a friend's husband. The husband was the librarian of the West Point library and the brother of the lost Frenchman. And so the books reached their destination in 1821. In the North End Cemetery is a stone memorializing the tragedy: "Sacred to the memory of Major Robert Sterry, who was wrecked and lost with the ship *Helen*, Jan. 17, 1820, aged 37 years."

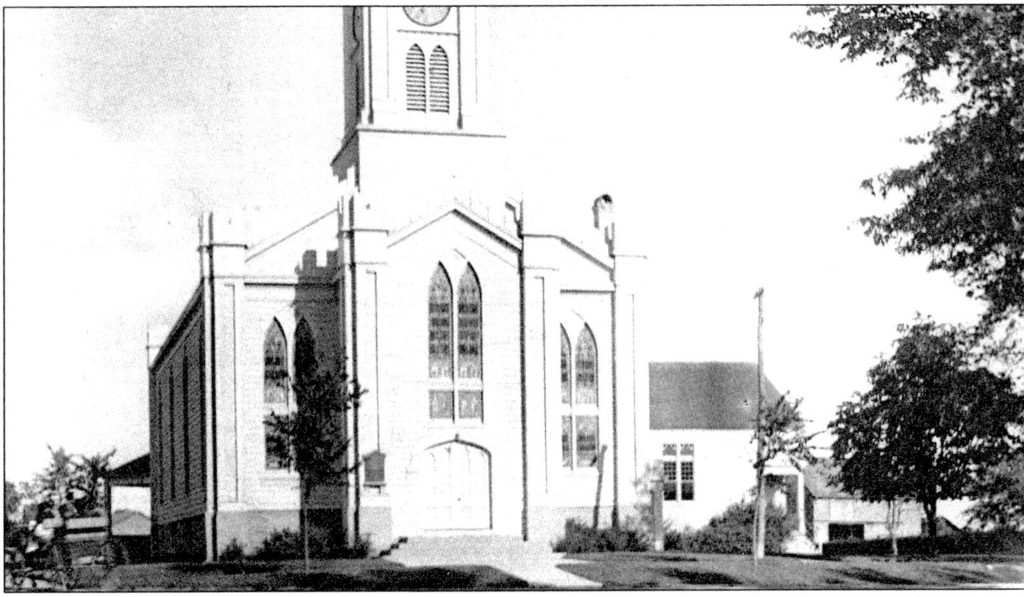

The Declaration of the Company of Men Who Founded Southampton reads as follows: "Our true interest and meaning if that when our Plantacon is laid out by those appointed that there shall be a church gathered and constituted according to the mind of Christ, that there we do freely lay downe our power of ordering and disposing of the Plantacon and of receiving inhabitants or any other Thinge that may tende to the good and welfare of ye inhabitants at the feet of Christ and His Church." (Courtesy Suffolk County Historical Society.)

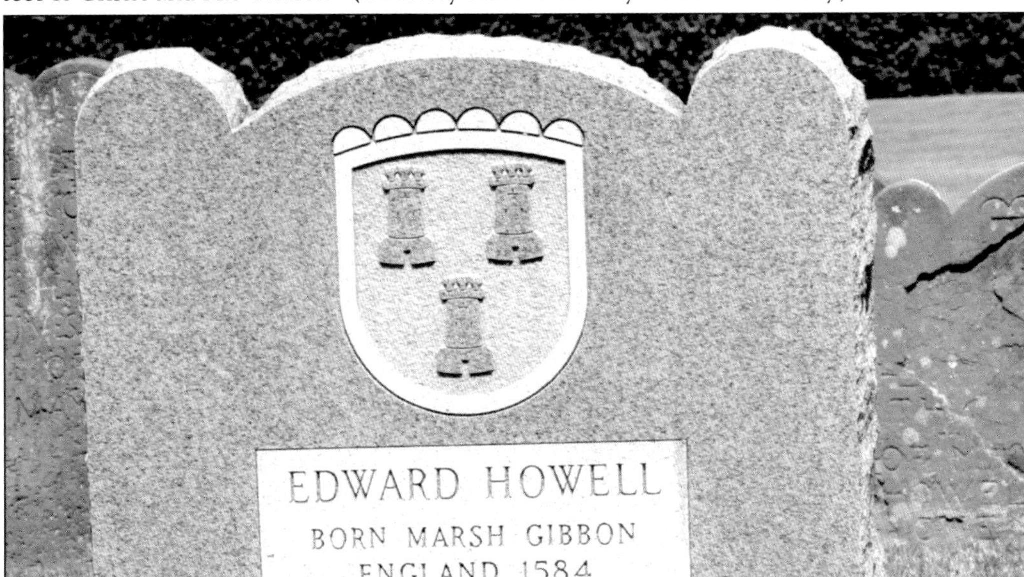

The colonists were led by Edward Howell. The "undertakers" were greeted at their landing place in North Sea by a group of friendly Shinnecocks. They made a treaty with the American Indians, under which, "for due consideration of sixteen coats and also three score bushels of corn to be paid upon lawful demand September, 1641, and further that the above named English shall defend us from the unjust violence of whatever. . . ." The Howell stone is carved with the family crest, a common practice at that time in England.

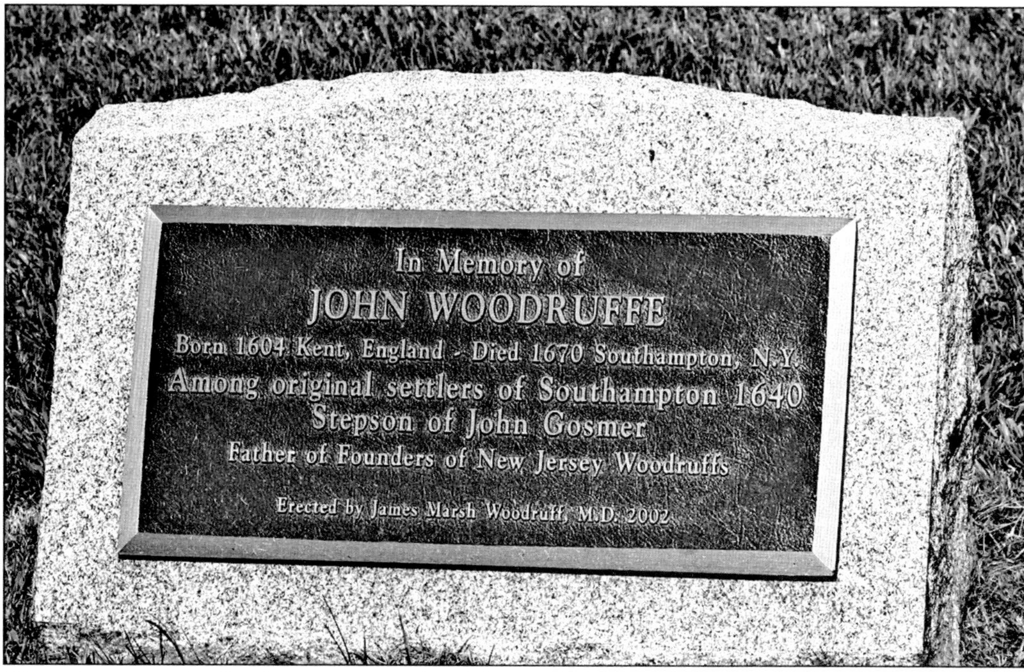

This plaque reads, "In Memory of John Woodruffe, born 1604 Kent, England – died 1670 Southampton, N.Y. Among original settlers of Southampton 1640. Stepson of John Gosmer. Father of founders of New Jersey Woodruffs. Erected by James March Woodruff, M.D. 2002."

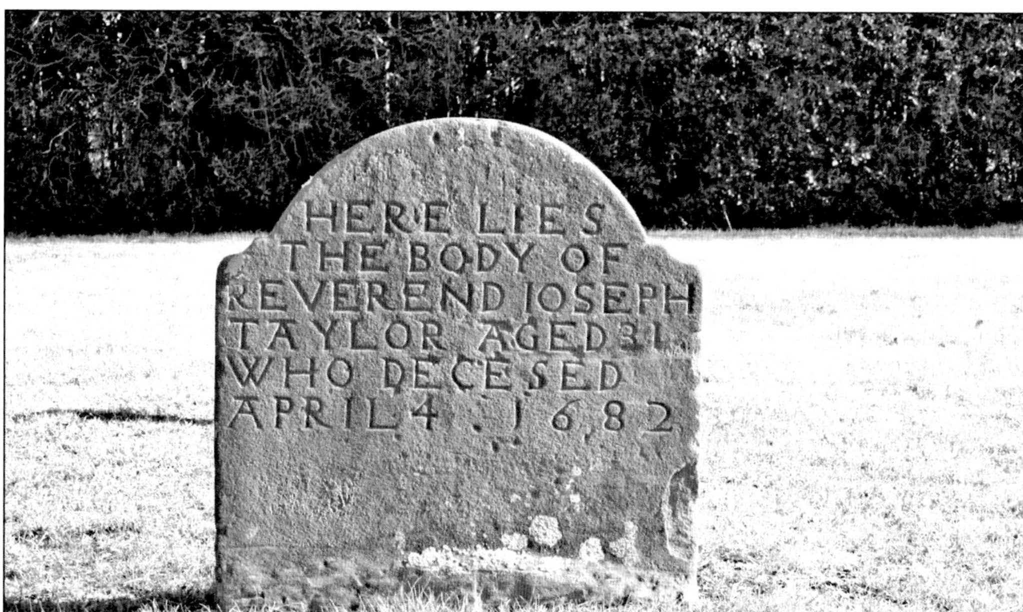

Rev. Joseph Taylor died in April 1682 at age 31. He was the fourth minister of the Southampton church. His salary statement reads, in part: 100 pounds per annum, to "bee paid either in winter wheat at five shillings per bushel or summer wheat at five shillings sixpence per bushel, or Indian corne at two shillings sixpence pr. Bushel, . . . or whalebone at eight pence per pound." In any event, it was to be collected by the constable.

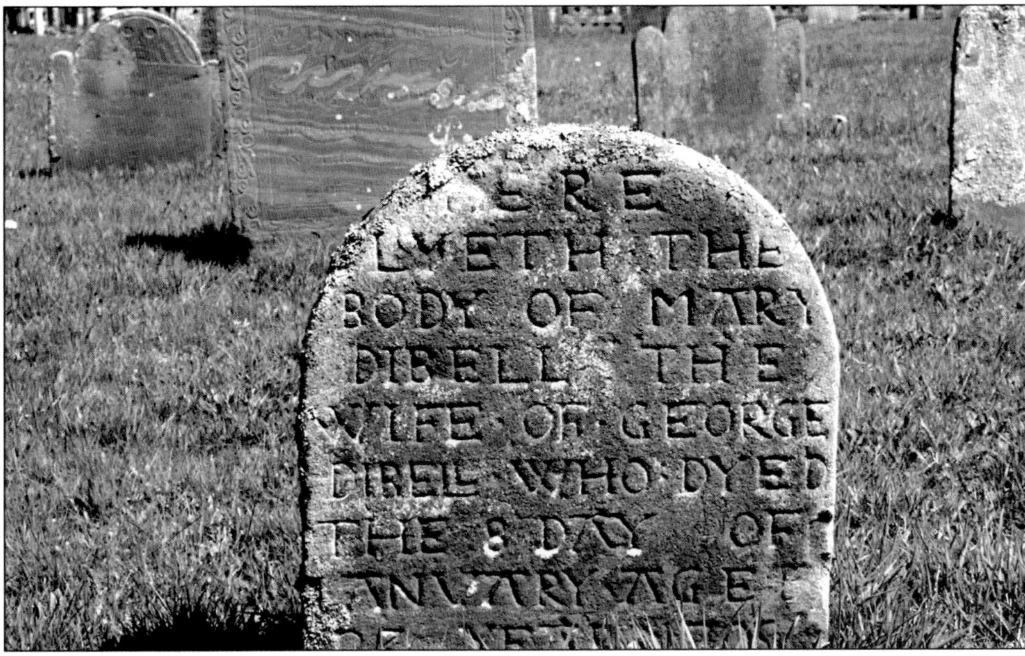

The tombstone of Mary Dibell, who died in 1706 at age 23, has the bold lettering typical of the Connecticut Valley style of the late 1600s. The deep carving was possible due to the soft red sandstone used for the gravestone. The letter A is the signature style of James Stanclift (d. 1712). Also typical is the dot used to separate individual words.

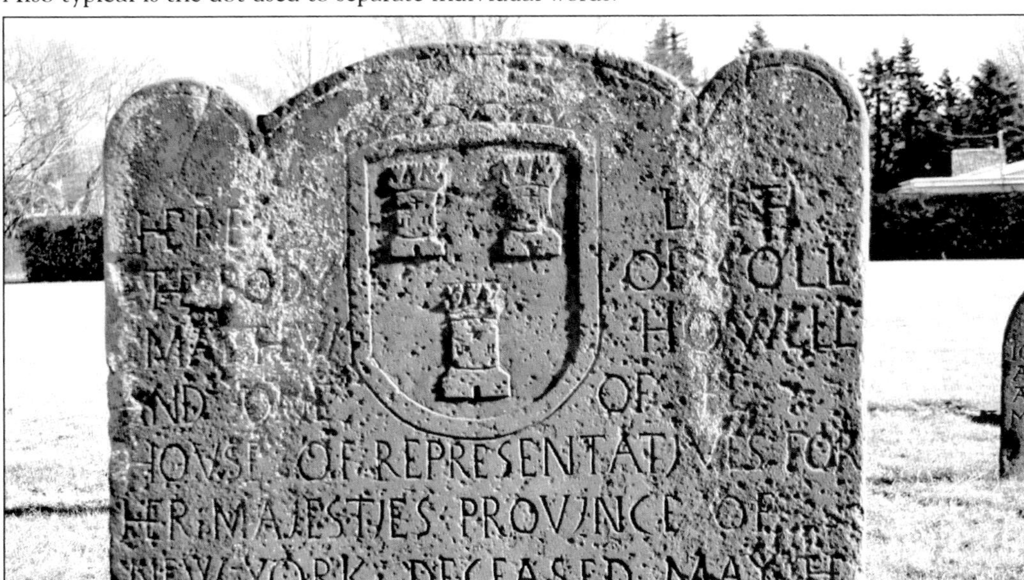

Col. Matthew Howell was a representative for Suffolk County in the Colonial legislature. On April 17, 1701, he was "honored with an expulsion" for presenting a paper considered "disloyal to His Majesty." The paper "we should now regard simply as breathing only the sentiments of a larger liberty than that vouchsafed to the colonists at that day." Howell was promptly returned by his constituents to the legislature, where he continued to fight for the rights of the colonists. The seeds of the rebellion were planted early.

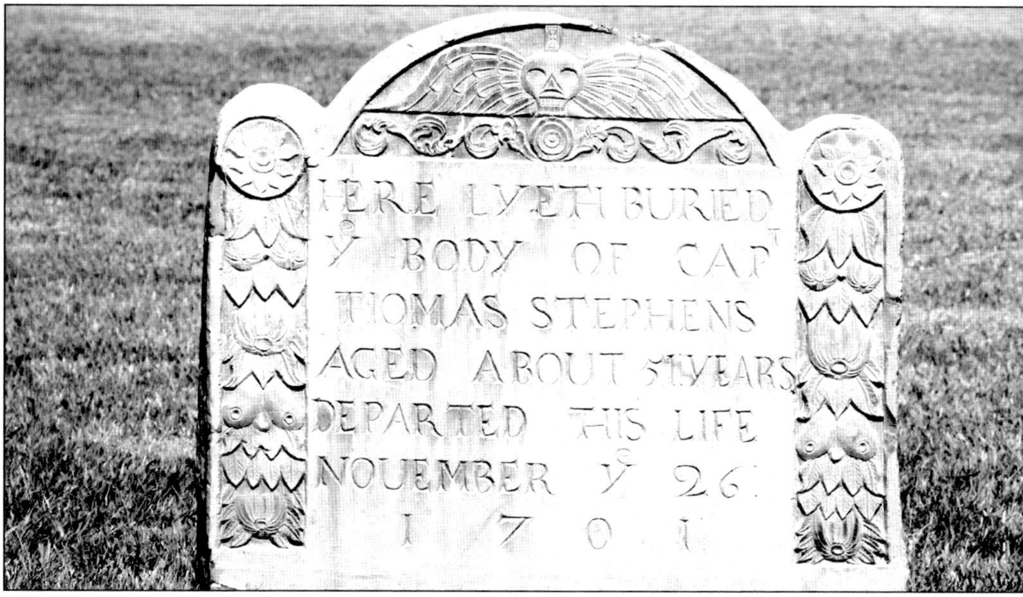

The negative view of death in the early Colonial days was commonly reflected in the use of the winged death's head. In this example the view is further enhanced by an hourglass perched atop the skull. Capt. Stephens had a duty to report the status of the drift whale catch to the chief secretary at New York when the governors attempted to cash in on the growing industry.

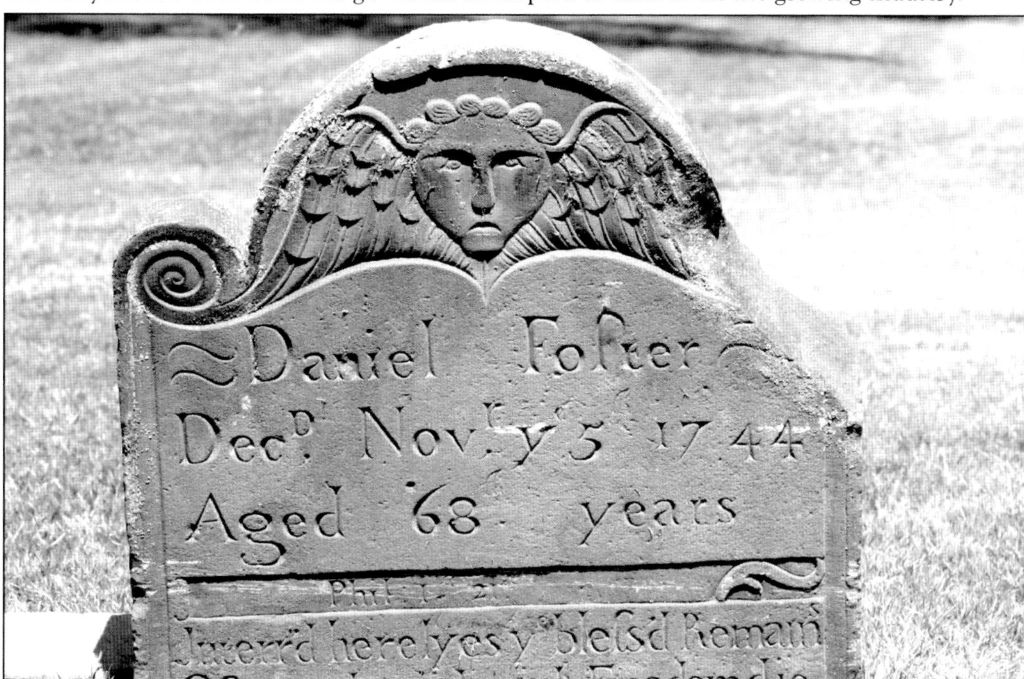

Daniel Foster's tombstone is carved in the Jamaica style. Foster was on "ye Suffolk Muster Roll Regiment of Anno Don 1715." He served in Southampton Company No. 2, under Capt. Isaac Halsey. Foster died in November 1744 at age 68. The gravestone is sinking, but the inscription at the bottom can still be identified as Philippians 1: 21.

Five

Flying Point to Poxebogue

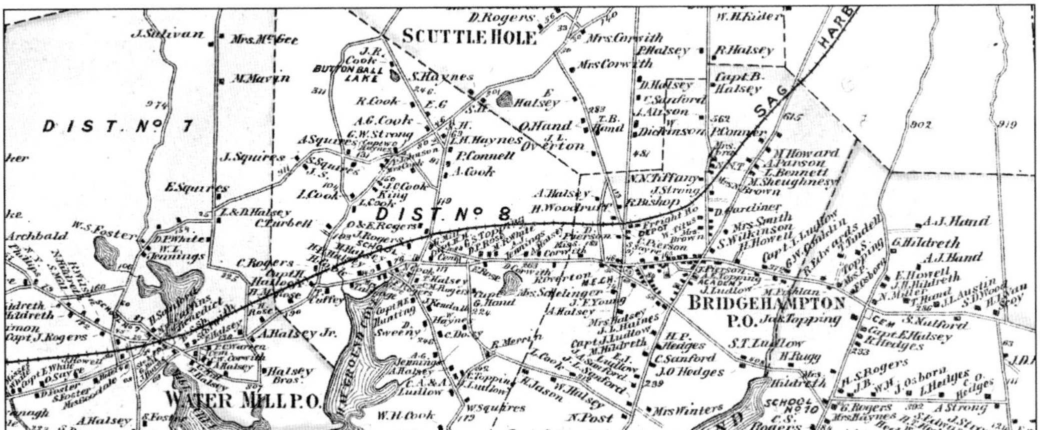

The settlers who had first landed at Oyster Bay told the Dutch who had detained them that "if the land were good" many more would come. And out east it was found to be "Good Ground." As a result, it was not long before the limits of "Old Town" expanded eastward. In fact, "Undeterred, by the constant danger of savage foes [the Narragansetts & Pequots], the little settlement continued to push on and extend its limits, and in January 1653 there was made the 'Division of lande called Sagaponack,' the land was so laid out extending from Flying Point to the East Hampton boundary line, and lying mainly between Mecox Road, Fairfield and Bridge Lanes on the north and the ocean on the south, on this tract, undoubtedly the first settlement was made at Sagg. . . ." —*History of Southampton Town*. There are many old cemeteries in the eastern portion of the village. The first at Flying Point is a well-maintained burial ground just south of Montauk Highway. (Courtesy Stony Brook University, Special Map Collection.)

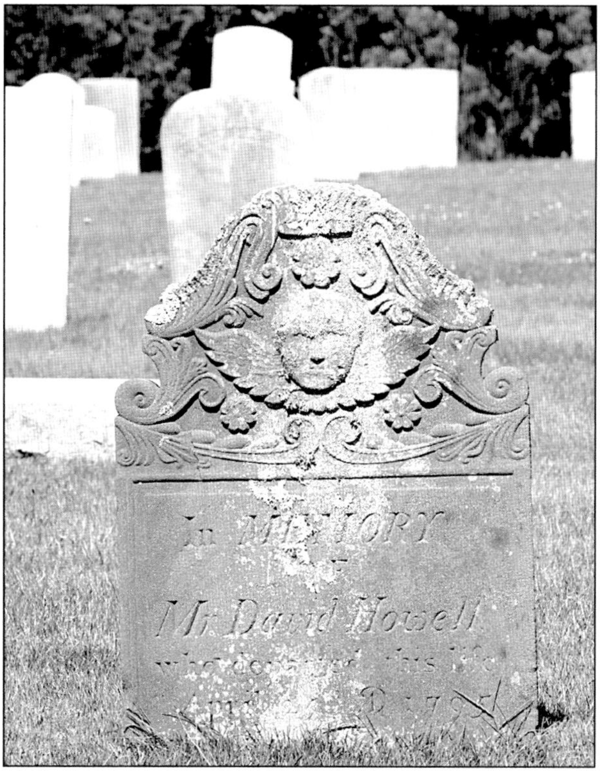

Historian Richard Welch notes that there was a marked absence of the New England–style tombstones on the East End during the Revolutionary period. When the war ended and carvings reappeared, both the style and materials had changed significantly. The earlier popular slate no longer prevailed. The David Howell gravestone in the Flying Point Cemetery is an excellent example of the post-Revolutionary period. The red sandstone, softer and easier to engrave, encouraged a more elaborate carving. And the Connecticut Valley craftsmen took full advantage of the opportunity. Howell, a signer of the Articles of the Association, died on April 25, 1795.

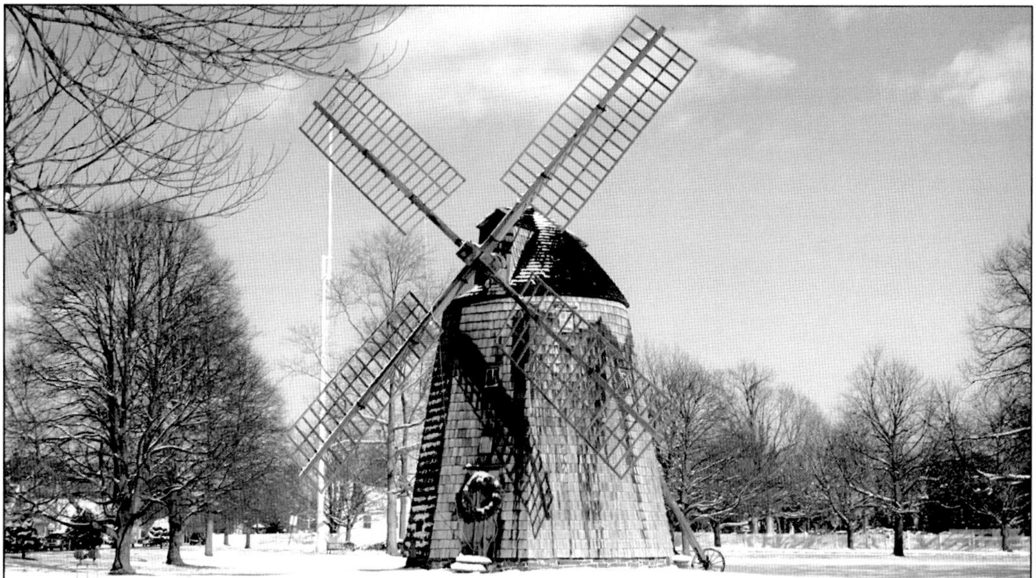

The early residents of Watermill engaged in many routine activities of the colonists. There were several types of mills in the village over the years. These included sawmills, gristmills, and fulling mills, which produced local woolen products. A windmill now stands on the commons, marking the entrance to the village. Also on the green is a monument to the local residents who served in the wars. The cemetery lies adjacent to the green. The land for the cemetery was part of a 40-acre grant from the Ludlam family.

Col. Edwin Rose was born in Hayground on February 14, 1807. He graduated from West Point in 1830 and served in the Black Hawk and Seminole Wars. In May 1832, Black Hawk led his people from the Iowa Territory, hoping to return home to Illinois. The U.S. Army, however, pursued and defeated Black Hawk at Bad Axe, on the Mississippi River. (The chief was memorialized in 1926, when the Chicago hockey team took his name.) (Image of Black Hawk [P&S–1920.0557] Courtesy Chicago Historical Society.)

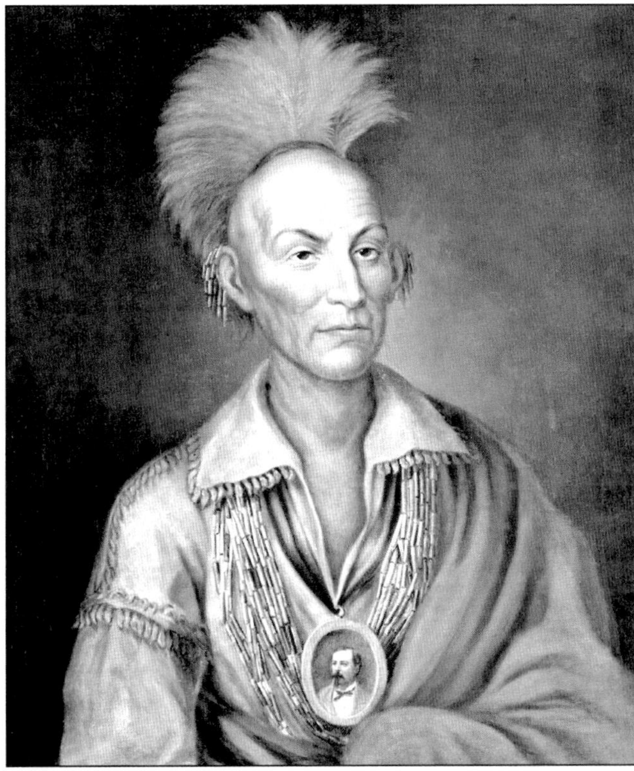

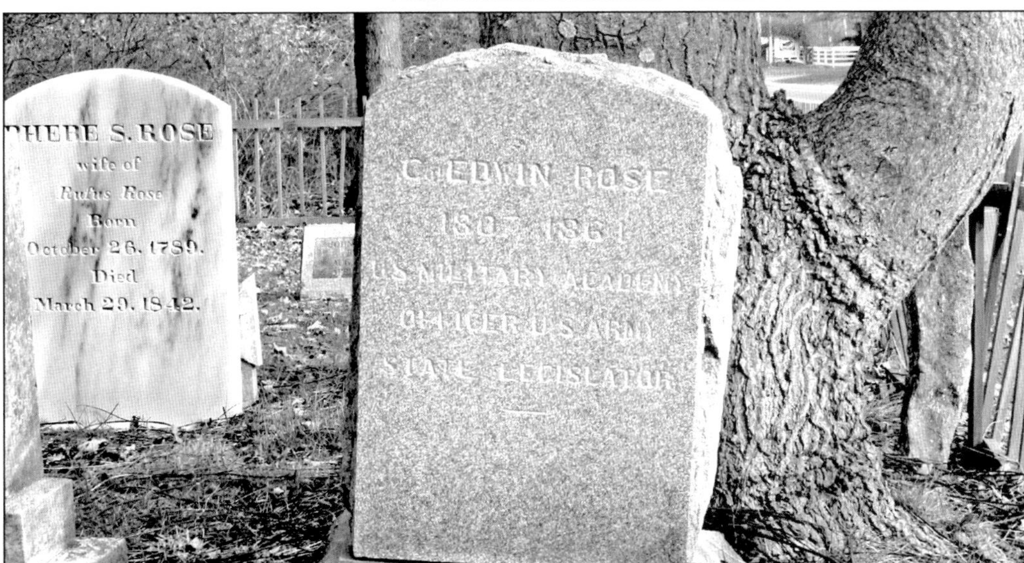

Edwin Rose later entered the service of the Territory of Michigan as a surveyor and did a survey for the Michigan Central Railroad. He then returned to Bridgehampton and served as a justice of the peace and a member of the legislature. At the outbreak of the Civil War, in 1861, he was commissioned colonel of the 81st New York Volunteers and participated in the Peninsular campaign. But his health prevented him from remaining at the front, and Pres. Abraham Lincoln appointed him provost marshal for the district of Long Island. Rose died on January 12, 1864.

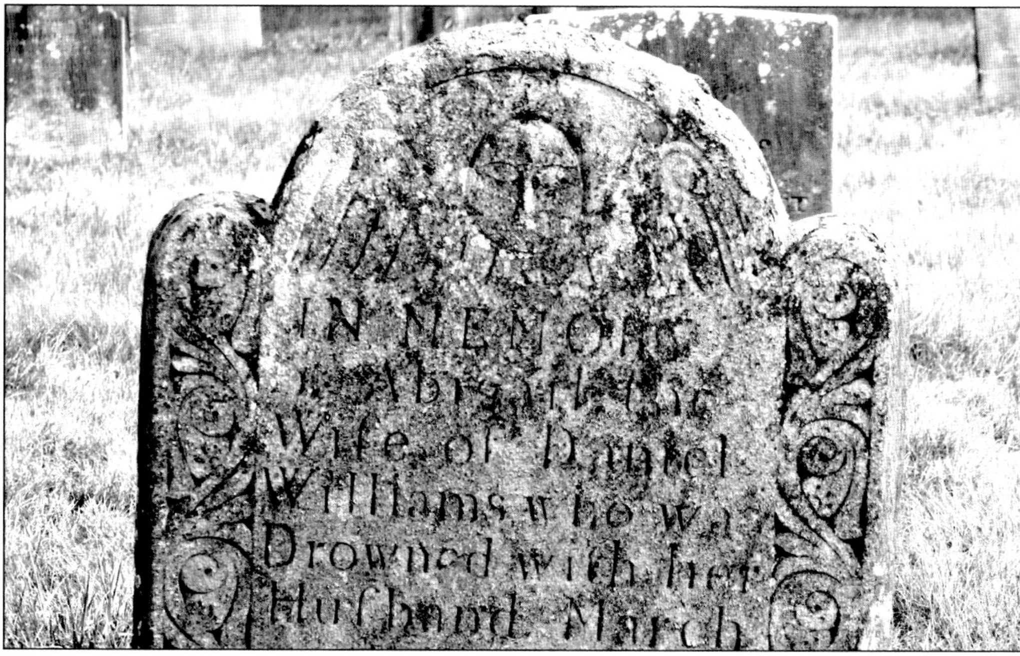

On March 25, 1764, Abigail Hand married Daniel Williams of Seabrook, Connecticut. The groom was taking his new bride to his home a few nautical miles north across Long Island Sound in a whaleboat when a squall developed and the boat foundered. The bodies were recovered, and the bride and groom were laid to rest side-by-side in the Hayground Cemetery.

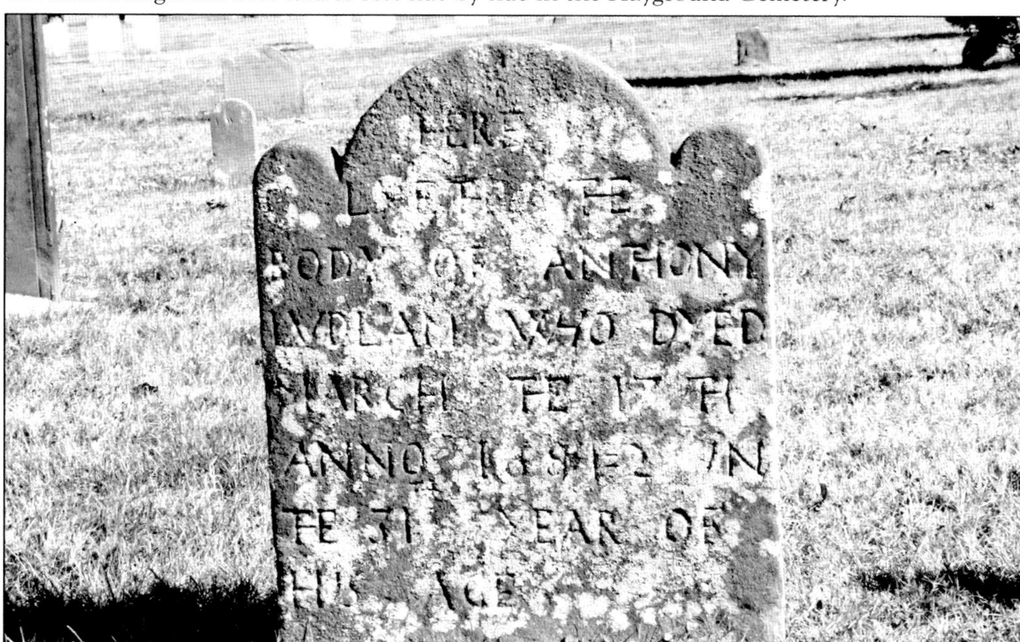

Anthony Ludlum was an early settler in Mecox. He is listed in the town records as one of the 10 "Eastern Men" in 1657. He owned about eight acres, and, as most men in the area, he engaged in shore whaling. In 1670, he hired several Shinnecocks, known for their skills in that endeavor. He died on March 17, 1681/2, and his gravestone is the earliest in Mecox.

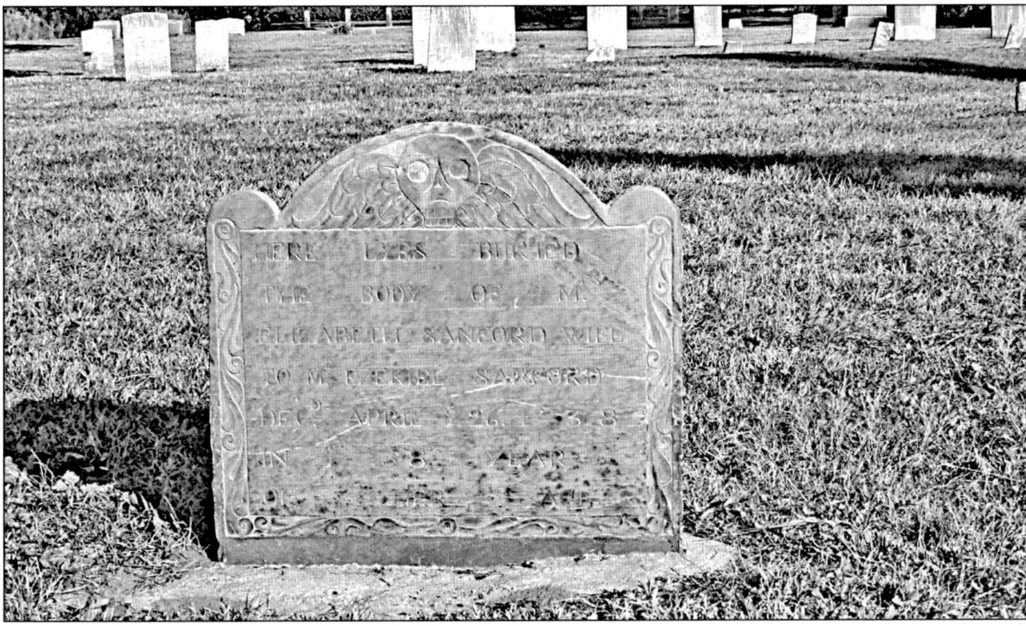

Ezekiel Sanford built the first bridge in Mecox in 1686. The Sagg Mecox Bridge is thought to have given the community its name. Sanford was another of the early residents of Mecox. Along with building bridges, he held a contract from the town to make cartwheels. The earliest Sanford tombstone in the Mecox burying ground is that of M. Elizabeth Sanford, wife of M. Ezekiel Sanford. She died on April 26, 1738, at age 58.

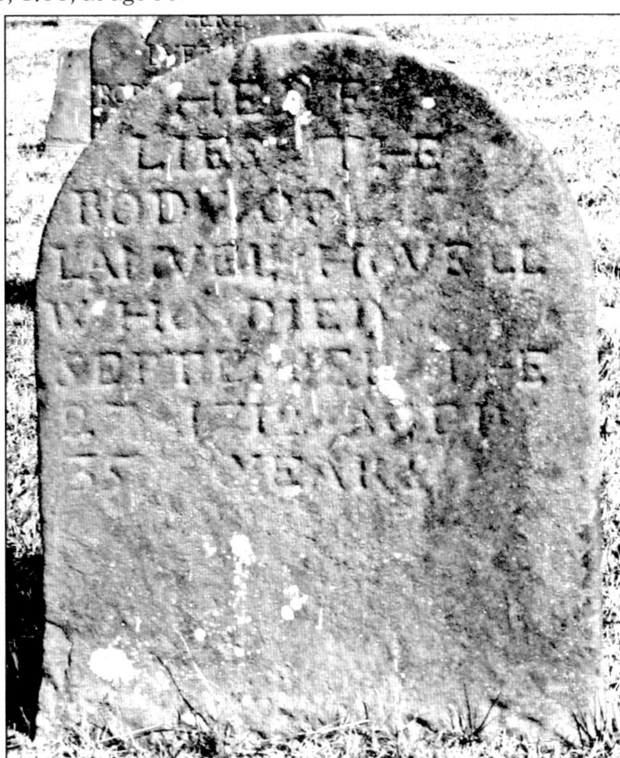

Lemuel Howell's name appears in the 1715 Bridgehampton Muster Roll. He was part owner of a windmill on the triangle. The local militia was required to drill three times a year on the triangle, which doubled as a parade ground. Each man was equipped with a flintlock musket with bayonet—perhaps not the best idea, since, "They used to have some jolly times in the afternoon . . . after they made sundry calls at the old Bull's Head Inn," according to historian James Truslow Adams.

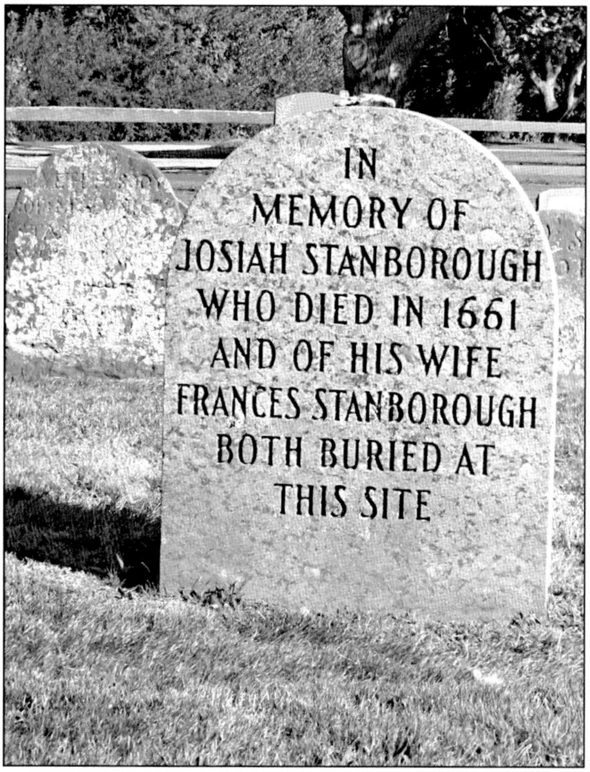

Josiah Stanborough, originally from Stanstead in Kent, England, came to Southampton from Essex County, Massachusetts, in 1643. Town records state that Stanborough was brought into court with his son Peregrine, who had been found guilty of stealing fruit from a neighbor. Josiah was placed in the stocks for refusing to whip his son in the presence of competent witnesses, and Peregrine was sent to the whipping post.

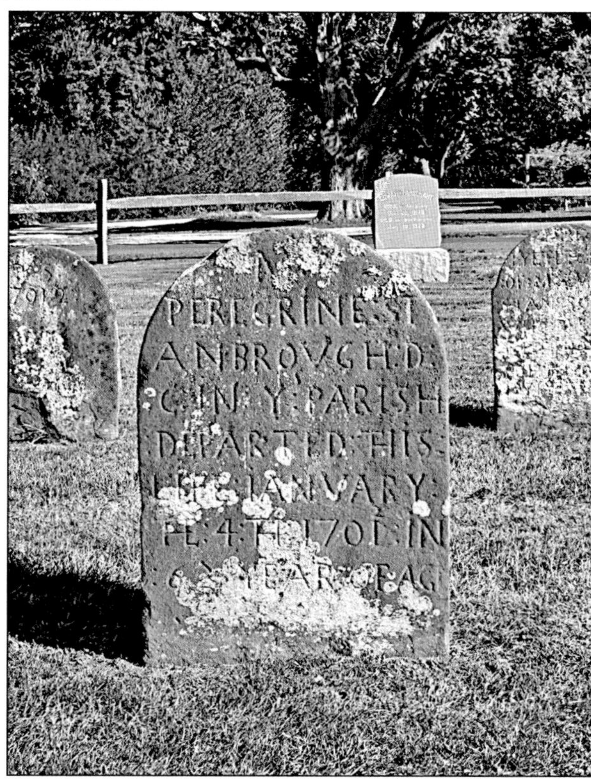

Peregrine Stanborough, son of Josiah Stanborough, was probably the first white child born in Southampton. His name appears in the Sagg census of 1698, along with the names of 118 other males and 103 females. The total population at that time was 222, which represented about one-third of the total population of Southampton Town. The census also notes a total of 83 blacks and 152 Native Americans living there as well.

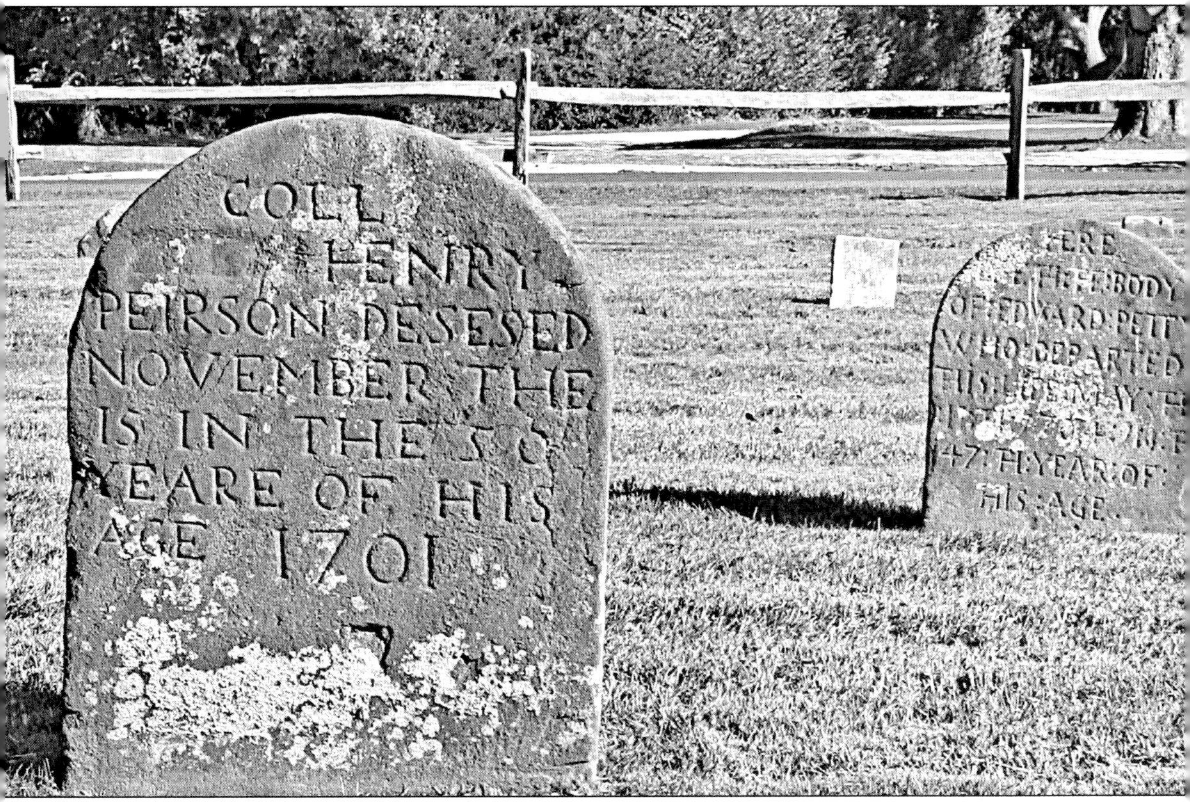

Lt. Col. Henry Peirson was a member of the Colonial Assembly as a representative from Suffolk County from 1691 to 1701 and Speaker of the House from 1693 to 1695. The governments of the 13 colonies had many elements in common. Each had an assembly, usually elected local citizens. Voting was restricted to free white males and often further restricted by property ownership and church affiliation. The assembly was responsible for initiating the budget, which was connected with support for the militia. It generally met for one brief session. As the Revolution grew nearer, conflicts with the governor increased, often resulting in the dissolution of the assembly. Peirson died in November 1701, at age 50.

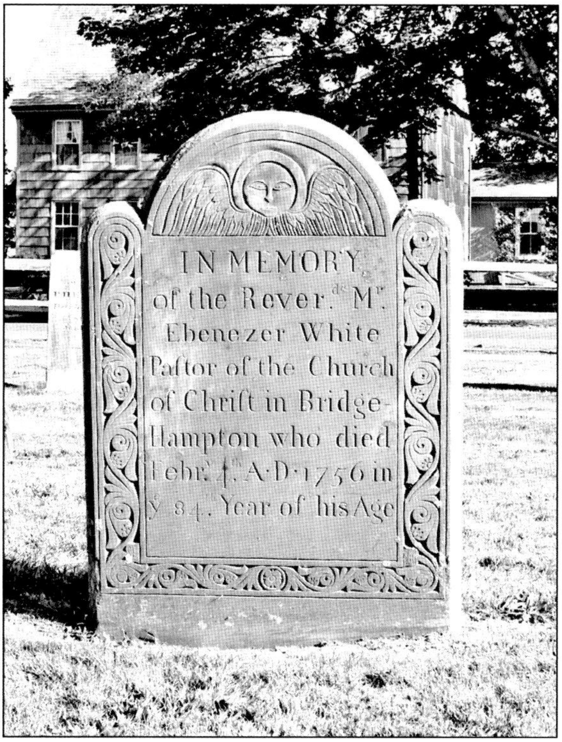

The Rev. Ebenezer White died on February 4, 1756, at age 84. He lived opposite the burying ground. In fact, it was common practice at that time to locate the cemetery near a residence out of concern that the graves might otherwise be subject to desecration. As previously noted, the early churches were of no particular denomination. White was the first pastor of the Church of Christ of Bridgehampton.

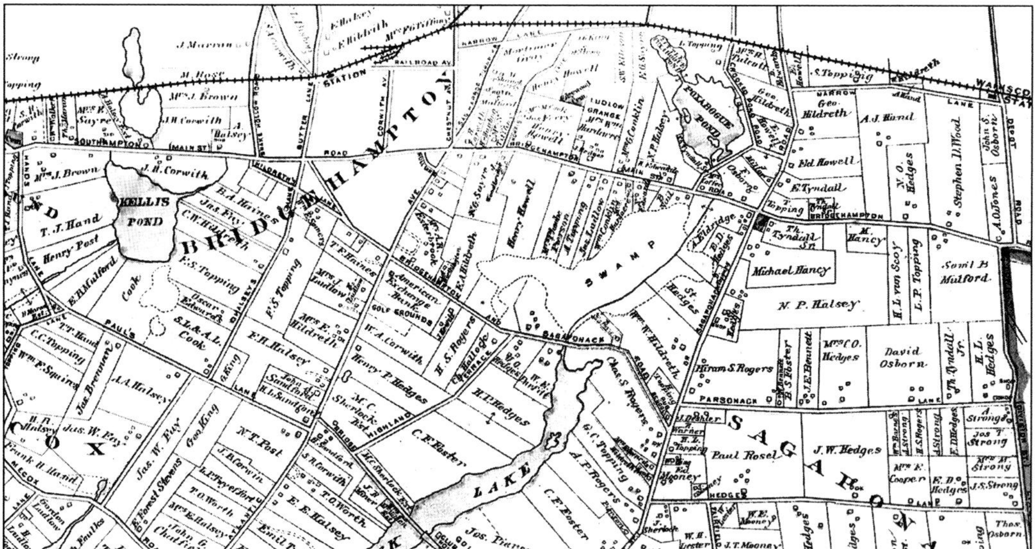

The village of Bridgehampton is located at the eastern extremity of the town of Southampton. The first reference to the name in the town records is in 1699 in regards to a land transaction. The original colonist's name for the area was Bull's Head. A man named John Wicks ran Bull's Head Tavern. When historian Richard M. Bayles visited the village in 1874, he observed that the name Bull's Head "is still used to some extent at the present time, but the refined spirit of the day has nearly abolished the frightful appellation." (Courtesy Stony Brook University, Special Map Collection.)

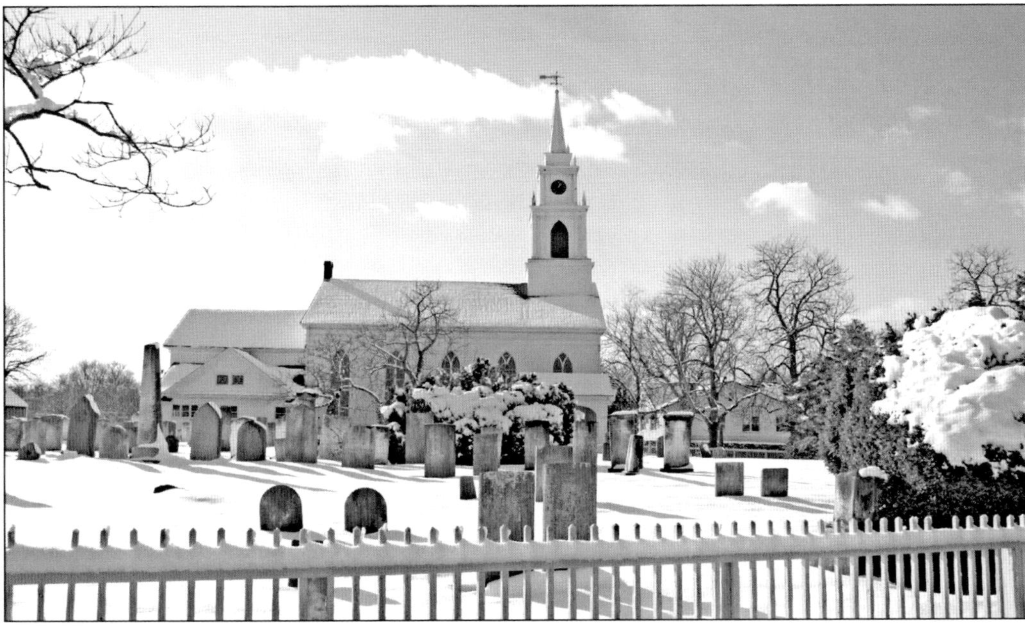

Poxebogue lies just east of Bridgehampton, virtually at the dividing line between the townships of Southampton and East Hampton. Bridgehampton has two cemeteries: Edgewood and an old burial ground adjacent to the Presbyterian church. The First Church of Bridgehampton is said to have been built in 1670. The Poxebogue Cemetery is located on the south side of Montauk Highway.

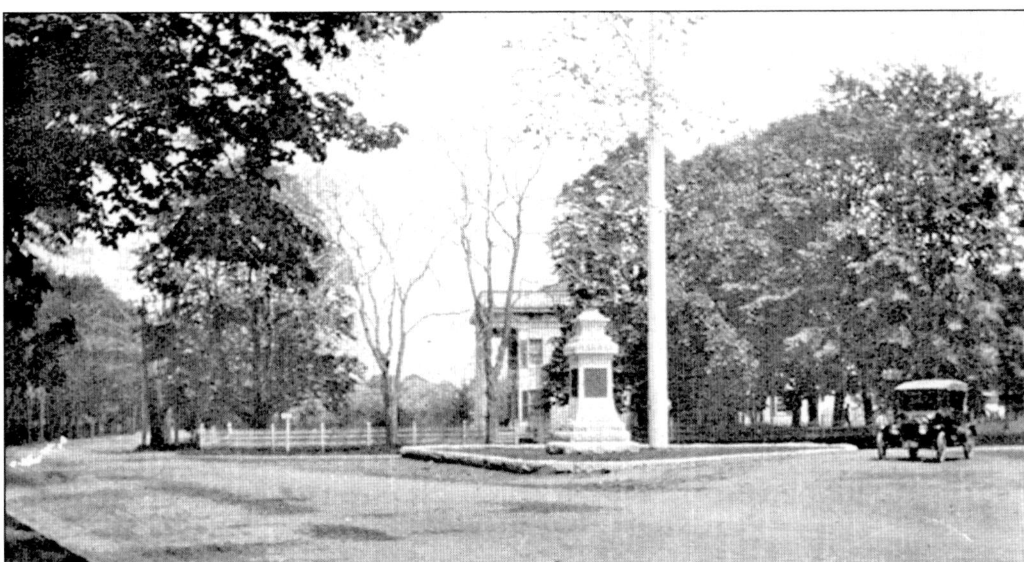

Virtually every village and hamlet in the Hamptons has a war memorial. The practice started after the Civil War. "What has occurred in this case must never recur in similar cases. Human nature will not change. In any future great national trial, compared with the men of this, we shall have as weak and as strong, as silly and as wise, as bad and as good. Let us therefore study the incidents of this, as philosophy to learn the wisdom from, and none of them as wrongs to be revenged." —Pres. Abraham Lincoln. (Courtesy Suffolk County Historical Society.)

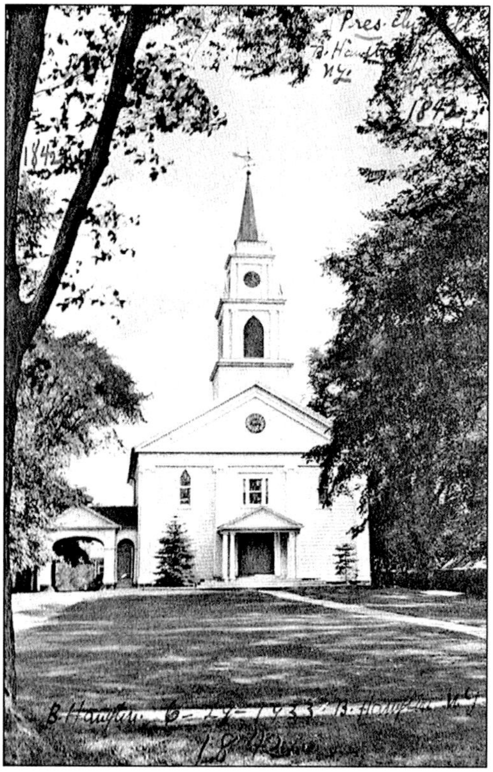

The Rev. Epher Whittaker wrote that the first churches were neither Presbyterian nor Congregational, as the terms are understood today. It was the civil government that established the church and gave a settlement to the pastors. The town, in turn, levied a tax from the citizens and paid the pastor's salary. If a townsman was found delinquent, his property was subject to seizure. A proviso of a grant in 1712 for 20 acres was to be used as "a parsonage for a Presbyterian minister and no other." (Courtesy Suffolk County Historical Society.)

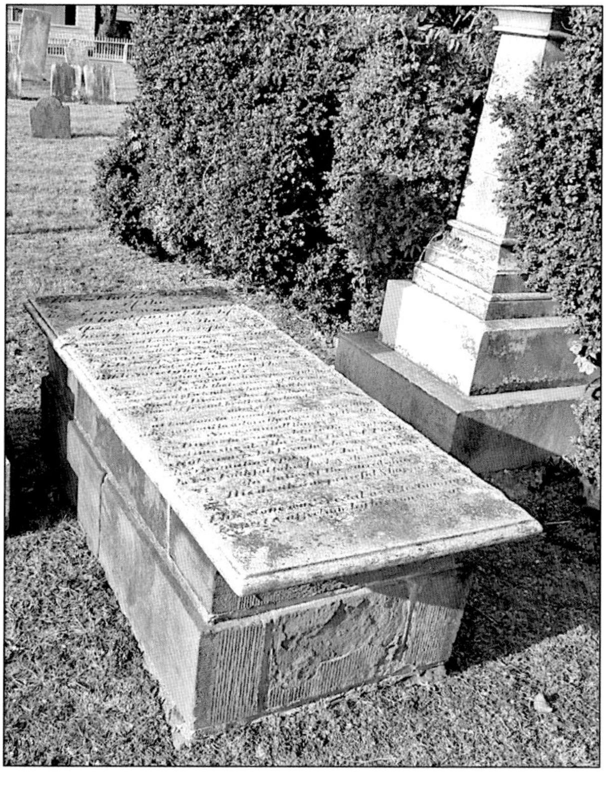

Judge Henry Hedges held, however, that the church was Congregational until 1747. In any event, engaging a minister needed to be ratified by the people of Bridgehampton. When the Rev. Aaron Woolworth was ordained, it was not by the Presbytery, but by a council. The agreement said, in part, "These presents Witnesseth an agreement made Betweene Mr. Aaron Woolworth, minister of the Gospel on the one part, and the subscribers Hereunto, inhabitants of the Parish of Bridge Hampton on the other part. . . ."

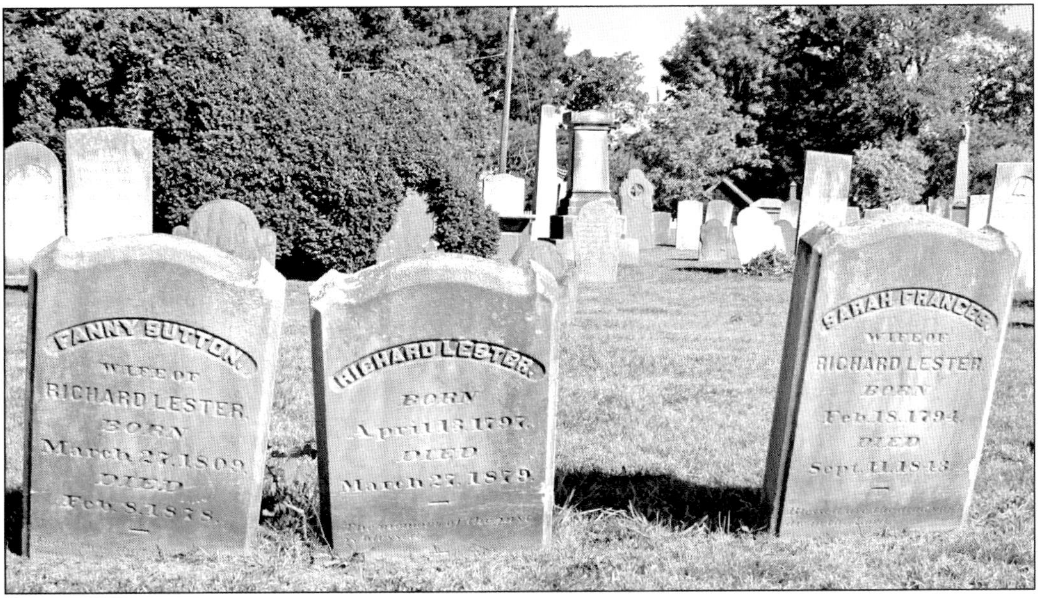

Judge Henry Hedges wrote, "When a man deprived of educational instruction, unlettered, can without books kept or a scrap of writing, . . . carrying in his head all the details of purchase sales, payment, sums, circumstances. That man is a born genius, and that Richard Lester could do. He could drive 150 cattle of a dozen different persons to Montauk, get them together at Montauk when the pasture season was ended, drive off to each owner out of the herd his quota, and do it all without with no memorandum, by sheer force of iron memory."

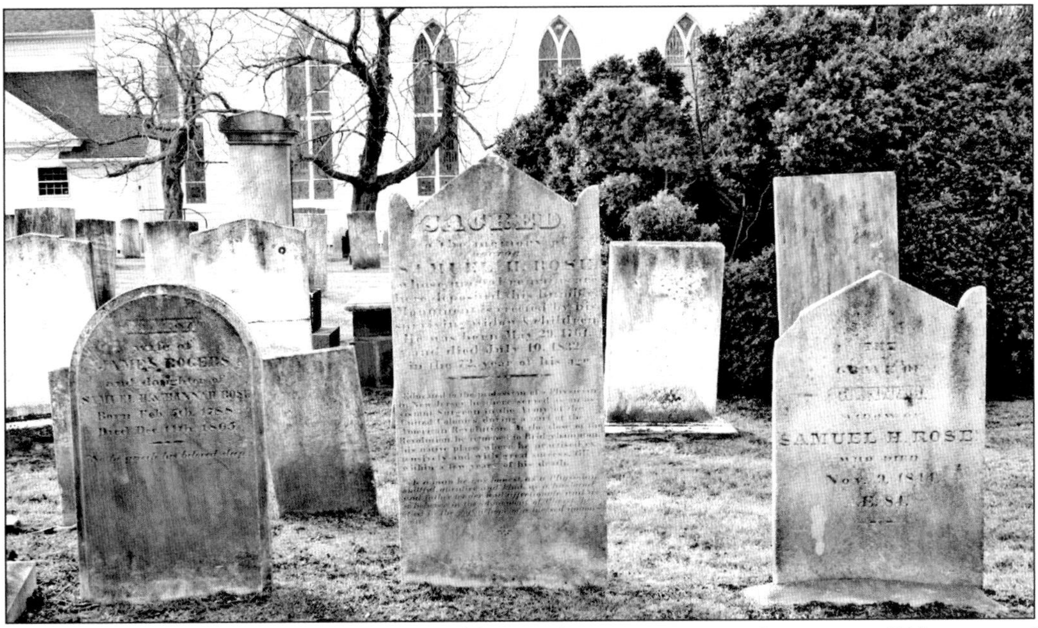

Dr. Samuel H. Rose (1761–1832) is buried here. The inscription reads, in part, "Education of a physician in New Jersey, he there served as an assistant surgeon in the Army of the United Colonies during a part of the American Revolution. At the close of the Revolution he returned to Bridgehampton, his native place, where he practiced extensively and with great success till within a few years of his death . . . he died in the joyful hope of a blessed immortality."

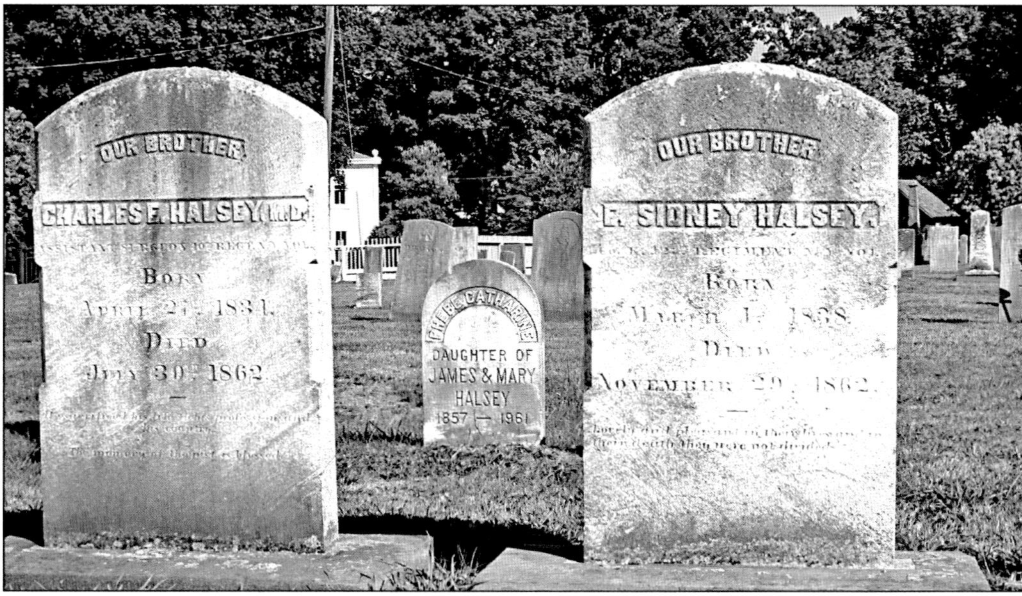

A Halsey family plot includes two members who died serving their country. Brothers Charles E. Halsey, M.D., of the 40th Regiment, and E. Sidney Halsey of the 127th Regiment New York Volunteers died within months of each other in 1862. Another Halsey, Capt. Elias Henry Halsey, died during the Massacre at Groton on September 6, 1781. The captain's name is on a monument at the site of the fort in Connecticut where Benedict Arnold led his army against a much smaller group of patriots and killed 84 men.

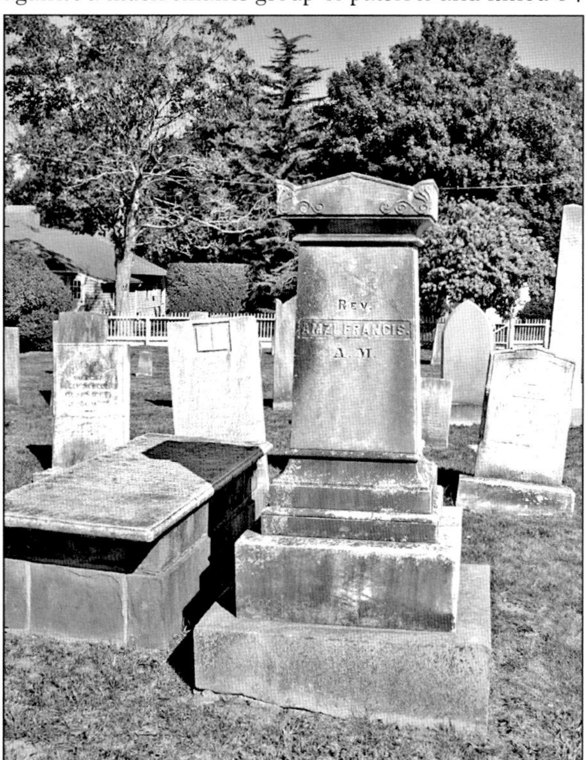

The Rev. Amzi Francis was born in West Hartford, Connecticut, in 1793. He was ordained in Bridgehampton on April 17, 1823. He died here on October 18, 1845. At his funeral, at 2:00 p.m. on October 20, the orator said, "Mr. Francis was of small stature, nervous temperament, his large black eyes denoted intellectual and spiritual action. He was scholarly in habit and appearance, studious, industrious, devout, intensely in earnest, spiritual, meditative, logical, small, one of God's uncomplaining, patient, self-denying saints."

Judge Henry P. Hedges was born in Wainscott on October 13, 1817. He attended the highly respected Clinton Academy and graduated from Yale Law School. He was a member of the New York State Assembly (1852), served as Suffolk County district attorney (1865–1870), and served as county judge and surrogate (1865–1870 and 1873–1880). Most importantly to East Hampton, he was deeply interested in the history of the town, and his writings are an invaluable source of documents for historians of East End history. He died on September 26, 1911.

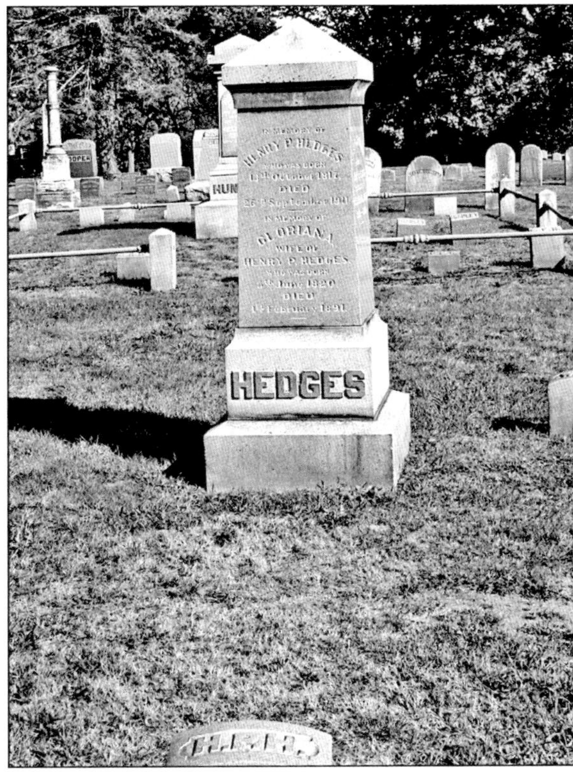

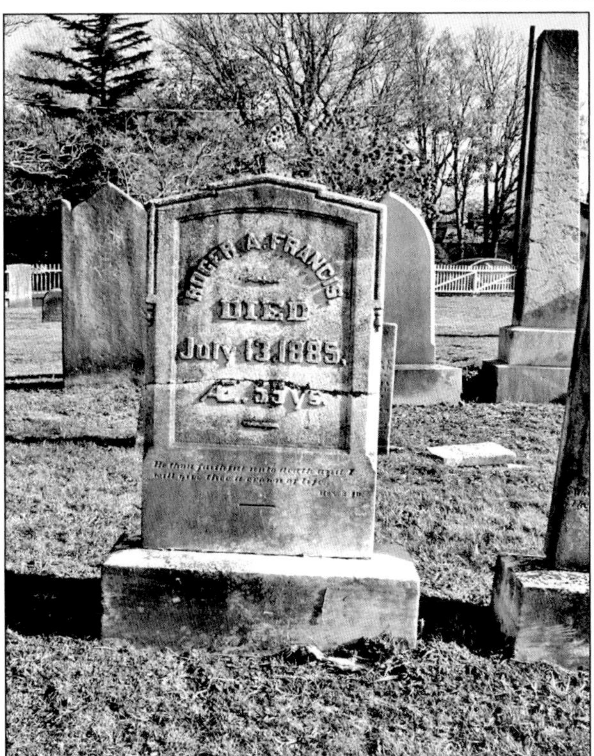

Roger A. Francis owned a stream mill on the commons in 1851. Finding it unprofitable, he moved it down the road to Mecox. More the poet than the merchant, his annual Christmas message concludes, "One theme remains – and then we're through / tis our plan for fifty-two, / Long may you live, long may you buy / Atlantic flour for a Christmas pie, / While every year at this same season, / We'll have a dish of rhyme and reason."

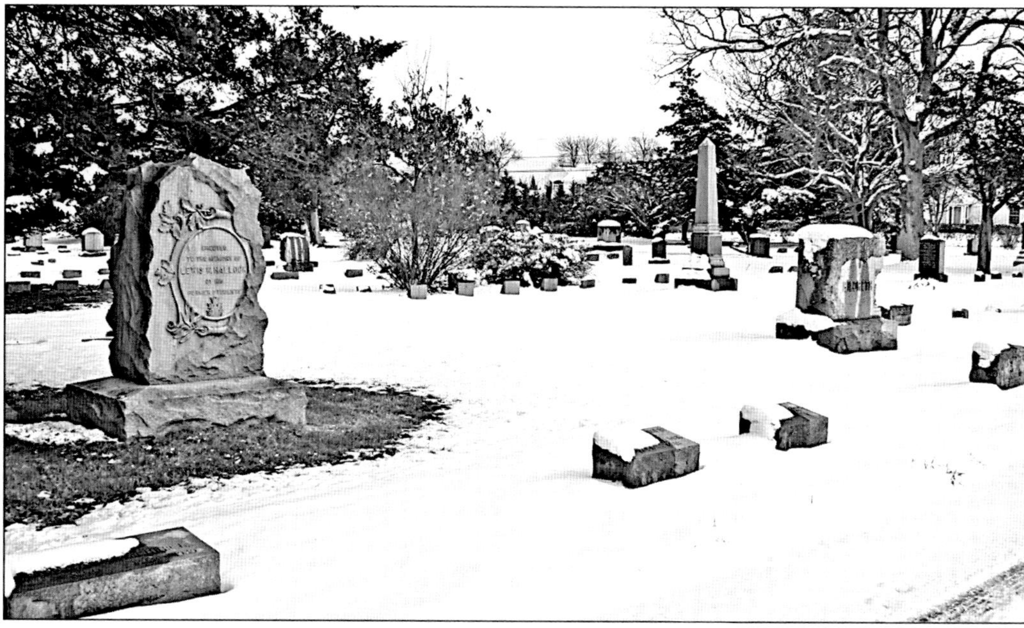

The Edgewood Cemetery is so new (the first interment was on August 17, 1894) the book *Memorials of Old Bridgehampton* chose not to incorporate it in the burial list of the area. One tombstone here predates the cemetery by 114 years. Lemuel Howell died of smallpox and was buried in the woods that are now included in the cemetery. The inscription reads, "Lemuel Howell, born Sept. 18, 1718, died Feb. 22, 1781."

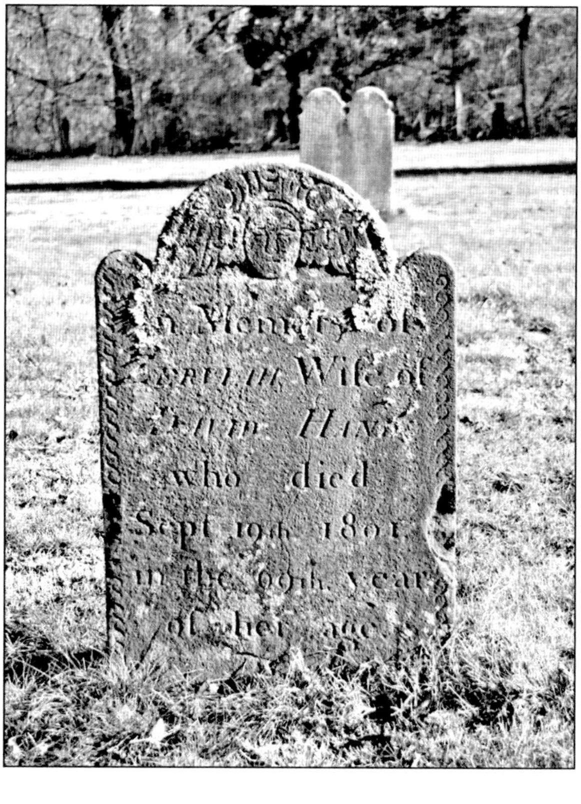

The Hands lived in Poxebogue and had a home on Poxebogue Pond. One night David Hand's wife, Lerviah, heard screams coming from a nearby wigwam and went to see what was wrong. She found a neighbor who had been drinking, holding his wife by her hair with one hand, a long black stone grasped in the other. She ran up behind him, snatched the stone from his hand, and then ran home. The stone was used in the Hand family for generations as a pestle.

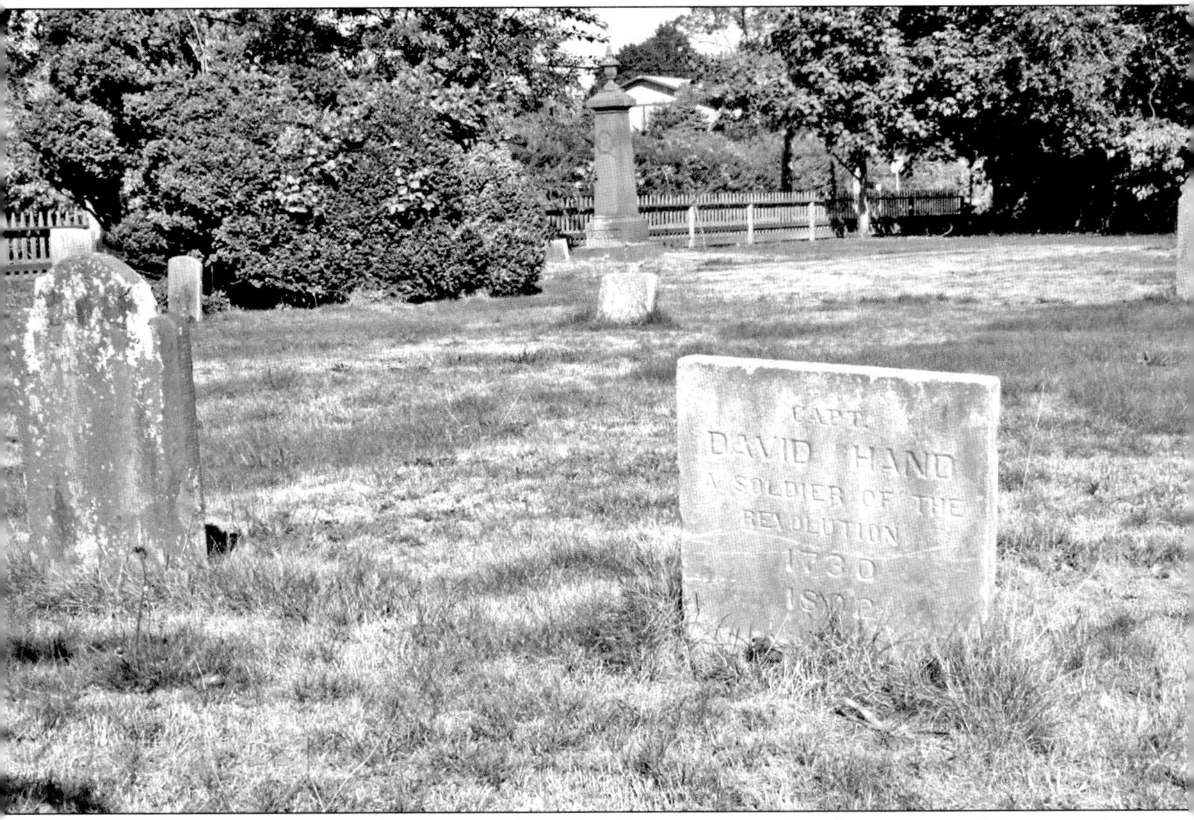

To call Capt. David Hand (1730–1802) daring is to be a master of understatement. He was with Gen. George Washington at the Battles of Long Island and Trenton. As a prisoner of war during the Revolution, he escaped five times. When ordered by a British major to hitch up a team to haul a load of fodder, he refused. The major drew his sword, and Hand responded, pitchfork in his grasp, "I've fastened many a whale, and I'll fasten you too if you don't get out of here." The major replied, "Well then, I guess you and I had better be friends." In a port in South America, Hand's men and those of a Spanish ship got into a quarrel. Each captain took the side of his men, leading the Spanish officer to challenge Hand to a duel. Hand, as the challenged party, chose his weapon: a harpoon with a line attached. As he balanced the whaling iron in his hand, he turned to his second and said, "When I strike, haul in the slack." And when he turned back to face his nemesis, there was no one in sight.

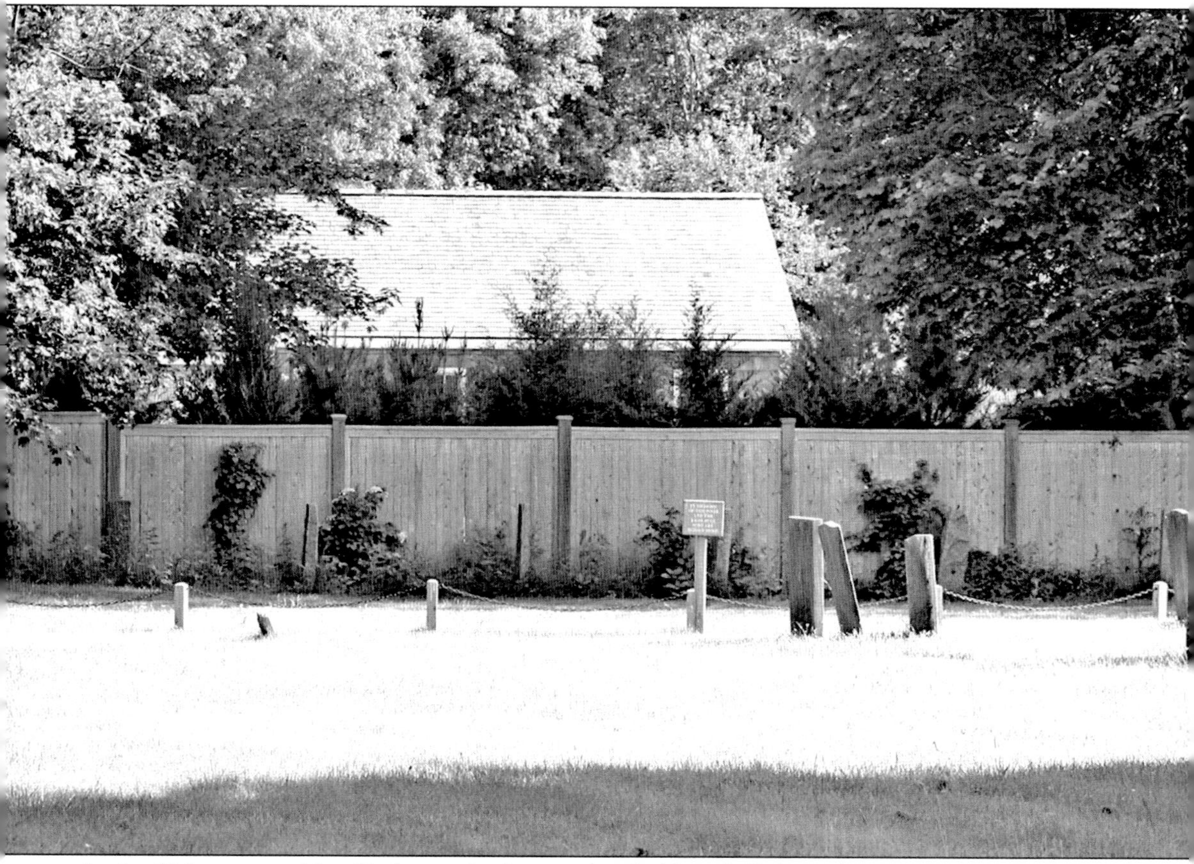

In the 18th century, New York was the largest slaveholder of all the colonies. Among New York counties, Suffolk had the largest slave population—up to 13 percent. In the rear of the cemetery in Poxebogue is a rope-enclosed slave burying ground. The sign says simply, "In memory of the poor and the ex- slaves who are buried here." Slavery was abolished gradually in New York, until it officially ended in 1828. It is noteworthy that from the earliest times, the colonists recognized their obligation to the poor. Each year, individuals were reimbursed for providing food and lodging to the town poor. Josiah Stanborough's will included five pounds for the poor. John Cooper left "unto the poor of said town a mare foal, the best that one of the first come up."

Six

Wainscott to East Hampton Village

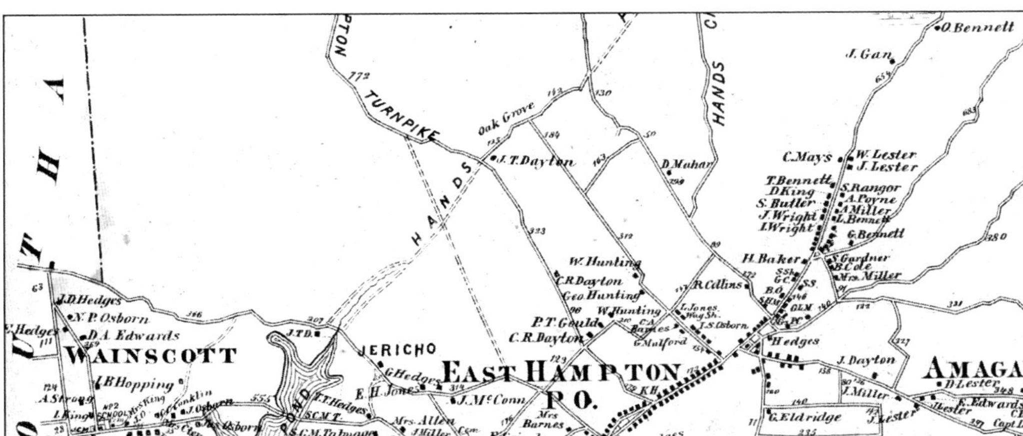

The town of East Hampton was settled in 1649, eight years after Southampton. It was originally named Maidstone, where the colonists had lived in England. The boundaries extend from its western end at the town line shared with Southampton eastward to Montauk Point. The northern shores are washed by Gardiner's and Peconic Bays. The South Shore beaches, fronting on the Atlantic Ocean, are a major attraction to the summer tourists. The village of East Hampton is the center of East End nightlife. The name Wainscott is not, as is often supposed, of Indian origin. According to historian William Wallace Tooker, the hamlet got its name from an ancient method of preparing wainscot (oaken timber or boarding). The process involved putting a tree in a muddy place in a river for a time until it was sufficiently seasoned. It was then cut into boards exported for wainscot. More recently it has been suggested that the village was named after a small village in Kent, England. (Courtesy Stony Brook University, Special Map Collection.)

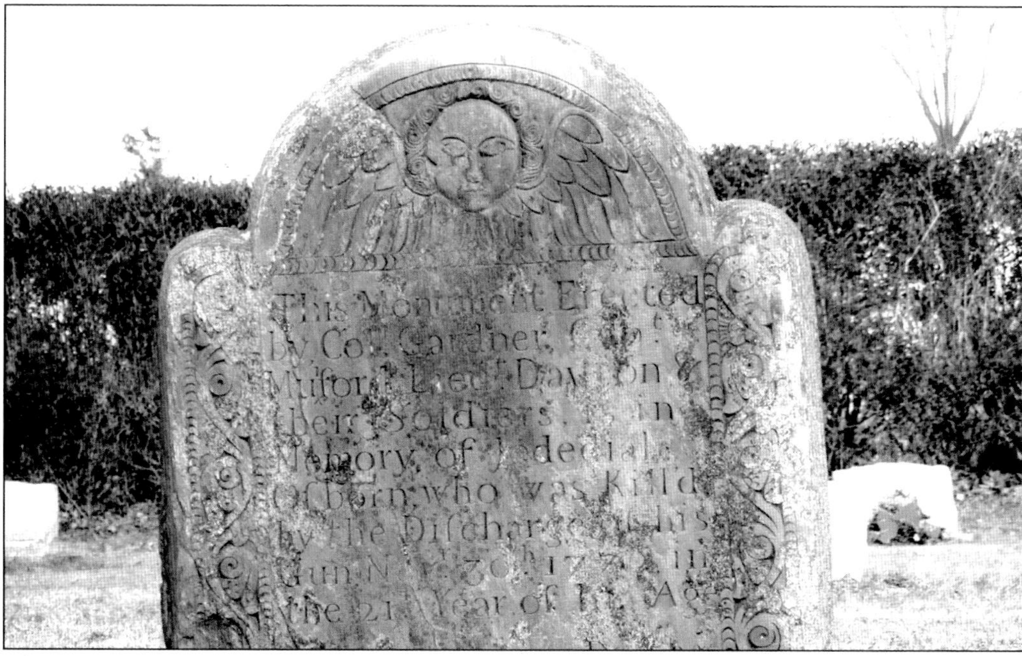

The inscription on this gravestone reads, "This monument erected by Col. Gardiner, Capt. Mulford, Lieut. Dayton and their soldiers in memory of Jedediah Osborn, who was killed by the discharge of his gun, Novr. 30th, 1772, in the 21st year of his age. 'How sudden was my death / Life is but fleeting breath.' "

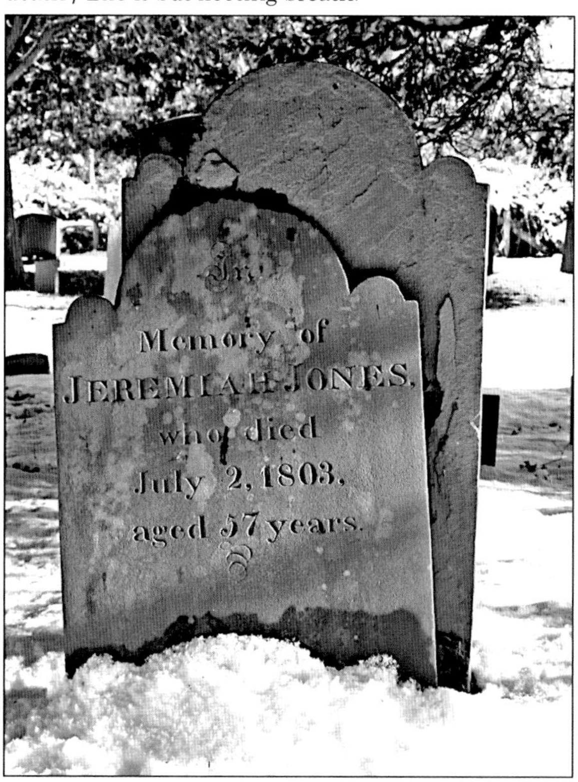

Ithuel Hill was the only known Long Island stonecutter from the late 1700s to the early 1800s. He moved from Connecticut to Sag Harbor and married Isabel Cornwall. His stones can be identified by his distinctive "signatures," like that on this Jericho Cemetery stone for Jeremiah Jones. Hill lived with his family in Sag Harbor and died in Tarpaulin Cove at age 54. Isabel Hill died at age 71 and is buried in the Oakland Cemetery in a grave with a plain stone.

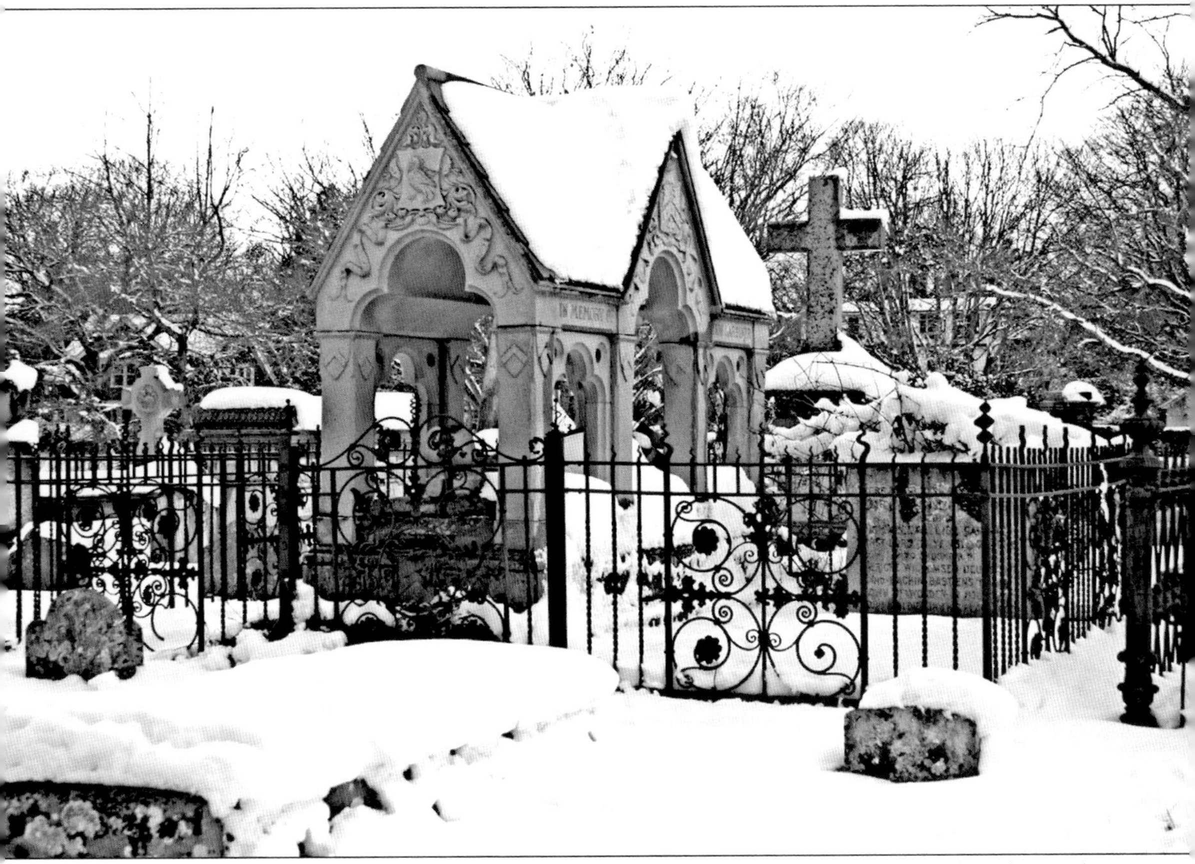

Lying within the fence surrounding the monument of Lion Gardiner (1599– 1663) is the modest grave of his wife, Mary Gardiner. Their daughter, Elizabeth, was the main character in the only story of witchcraft on the East End. In 1657, as a young bride, Elizabeth Howell was taken ill while home with her newborn. Passing in and out of delirium, she suddenly cried out that she had seen standing in the corner a witch, whom she identified as Goodwife Garlicke. She died two days later. The village was rife with accusations of witchcraft, and eventually an inquest was held as to the cause of Elizabeth Howell's untimely demise. The local magistrates were unable to unravel fact from fiction and decided to send the case to the more experienced Connecticut jurisdiction. It did not look good for Garlicke, since six of eight prior trials had ended with the hanging of the accused. Reason eventually prevailed, however, and the Hartford jury concluded there was insufficient evidence to find the defendant guilty. Garlicke was once again a free woman.

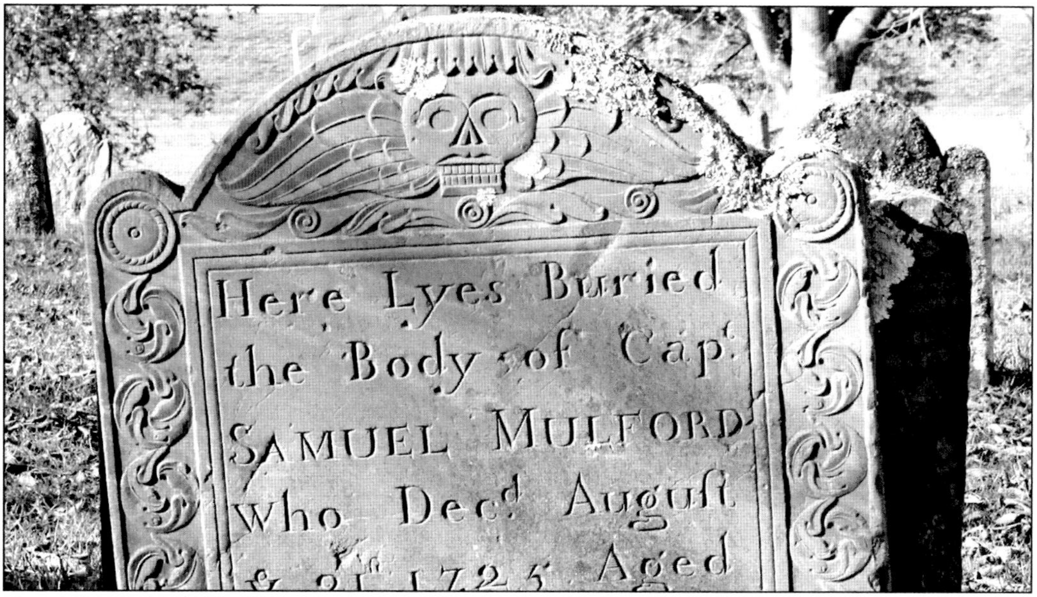

Capt. Samuel Mulford was a member of the assembly in 1705 and was known locally as "Honest Sam." He opposed "prerequisites" (read graft) and bitterly opposed taxation without representation, for example, the tax on whale oil. He took his case to London in 1716, where he dissuaded pickpockets by sewing fishhooks into his coat, earning him the nickname "Fishhook." His efforts led parliament to repeal the obnoxious levy. Mulford died on August 21, 1725, at about age 80.

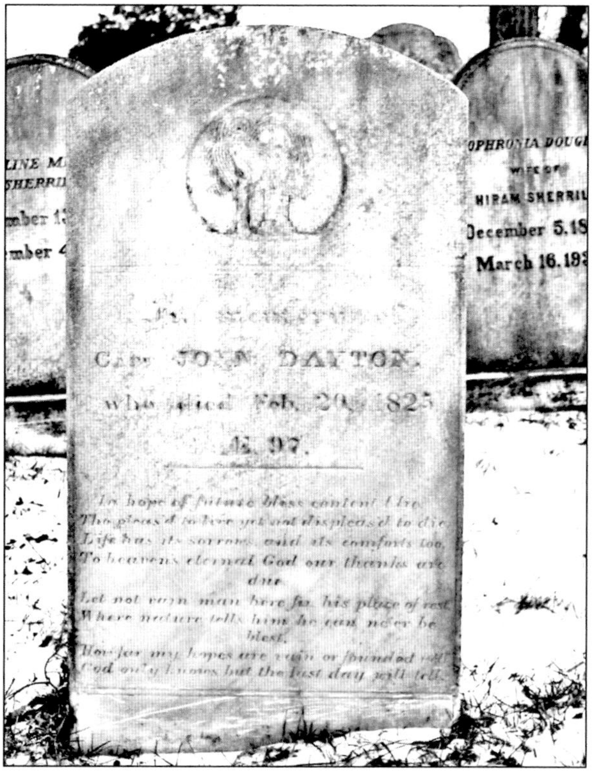

Capt. John Dayton earned great respect for his boldness in the face of the enemy. When a British ship was sighted off Montauk, he marched his small company of men to the area and had them parade, single file, along the crest of a hill, in full view of the enemy. Out of sight, they turned their coats inside out and again marched along the top of the hill. Convinced that Montauk was strongly defended, the British commander, choosing discretion over valor, sailed off. Dayton died on February 20, 1825, at age 97.

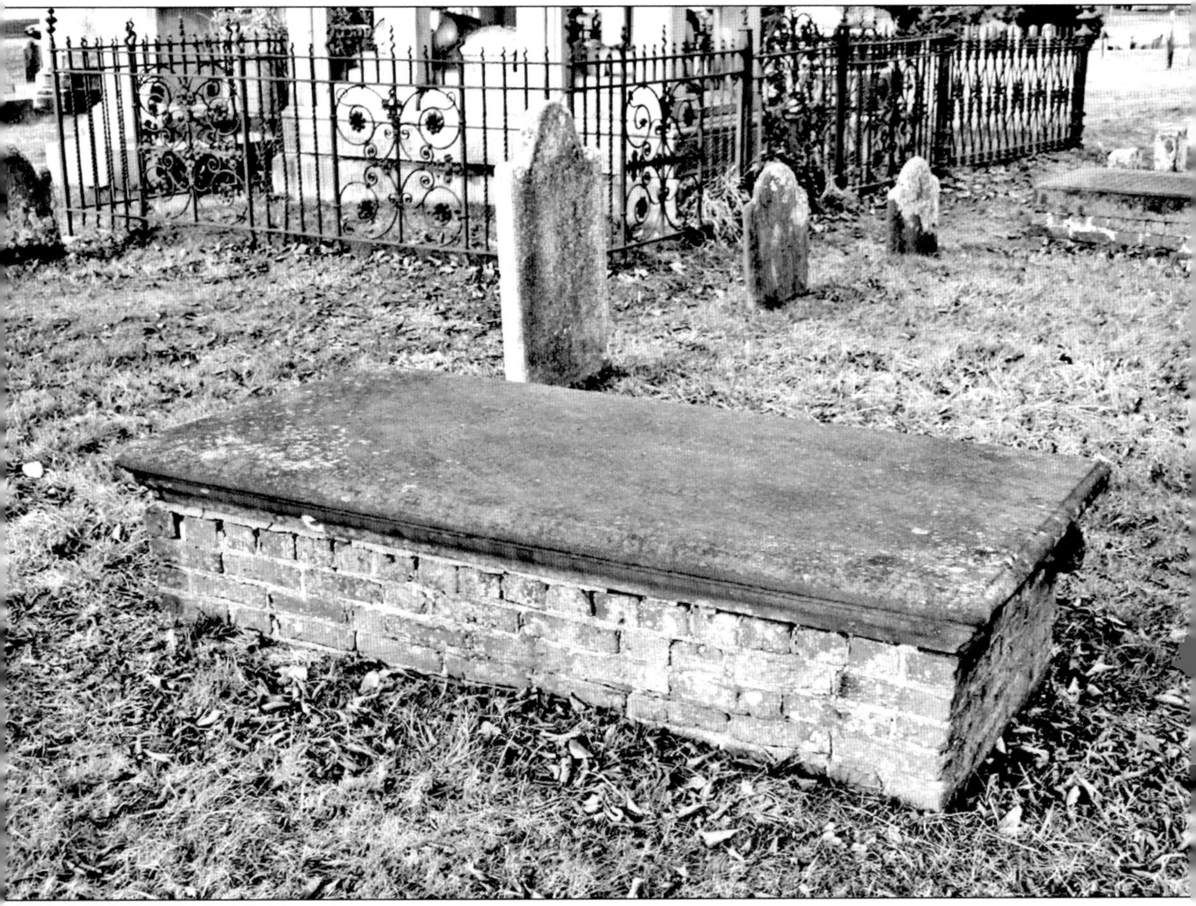

After the patriots' loss in Brooklyn, the entire island fell under the occupation of the British Army. The East Enders were faced with a Hobson's choice: seek refuge in Connecticut and risk loss of their possessions, or stay and face the vengeance of the Loyalists. Many chose to go. Those who stayed were forced to take the oath of allegiance to the king. Col. Abraham Gardiner chose at first to stay. In doing so, he faced a further indignity. Although he was a signer of the Articles of the Association in 1775, he was now a colonel in His Majesty's service. Gardiner was required by Gov. William Tryon to extract the oath from all males who had chosen to stay in East Hampton. The Honorable Henry P. Hedges stated that the man had no other option and urged that Gardiner not be judged too harshly. Eventually, on September 9, 1776, Gardiner himself chose to seek asylum in Saybrook, Connecticut. During the year he was gone, his house served as Tryon's headquarters. If further evidence of his loyalty is needed, it may be pointed out that Gardiner's son also served the patriots' cause.

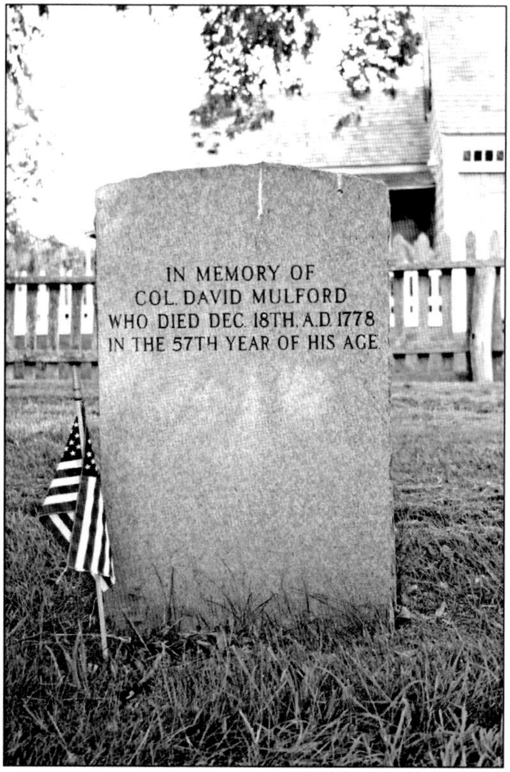

Some men like Col. David Mulford chose to stay. In order to stay, Mulford had to swear allegiance to the king, by saying, "I do swear upon The Evangelist of Almighty God, that I hold true and faithful allegiance to his majesty King George the Third of Great Britain, his heirs and successors; and hold an utter abhorrence of congresses, rebellions, &c; and do promise never to be concerned in any manner with his majesty's rebellious subjects in America. So help me God!" Mulford died on December 18, 1778, at age 57.

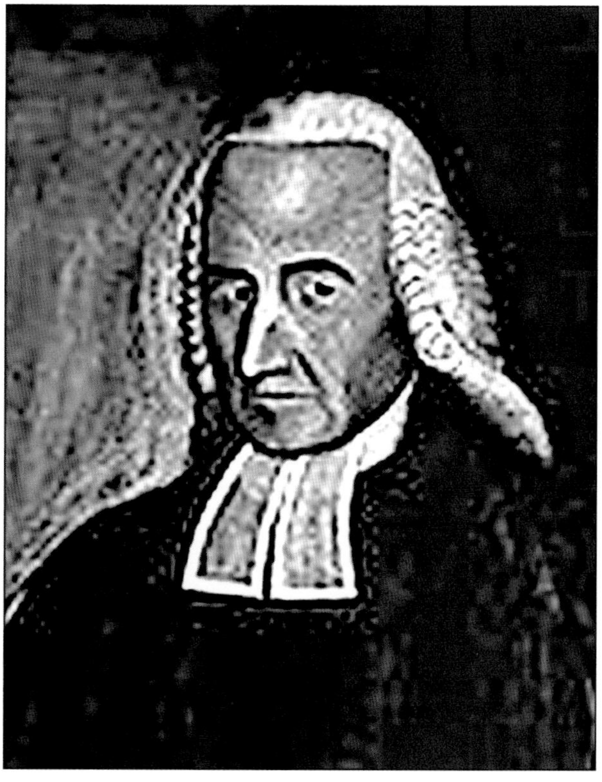

Dr. Samuel Buell was installed in 1746 as the third minister of the town of East Hampton. He was a supporter of the king's cause in the French and Indian War, and then an ardent supporter of the patriots' cause in the Revolution. Indeed, he defied the British commander who informed Buell of his order to assemble the townspeople on the coming Sabbath. Buell replied "[I] am myself commander and chief on that day and have annulled the order." The order was, indeed, revoked. (Courtesy East Hampton Library, Long Island Collection.)

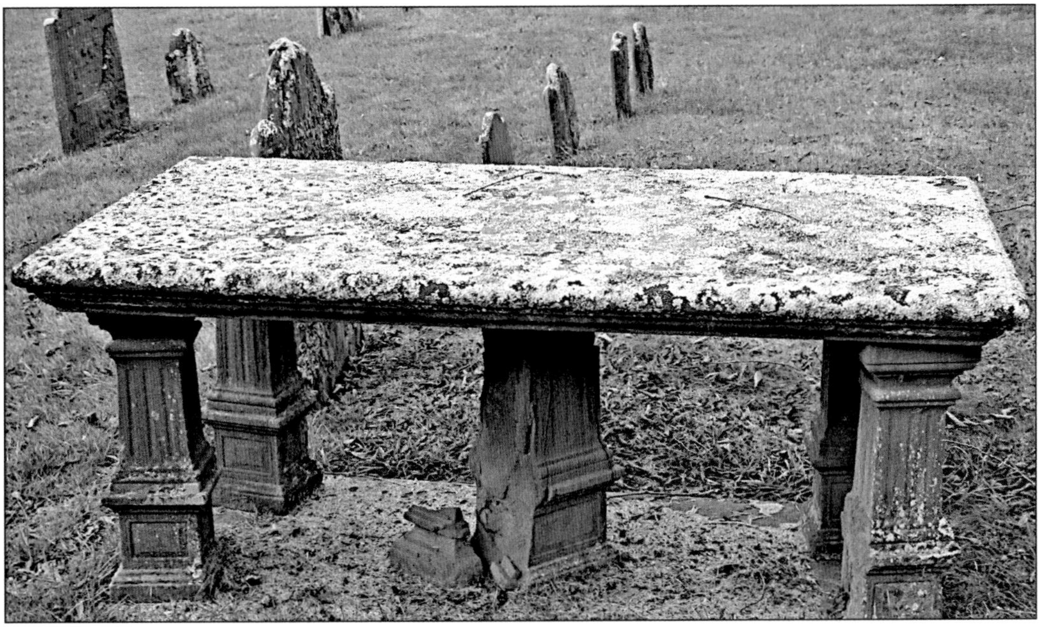

The year was 1756. The place was the First Presbyterian Church in East Hampton. The Reverend Samuel Buell stood in the pulpit facing 38 men about to leave for Lake George to take part in the French and Indian War. He read from 1 Chronicles 19:13 and then told them, "The cause is just and good . . . that a defensive war is frequently necessary as well as lawful, and that an offensive sometimes so. . . ." These words he could have delivered to any army, any time, in any war.

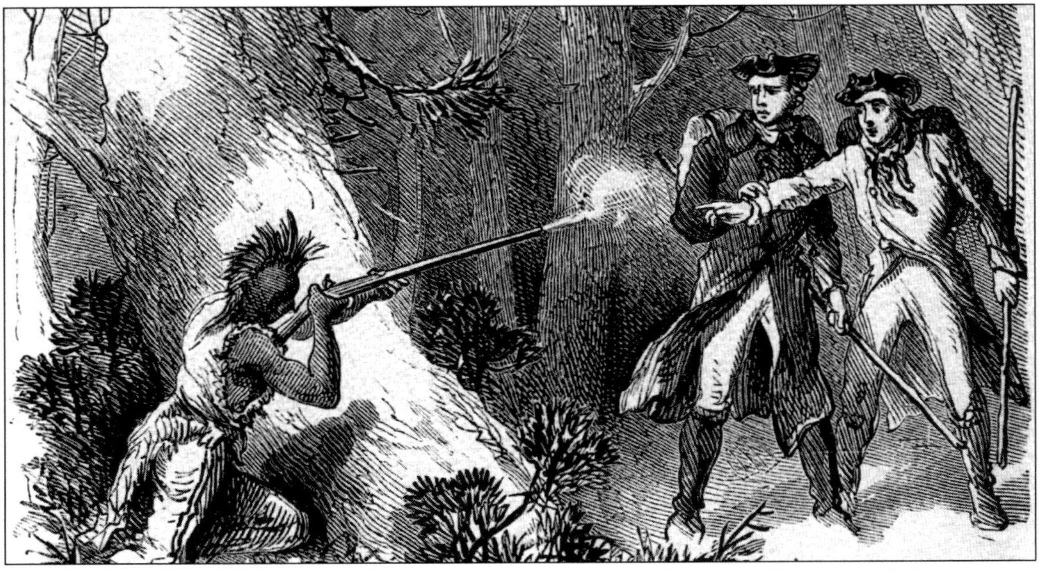

The French and Indian War took place in North America between Britain and France from 1754 to 1763. The war served as a training ground for George Washington. In 1754, at age 22, Washington led a mission into the Ohio Country. He ambushed a French Canadian search party, killing 10 men, including its leader. The next year, he accompanied Maj. Gen. Edward Braddock in the disastrous Battle of the Monongahela. Washington distinguished himself by arranging a successful retreat, foreshadowing his brilliant tactical retreat at the Battle of Long Island 21 years later. (Courtesy Picture History.)

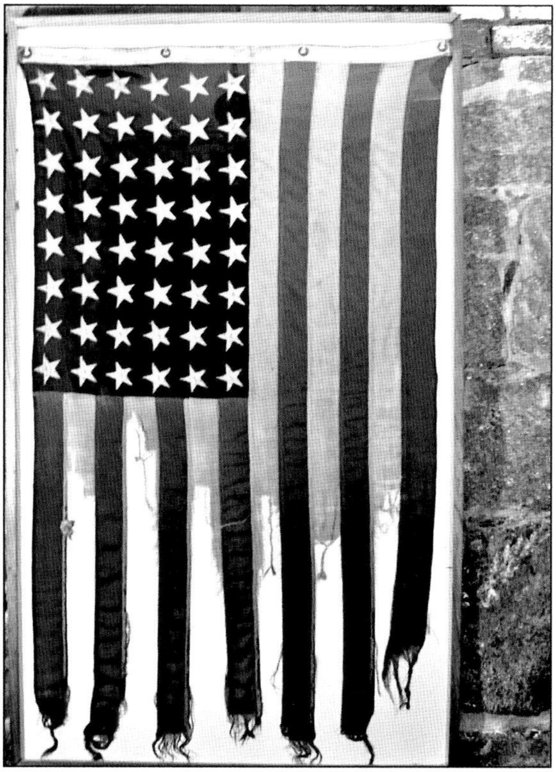

Iwo Jima was strategically located 650 miles south of Tokyo, Japan. During World War II, in their buildup to defend the island, the Japanese constructed an elaborate system of tunnels and bunkers, manned by 21,000 to 23,000 men. The plan was to lay down a withering spray of gunfire as the landing force advanced up the beach. On February 9, 1945, the first of 30,000 Marines landed on Iwo Jima. Navy Lt. Jerome Grattan of Southold was communications officer aboard LLCFF 994. This flag, which Grattan later acquired, flew proudly on a landing craft during the invasion. (Courtesy Southold Historical Society.)

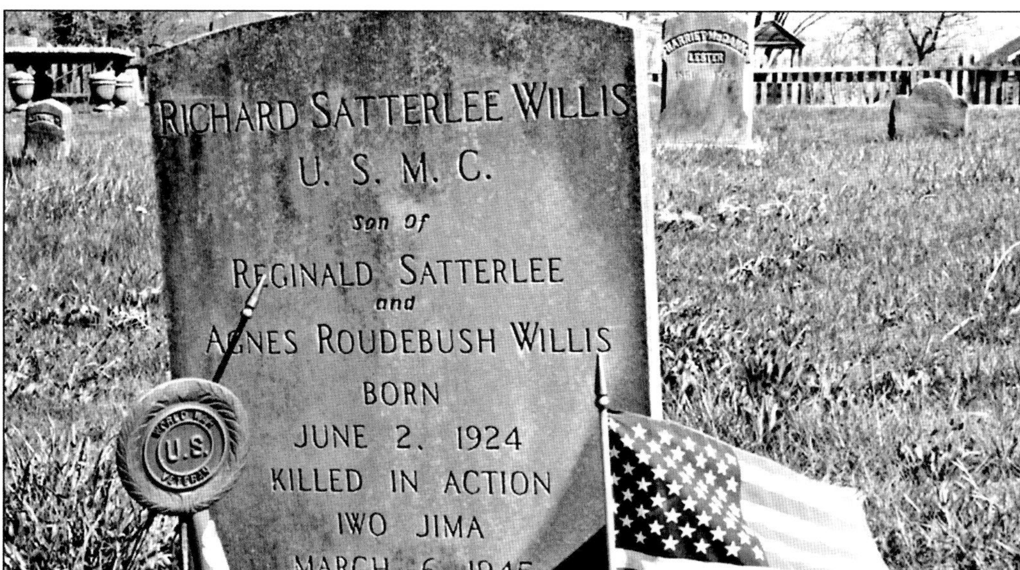

The 3rd, 4th, and 5th Marine Divisions took part in the assault on Iwo Jima. Their gunfire was ineffective. Finally, flame-throwing Sherman tanks drove the Japanese out of their bunkers. On February 23, 1945, four marines raised a flag atop Mount Suribachi. The moment was captured in a Pulitzer prize–winning photograph. The fighting raged until March 26, when Iwo Jima was declared secure. The final numbers are staggering: 7,000 marines were killed, and 19,000 were wounded. The Japanese lost 21,800 of a total force of 22,000.

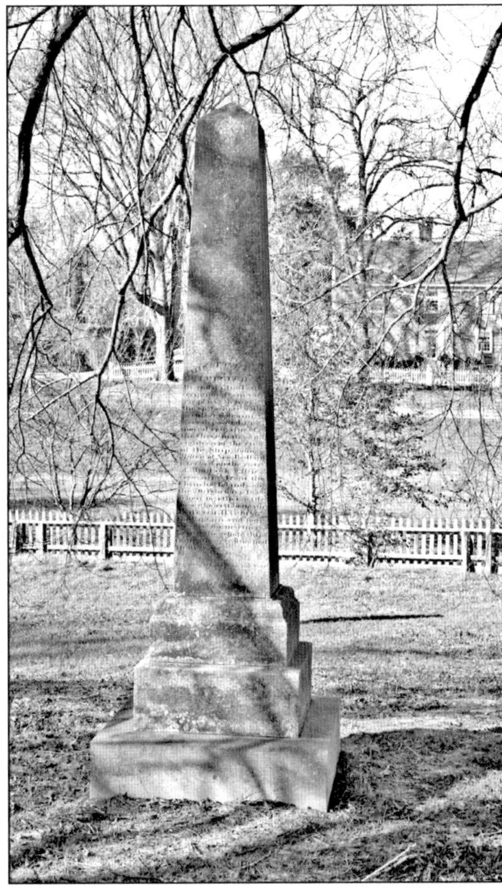

"But like the reef of 'Norman's woe,' / Where sank the *Hesperus* of old; / So this spot, 'mid night and snow / Shall the sad *Milton*'s tale be told." —Dr. John Huntington. A blinding snowstorm enveloped the East End on the night of February 19, 1858. Crewmen of the *John Milton*, thinking the ship far offshore, went about their duties. Too late they heard the sound of waves crashing on the shore of Montauk. The *John Milton* ran up against a reef. The news came the next morning. That evening, two wagons rolled up to the coroner's house with 14 frozen bodies. More bodies followed. The tragedy struck a sad chord in the hearts of the East Hampton community, for these were local seamen. Capt. Ephraim Harding and his young son were lost, along with all of the crew. On a man-made mound in the South Cemetery stands a tall obelisk. Beneath it lies a mass grave containing the remains of 21 men. For many years the bell from the ship rang from the church belfry. (Courtesy Suffolk County Historical Society.)

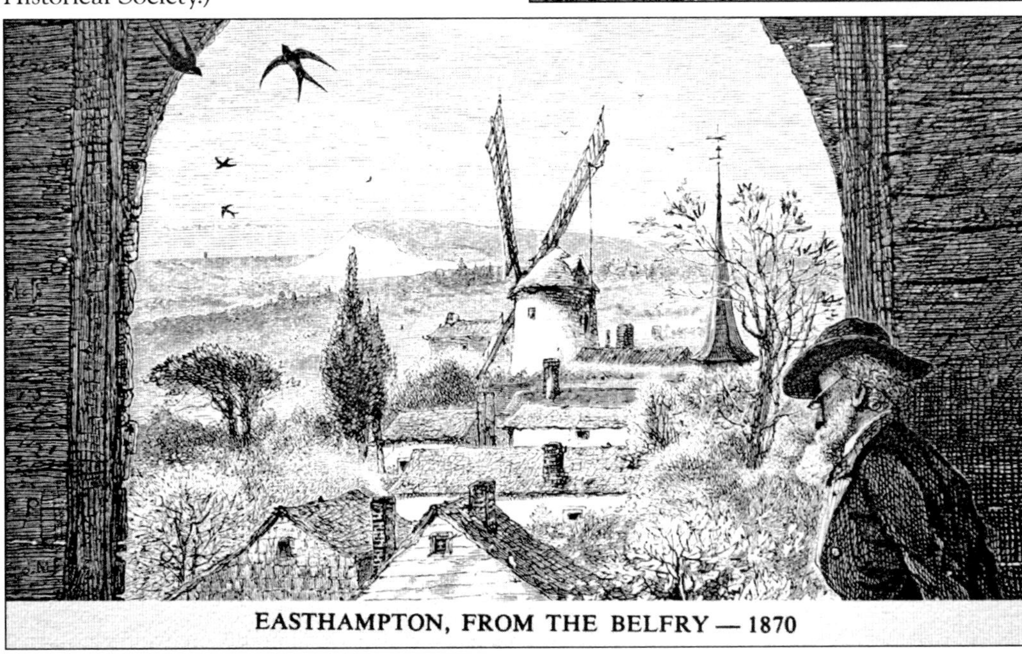

EASTHAMPTON, FROM THE BELFRY — 1870

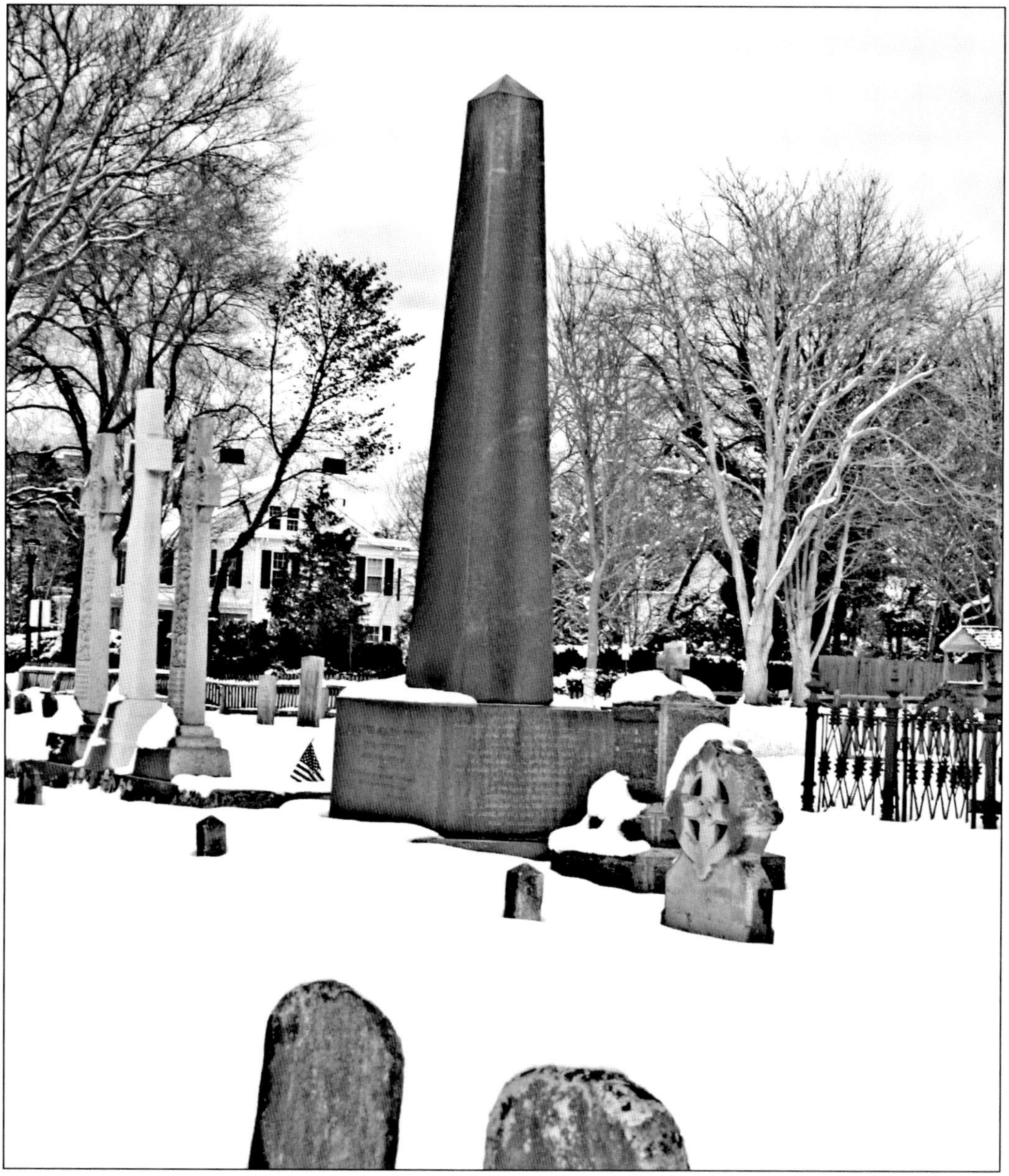

One of the largest monuments in the East Hampton burial ground is that of David Gardiner. Gardiner, a senator from the state of New York, died on February 28, 1844. On that day he sailed aboard the frigate USS *Princeton*, at the invitation of Pres. John Tyler (1790–1862). Former president William Henry Harrison had died a month after taking office. Tyler then became the first vice president to become commander in chief upon the death of the chief executive. Tyler, a southern Democrat, had a stormy career. His own party suggested he be designated "acting president," but their bid failed. He was a man without a party and became the first president to be threatened with impeachment. Initially called by many a mediocre president, most historians viewed him as a man of courage who was devoted to the principles of Thomas Jefferson. Ultimately, his administration lasted four years (1841–1845). In 1845, as his term drew to a close, Tyler signed two bills, admitting Texas and then Florida into the Union.

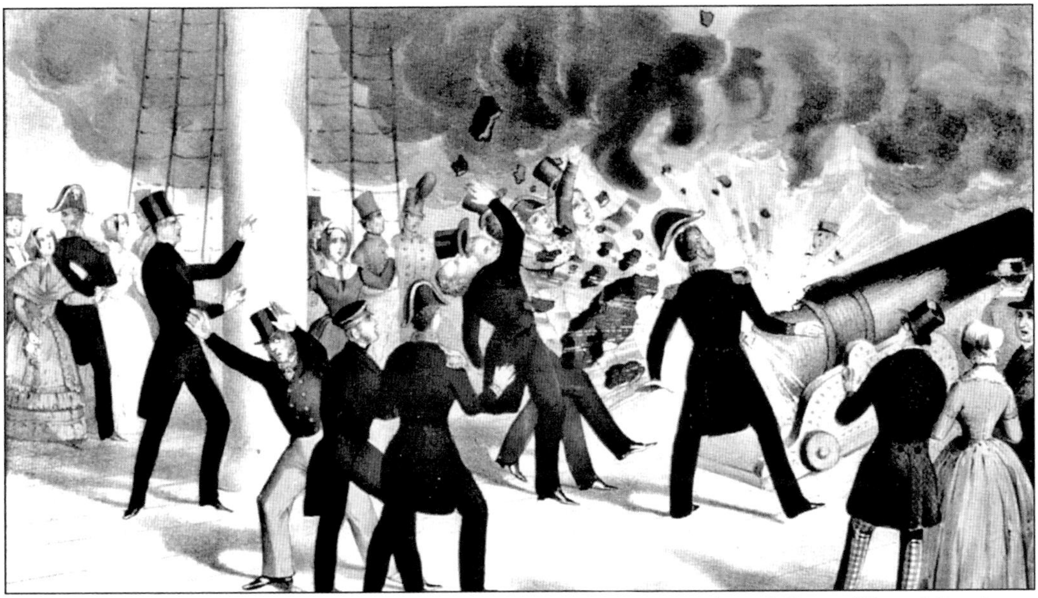

The inscription on David Gardiner's 20-foot-high monument reads as follows: "David Gardiner, born May 2nd 1784, died Feb. 28th, 1844, he was stricken with instant death by the bursting of the great gun [the Peacemaker] on board the steam frigate *Princeton*, on the river Potomac. A national calamity which wrung many hearts and deprived the country of some of its most distinguished and valuable citizens. Eight people, including the former state senator Gardiner were killed in the explosion." (Courtesy Picture History.)

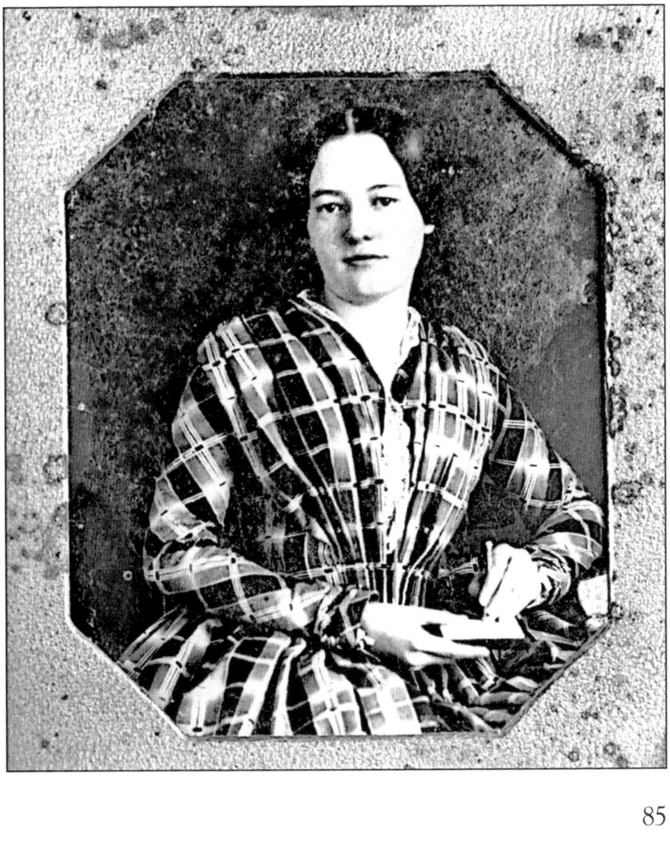

Below deck at the time of the disaster were David Gardiner's daughters Julia (pictured) and Margaret and their host, Pres. John Tyler. At the time, the president was mourning the recent loss of his wife. However, following a four-month courtship, which began after her father's death, Julia Gardiner became Tyler's bride and the new first lady. On September 25, 1845, she and Tyler visited East Hampton. (Courtesy Picture History.)

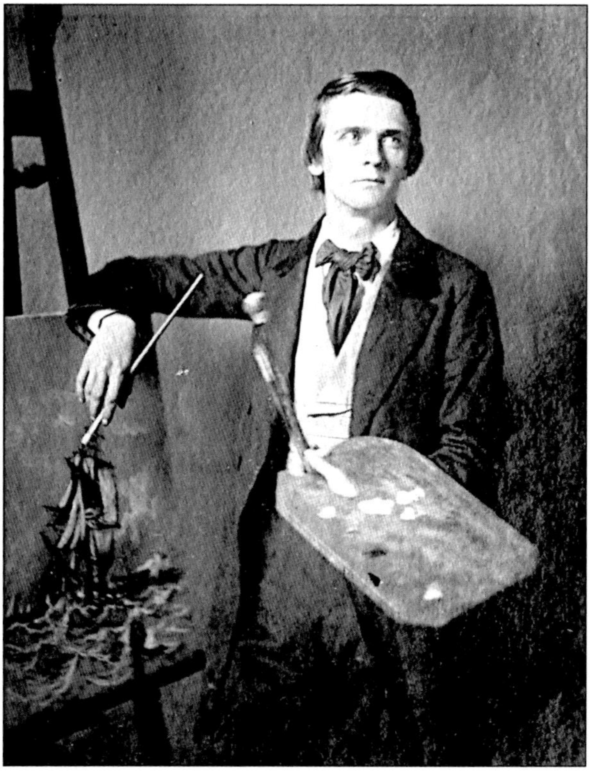

English-born Thomas Moran (1837–1926) was one of the foremost artists of the 19th century. His reputation as an outstanding American landscape painter was insured after visits to Yellowstone National Park in 1871 and the Grand Canyon in 1873. Moran moved to East Hampton in 1884 and built a cottage and large studio on Main Street, where he lived with his wife, Mary Nimmo Moran (1842–1899). The Morans are buried in the South End Cemetery with a large monument. (Courtesy Picture History.)

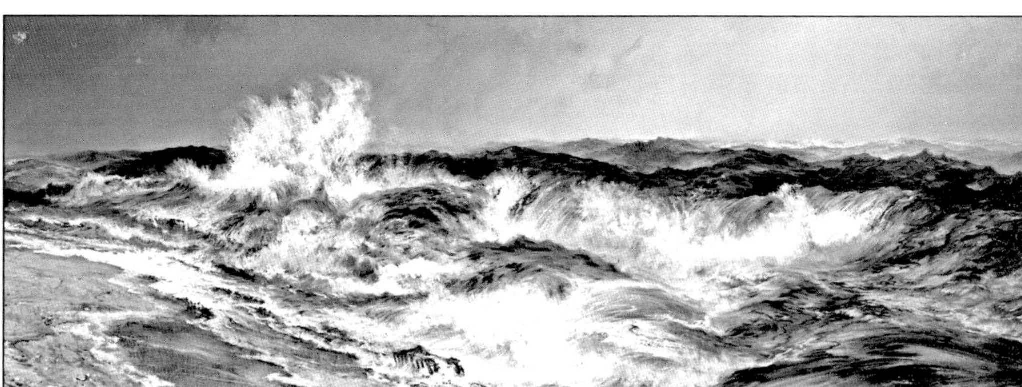

The Puritans who landed on the shores of the East End were confronted by an untamed wilderness and a too often "resounding sea." From his studio, Thomas Moran had easy access to the beach, where he captured the moods of the sea: the calmness, as in *Beach at East Hampton*, and the rage, as in *The Much Resounding Sea*. Mary Nimmo Moran was a well-known artist in her own right. (*The Much Resounding Sea* by Thomas Moran, Gift of the Avalon Foundation; image copyright Board of Trustees, National Gallery of Art, Washington, DC.)

Thomas James was the first minister of the East Hampton church, which was built in 1652. It was largely independent until 1748. James was incensed by many of the duke's laws and was jailed for three weeks after he delivered an impassioned sermon against a land tax. His pastorate lasted from 1650 until he died on June 16, 1696. It is said that James, a noted eccentric, was buried opposite his congregation so that he would face them on Judgment Day.

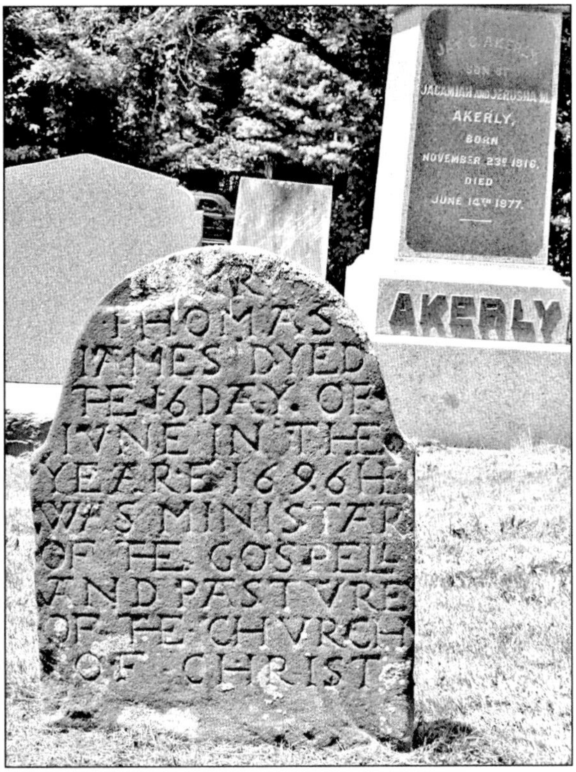

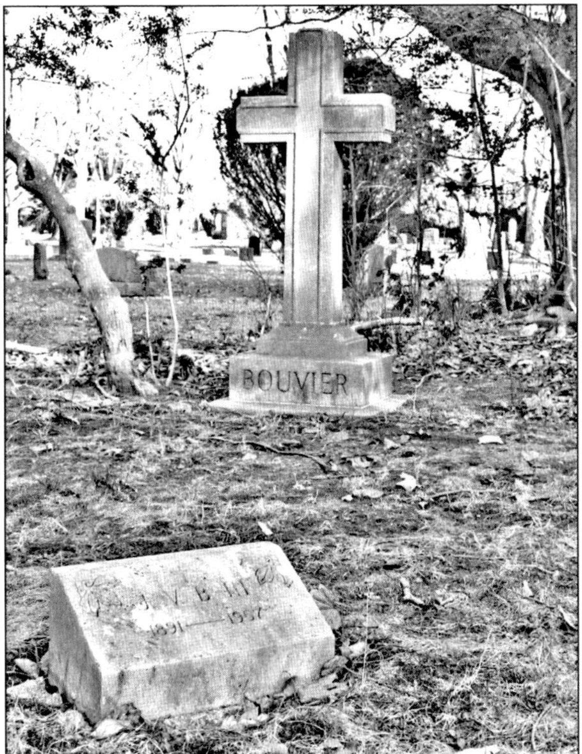

John Vernou Bouvier III (1891–1957), father of First Lady Jacqueline Bouvier Kennedy, was a Wall Street stockbroker with a reputation as a gambler and a drinker. Known as "Black Jack," he and his wife, Janet Norton Lee (1907–1989), ended up divorced, and he did not attend his daughter's wedding to John F. Kennedy.

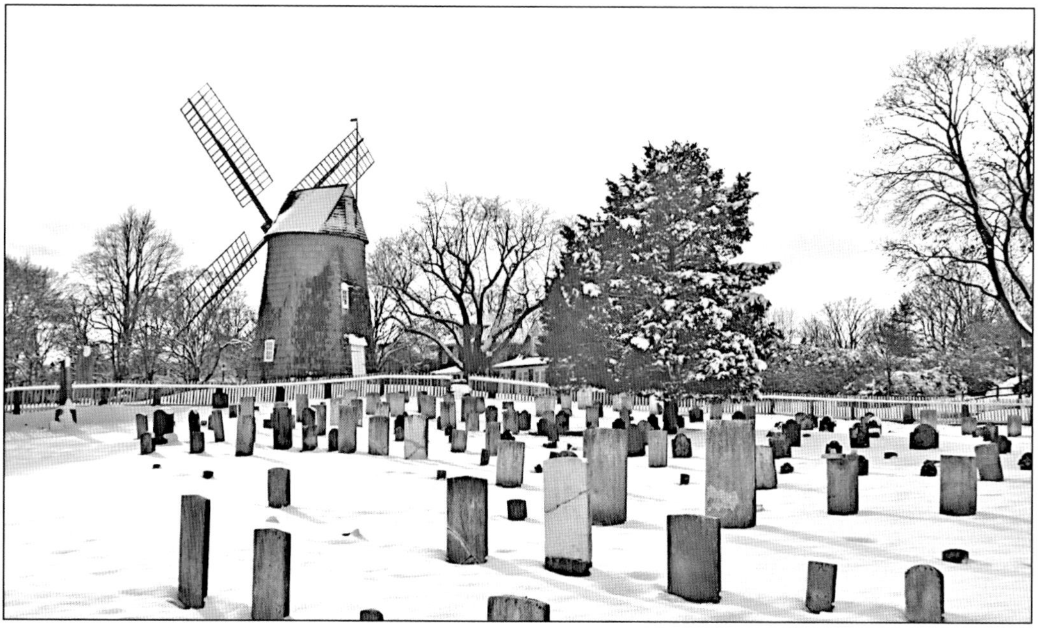

The Hook windmill is located on a man-made mound on the town triangle green. It was built in 1806 by Nathaniel Dominy V (1737–1812), one of the most prominent millwrights on the East End. It was the first to feature two pairs of millstones. The mill has been preserved by the town of East Hampton and is open to the public. It stands in front of the ancient North End Cemetery. The first to be interred in the cemetery was Joseph Post, who died in 1721.

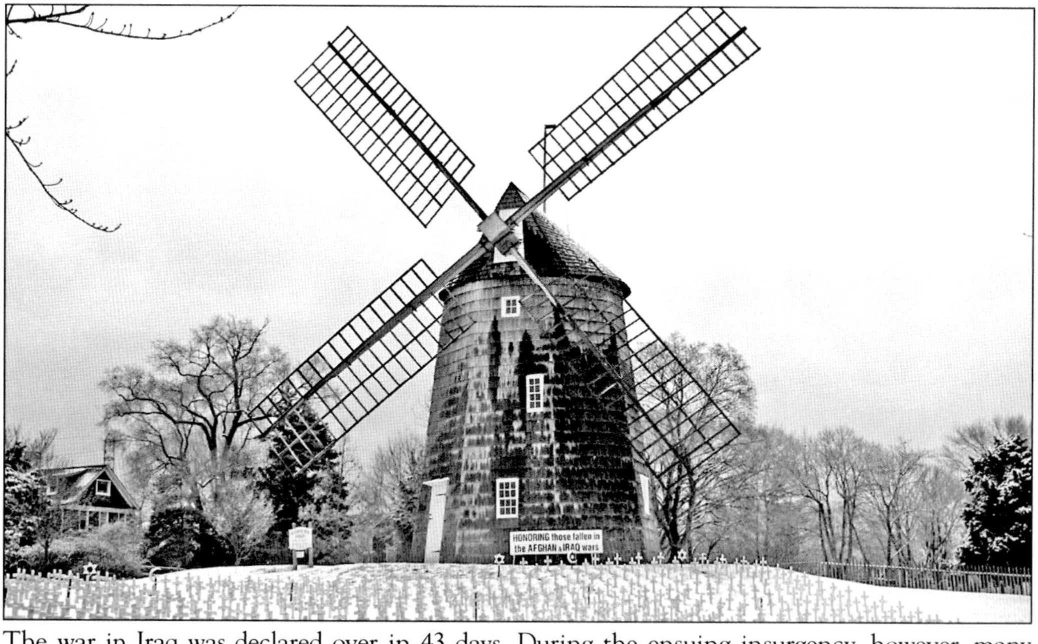

The war in Iraq was declared over in 43 days. During the ensuing insurgency, however, many soldiers continued to give their lives for their country while fighting the "War on Terror." In their honor, spontaneous, temporary memorials have been displayed across the country. Crosses, Stars of David, and Crescents have been erected, as appropriate. In January 2005, this memorial appeared on the triangle in East Hampton, the site of several memorials to veterans of previous wars.

Seven

Sag Harbor

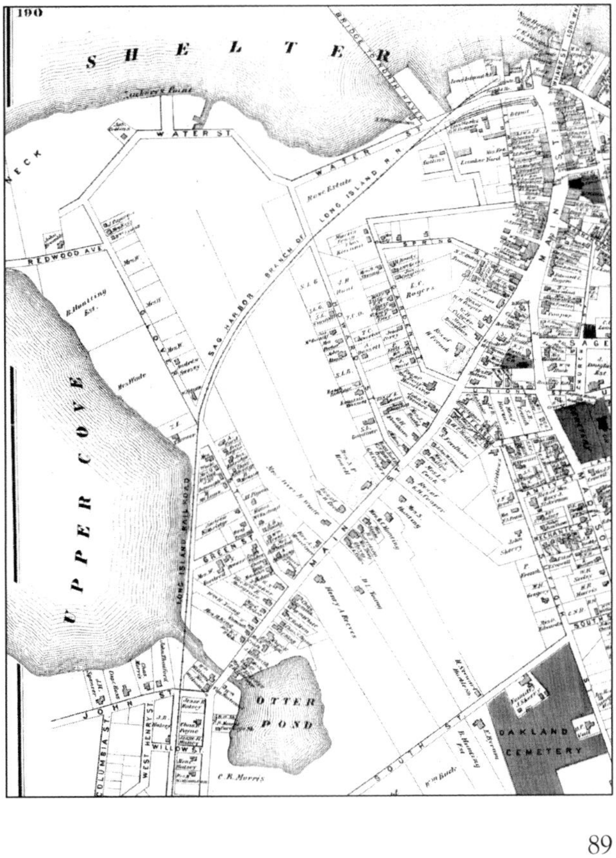

The village is first mentioned in the Southampton town records in 1711 as Bridge Hampton Harbor. Several years later, in 1715, it is mentioned as Sag Head. Finally, in 1730, the settlement becomes Sag Harbor. Located on the north shore of the South Fork, on Peconic Bay, it offers a sheltered, deep-water port. The western portion of the village is in the town of Southampton, and eastern Sag Harbor is in the town of East Hampton. The two largest cemeteries are in Southampton. During the heyday of the whaling era, the streets of Sag Harbor teemed with not only East Enders but also Portuguese, Scandinavians, and Native Americans. Although the last whaler left port in the 19th century, the myriad tales of success and tragedy are preserved, carved in the stones of the ancient burial grounds. (Courtesy Stony Brook University, Special Map Collection.)

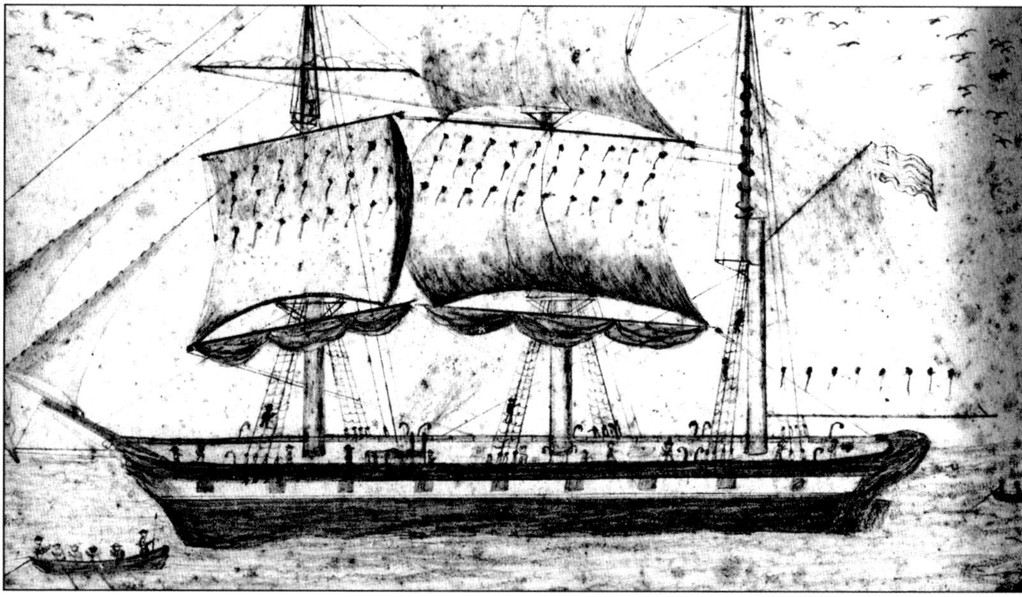

The bark *Trident* sailed out of New Bedford in 1865. The ship's log lists Capt. Jetur Rose as master, Moses Walker as second mate, and Melvin Halsey as keeper of the log. The *Trident* departed for the Arctic Ocean on November 16, 1865. Thus begins the tale of a family and crew of a whaler on a journey to meet the challenge of the sea and its leviathans. The journey lasted two years, four months, and one day and included a near-death experience of the keeper of the log. (Courtesy Southampton Historical Museum.)

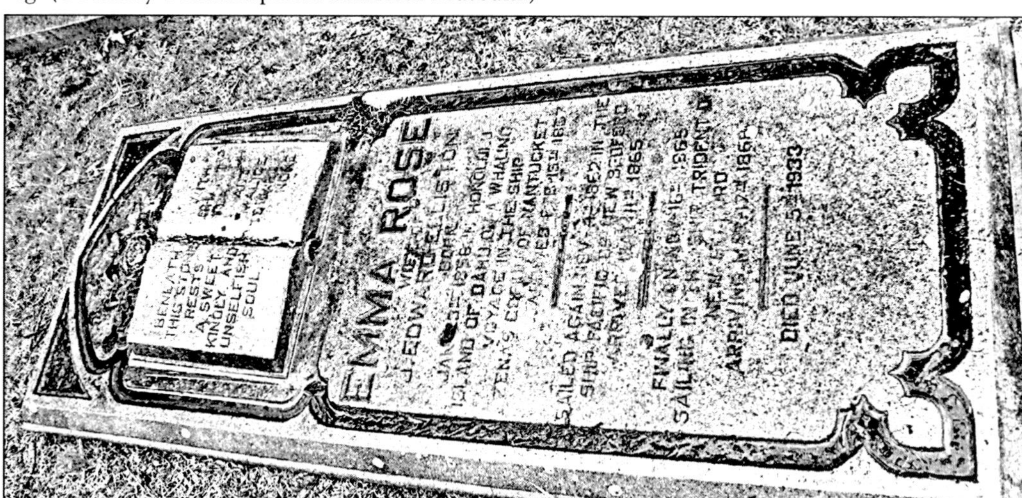

Whaling was a family affair with the Roses. Wife, C. B. Rose, and daughter, Emma Rose—who was born in Honolulu on January 23, 1856, when her father was captain of the whaler *Pacific*—often sailed with Jetur Rose. A verse from an old whaling song concludes:

> In fact I asked a little boy
> If he could tell me where he was born
> He answered, with a mark of joy
> "Round Cape Horn!"

In 1900, the daughter transcribed the log. It tells of rounding Cape Horn, of spending months frozen in the Arctic ice, and of the second mate's harrowing encounter with a whale.

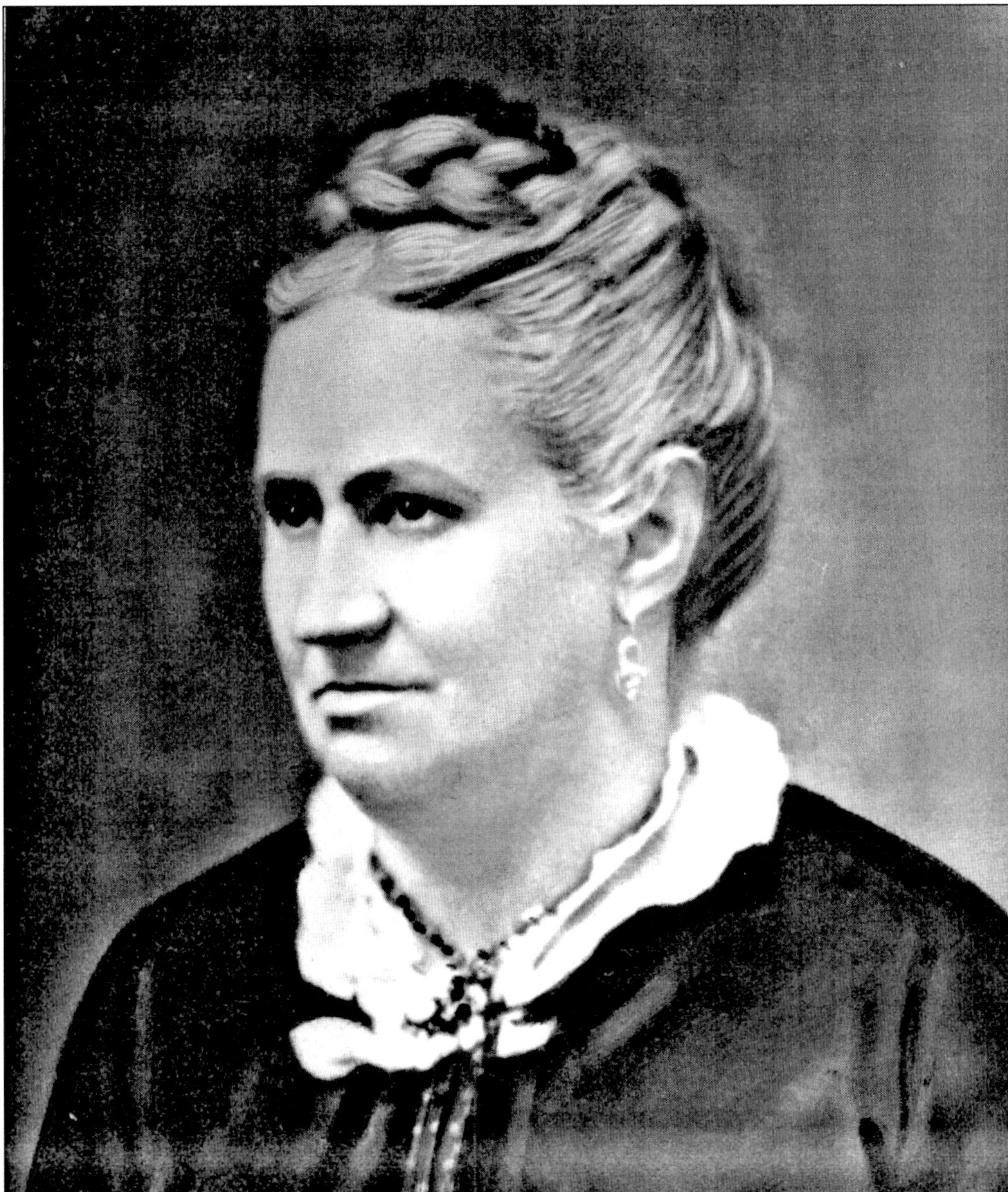

Emma Rose was an eyewitness to the chilling incident that happened sometime after 3:00 p.m. on September 15, 1866. The *Trident* raised a whale and the boats were lowered. Then, Moses Walker, the second mate, harpooned the whale. "The whale struck the boat, throwing him out & the line at the same time, the line was foul around his legs & the whale took him down, but came up letting Mr. Walker to the surface. He was near enough to the boat to grab the sheath knife that is always in the head of the boat. The whale took him down again. With extraordinary presence of mind, and supernatural strength, he managed to reach below his feet, and cut the line between him and the whale. Everything was dark, but he shot to the top when the weight was removed. Mother asked him what he thought when he was going down so fast, feet first. 'I thought that if I cut the line, we would not get the whale.' " Walker was not seriously hurt.

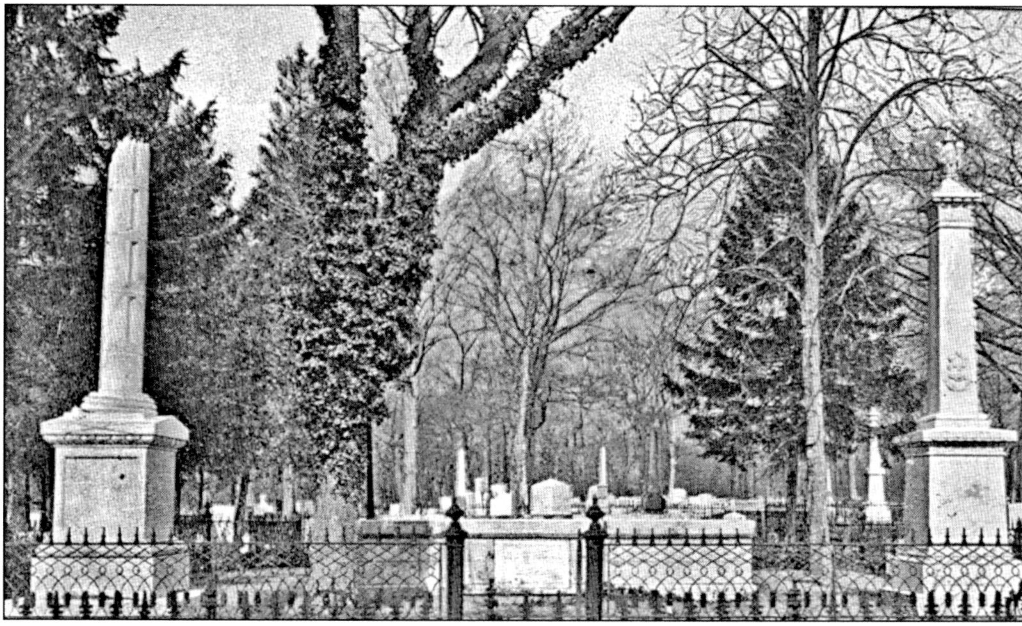

Inevitably, shore and offshore whaling diminished under the increased harvesting. The colonists had to build larger ships to pursue their quarry farther and farther seaward. It was a dangerous venture, as attested to by the Broken Mast Monument in the Oakland Cemetery in Sag Harbor: "Bold and enterprising ship masters . . . who periled their lives in . . . encounters with the monsters of the deep."

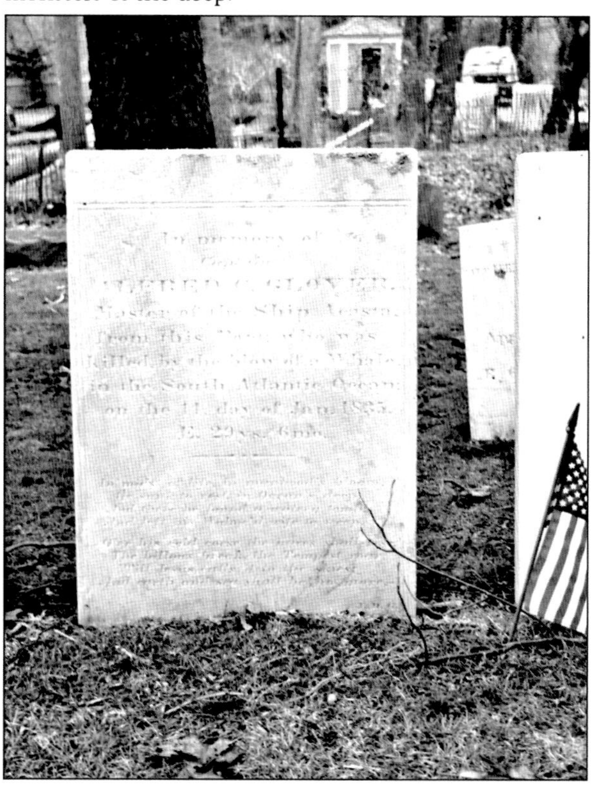

One did not need to have the obsession of Captain Ahab to stand in the bow of a whaleboat, harpoon poised to strike a leviathan. It was common practice for ship's captains to imperil their lives in the hunt and, often, to lose that ultimate gamble. This stone reads, "Alfred C. Glover, master of the ship *Anacosta*, from this port, who was killed by the blow of a whale, in the South Atlantic Ocean, on the 14th day of January, 1835, aged 29 years, & 4 months."

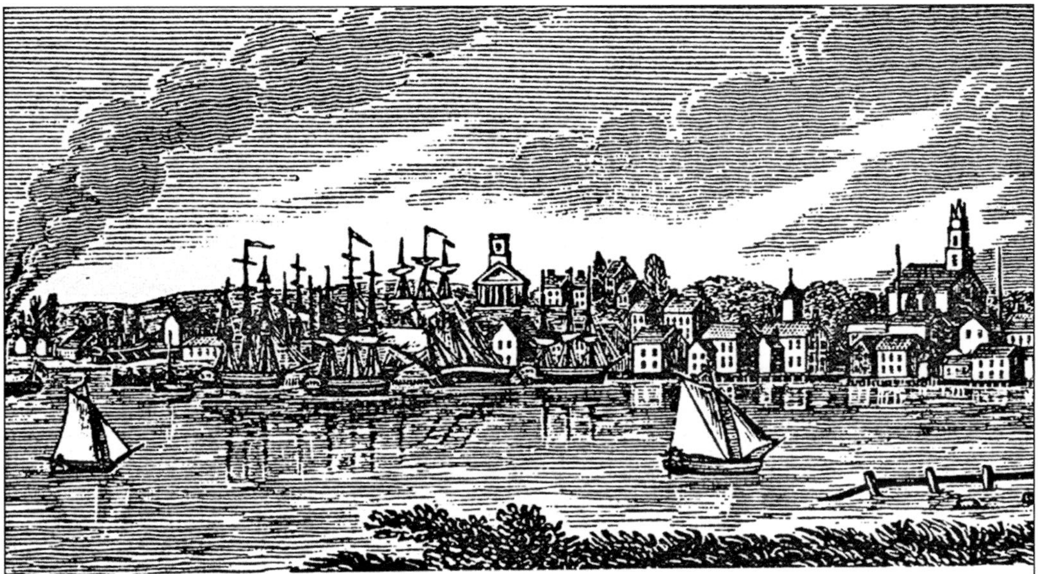

SAGG HARBOR IN 1841

The thriving village harbor was teeming with ships of every sort in the mid-1800s. The first wharf had been built in 1753 and included a triworks for processing the bounty of the returning whalers. The Long Wharf was constructed in 1770 and was gradually extended to its final length of 1,000 feet. Plans for a 1,100-foot-long wharf came to an abrupt end with the fire of 1848. (Courtesy Suffolk County Historical Society.)

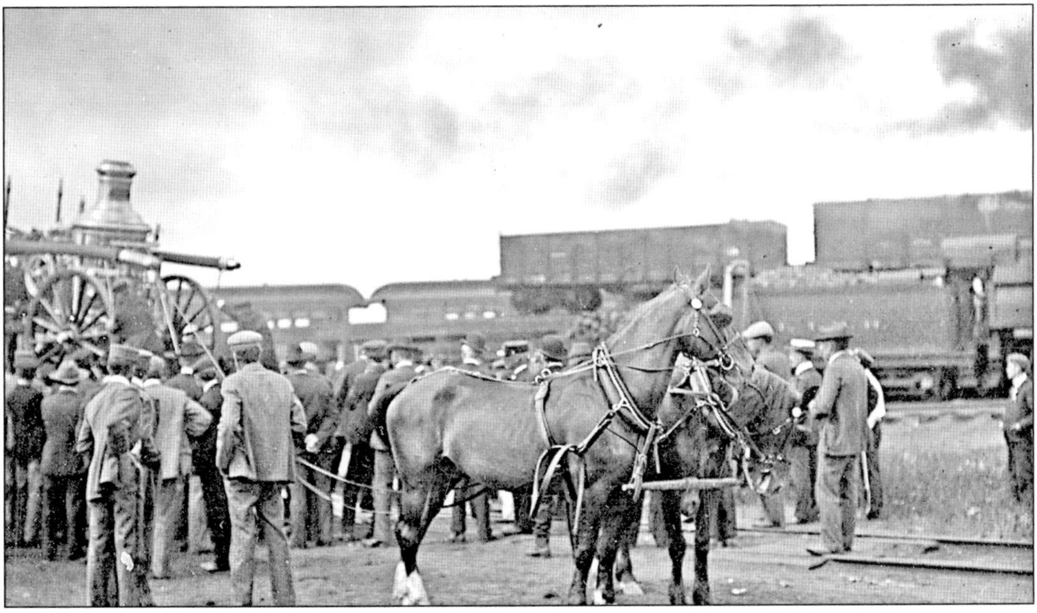

The railroad came to Sag Harbor in 1870. The mail, however, continued to be delivered by rail to Greenport and then by stagecoach across Shelter Island to the village. It took four years and a Committee on Mails to eventually change the system. The train brought sorely needed firefighting equipment to Sag Harbor. The wharfs and surrounding wooden buildings were an invitation to disaster—and fires were only too glad to accept. (Courtesy Suffolk County Historical Society.)

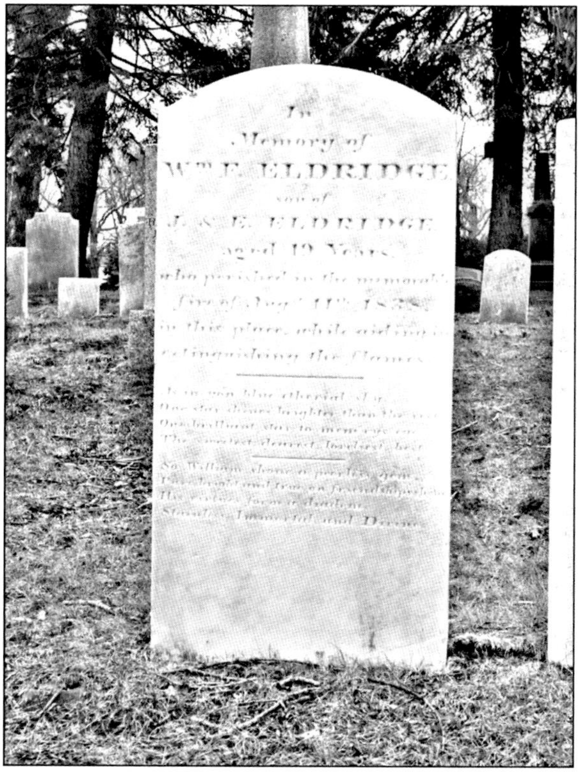

The village was devastated by fire on several occasions. In addition to 1838, other momentous fires raged in 1817, 1845, and 1877. The fire equipment brought by the railroad came too late for 19-year-old William F. Eldridge, who "perished in the memorable fire of 1838, in this place, while aiding in extinguishing the flames."

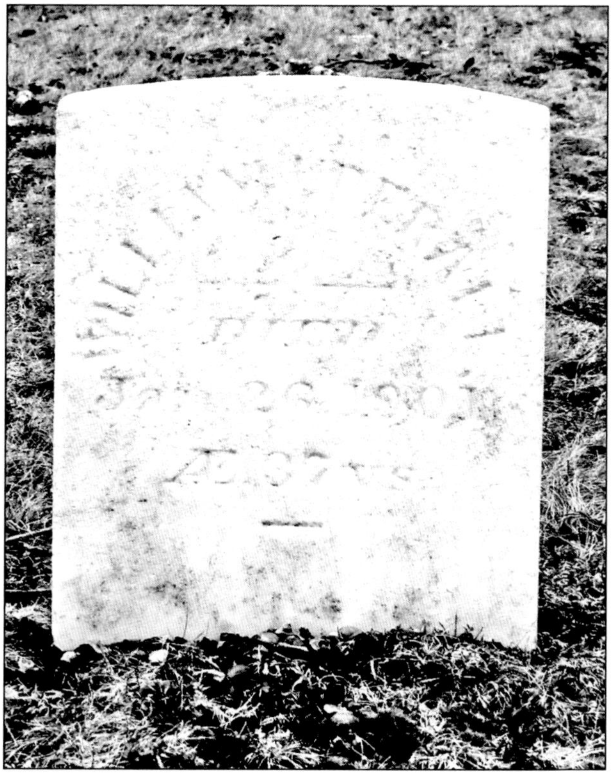

In 1859, Sag Harbor became the first village east of Brooklyn to be illuminated by gaslights. The gas facility was extensively damaged by fire in 1869, but gas remained the source of fueling heat and power until 1902. As is virtually always the case, progress is not without cost, often paid in human life. On January 26, 1901, when the electric plant was being installed, 37-year-old William Uberall was electrocuted while working on the electric line.

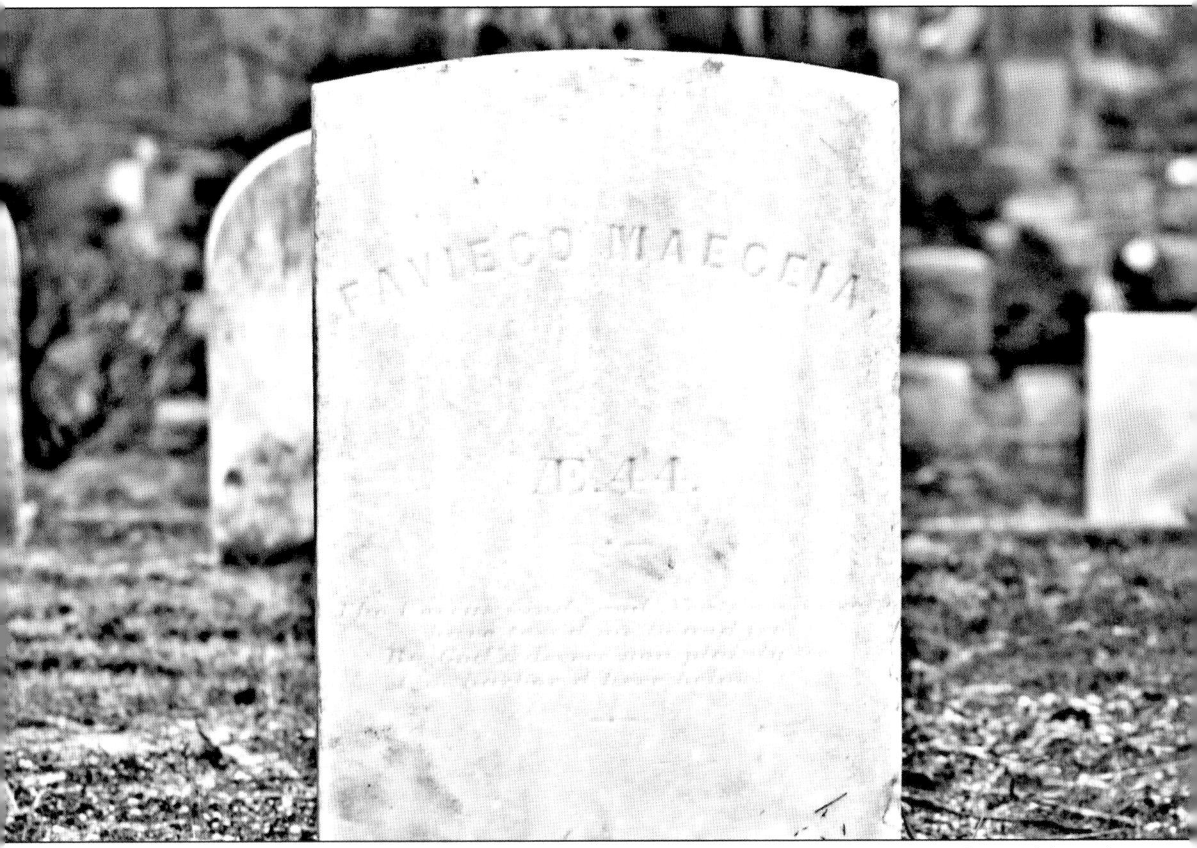

One night in September 1858, seven sailors appeared out of nowhere in Sag Harbor. Although Portuguese sailors were a common sight on the streets of this whaling town, these men stood out. Brandishing large amounts of Spanish coin, they aroused the curiosity of the locals. Stranger still, all but one of them were gone in the morning. Favieco Maeceia was mortally sick and died the very next day. The story slowly unfolded over the next few days. A marshal came to Montauk seeking information about a shipwreck off the Point. The picture that began to emerge was one of slave trade. The sailors were part of a crew that had recently sold 933 Africans in Cuba. The clipper ship was then scuttled five miles east of Montauk. All but Maeceia had made it safely to Connecticut. He was said to have left his caregivers more than enough coin for a decent burial in the Old Burial Ground. His remains, along with many others, were eventually moved to the Oakland Cemetery.

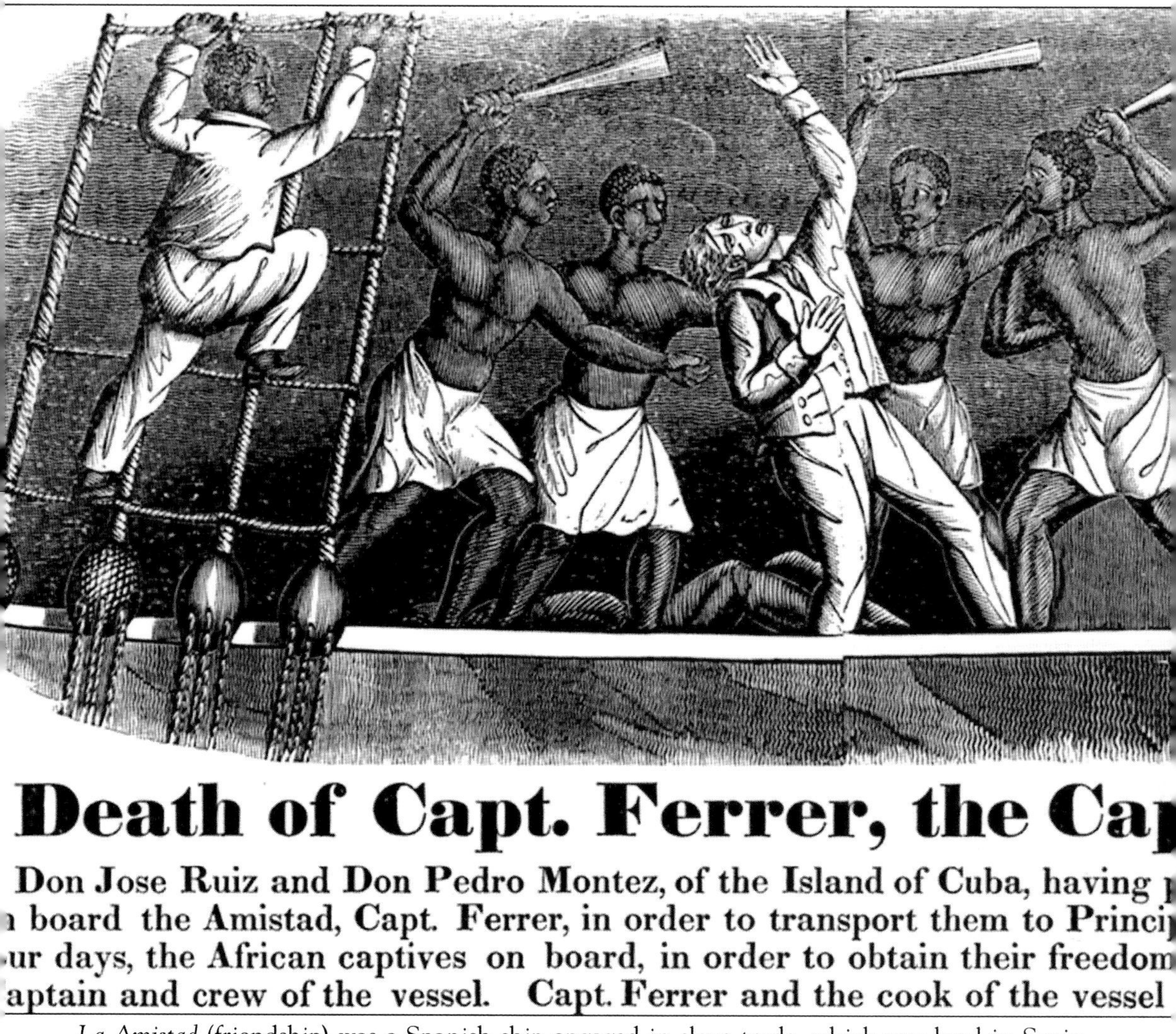

La Amistad (friendship) was a Spanish ship engaged in slave trade, which was legal in Spain. On June 28, 1839, it set sail from the Spanish territory of Havana, Cuba, with about 53 Africans who had been kidnapped in western Africa and sold into slavery. The schooner was on a course to Puerto Principe, Cuba. On July 2, Cinque, one of the slaves chained below deck, was able to free himself and then the remaining captives. The slaves stormed the deck and killed several of the crew, including Captain Ferrer. Two Africans also died in the struggle. Two other members of the crew managed to escape by jumping overboard. The lives of the two Spanish traders were spared, on the condition that they steer the ship on a course back to Africa, since the freed slaves did not know how to sail. The traders agreed, but instead steered the *Amistad* in the direction

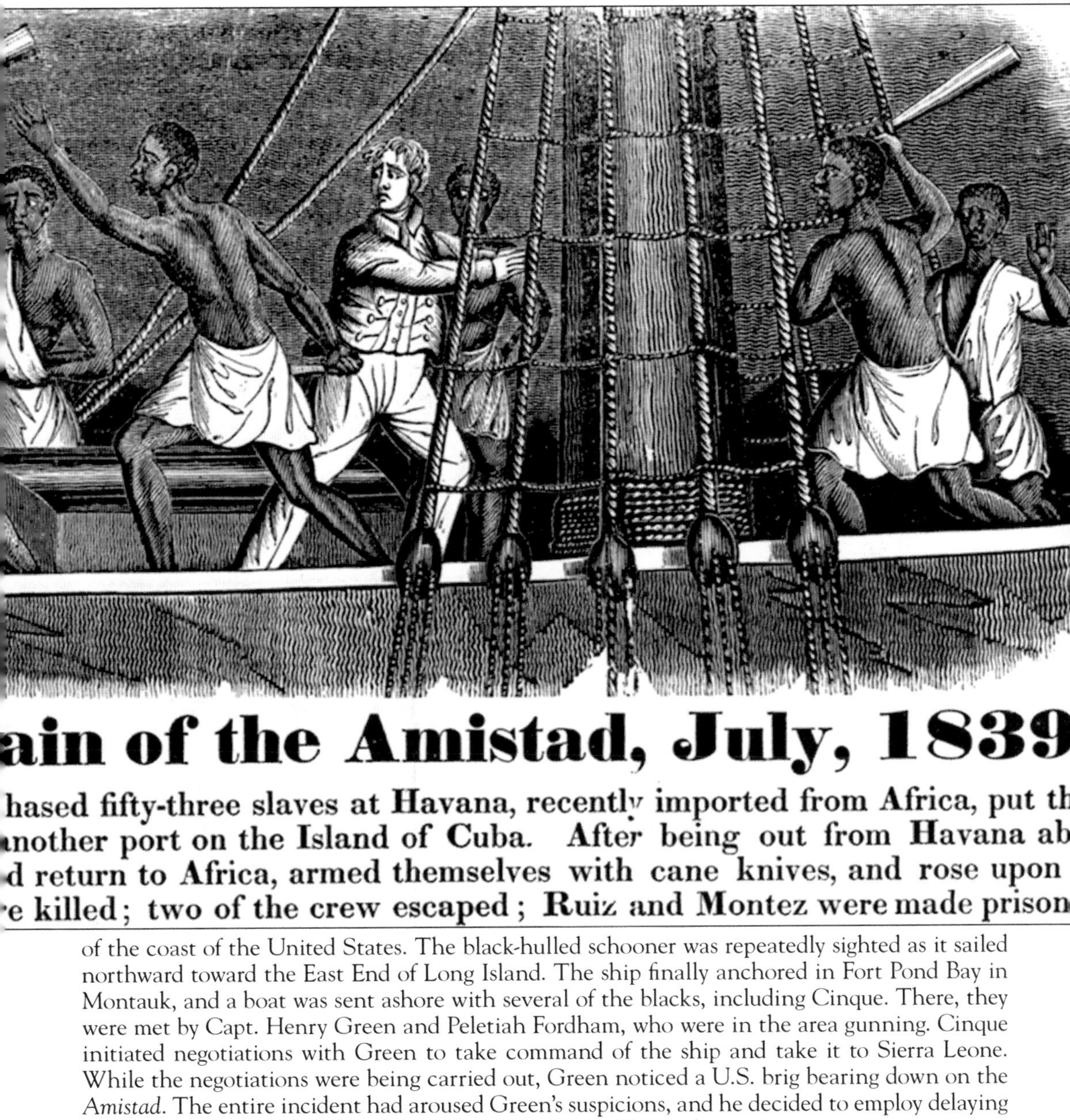

of the coast of the United States. The black-hulled schooner was repeatedly sighted as it sailed northward toward the East End of Long Island. The ship finally anchored in Fort Pond Bay in Montauk, and a boat was sent ashore with several of the blacks, including Cinque. There, they were met by Capt. Henry Green and Peletiah Fordham, who were in the area gunning. Cinque initiated negotiations with Green to take command of the ship and take it to Sierra Leone. While the negotiations were being carried out, Green noticed a U.S. brig bearing down on the *Amistad*. The entire incident had aroused Green's suspicions, and he decided to employ delaying tactics to see how things played out. (Courtesy Picture History.)

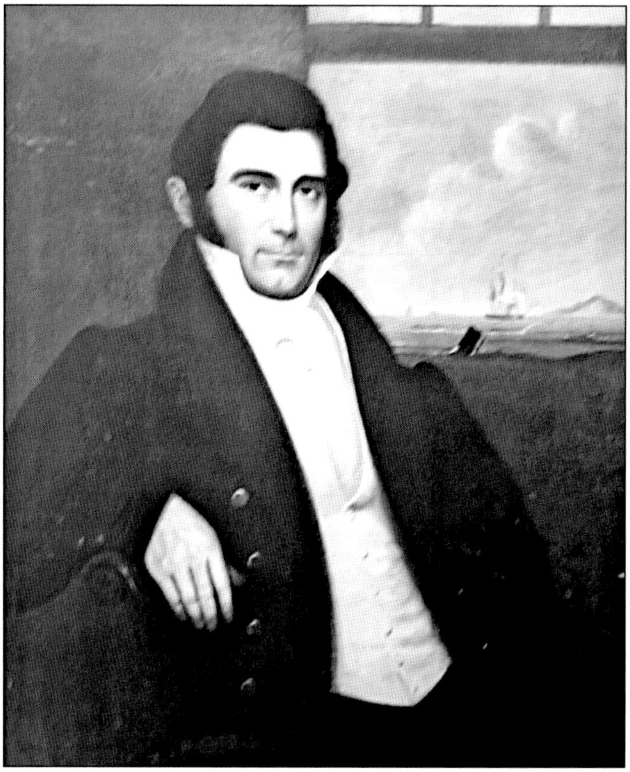

By the time the African Cinque became alerted to the situation, it was too late to avoid capture of the ship and his men. All were taken to New London and charged with mutiny and murder. Capt. Henry Green was a key witness at the trial, but his credibility was challenged on the basis of his claim to have conversed with Cinque, whereas the latter, along with his companions, had remained silent throughout the hearings. Eventually, it came out that Cinque could indeed converse in broken English, and the captain was vindicated. (Courtesy Southold Historical Society.)

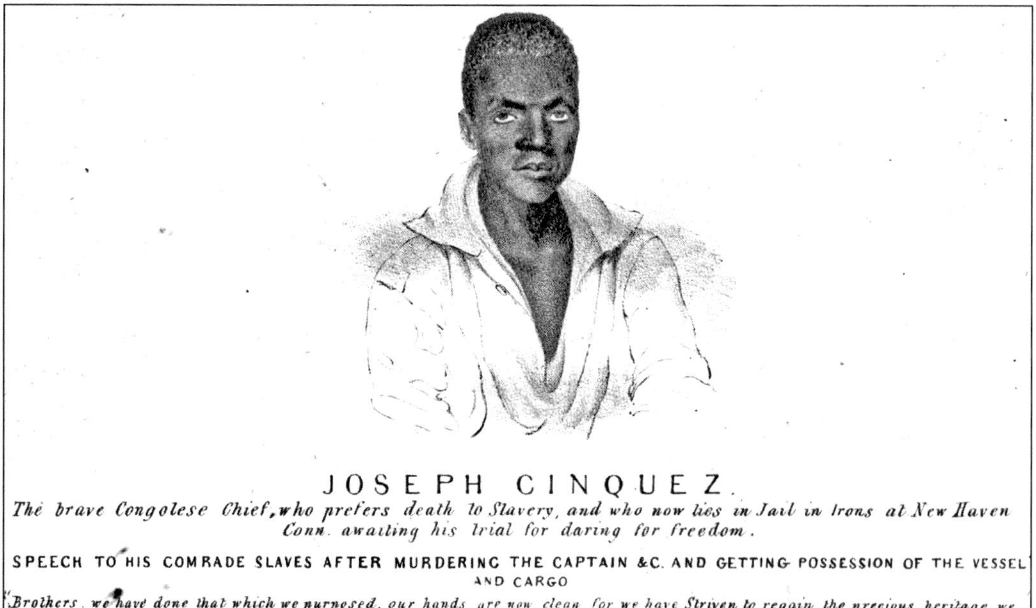

The abolitionists organized the defense for the African cause. Ultimately, the final disposition of the case was left for the Supreme Court in 1841. John Quincy Adams and Roger S. Baldwin were the attorneys for the defendants. The court ruled that the men were free and had the right to defend their freedom through violent insurrection. It is said, sadly enough, that upon his return to his homeland, Cinque himself became a slave trader. (Courtesy Picture History.)

Henry Green was one of the better-known whaling captains of his day. He was the captain of the *Sabina*, one of the first whalers to sail for California in search of gold. In 1816, a mysterious ship came ashore on a beach in Southampton. The wreck master took charge and stripped the ship of whatever could be removed. While gunning near the ship a few weeks later, Green, fresh from a voyage, took occasion to go aboard.

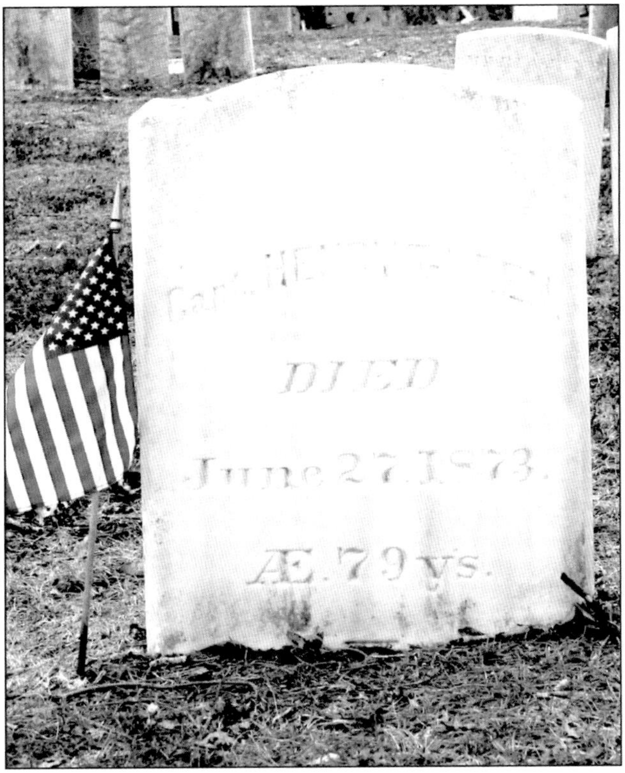

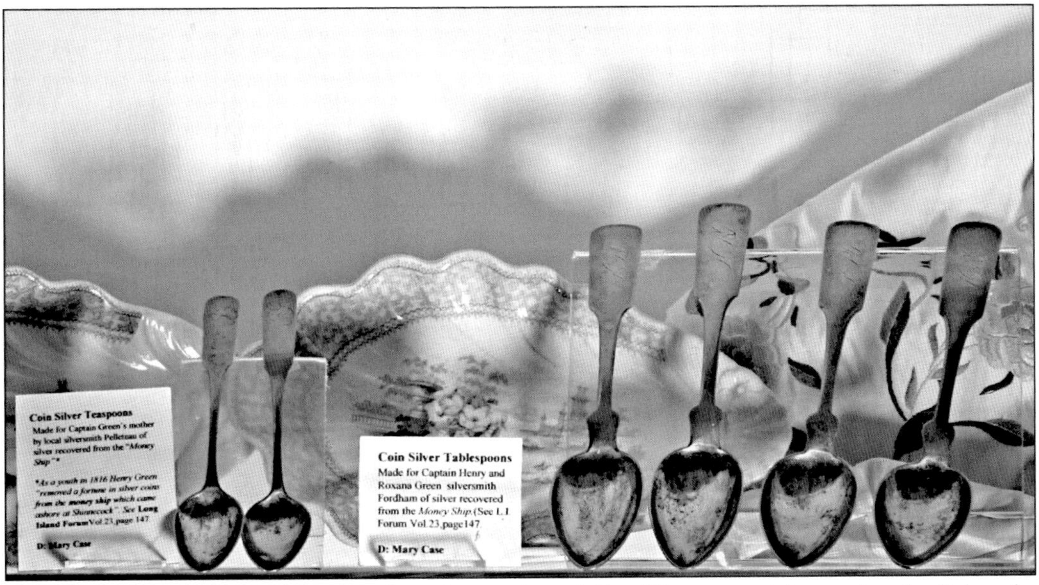

There, in plain view on the cabin floor, lay a silver dollar. The next night, under the light of a lantern, Henry Green began to search the cabin. He looked up and spied the edge of a silver dollar in the wooden ceiling. As he pried it open, he was showered with silver dollars raining on his head. His continued his "mining trips" until a storm hit and the wreck washed out to sea. Green gave his wife a set of teaspoons made from the silver dollars he collected on the "Money Ship." (Courtesy Southold Historical Society.)

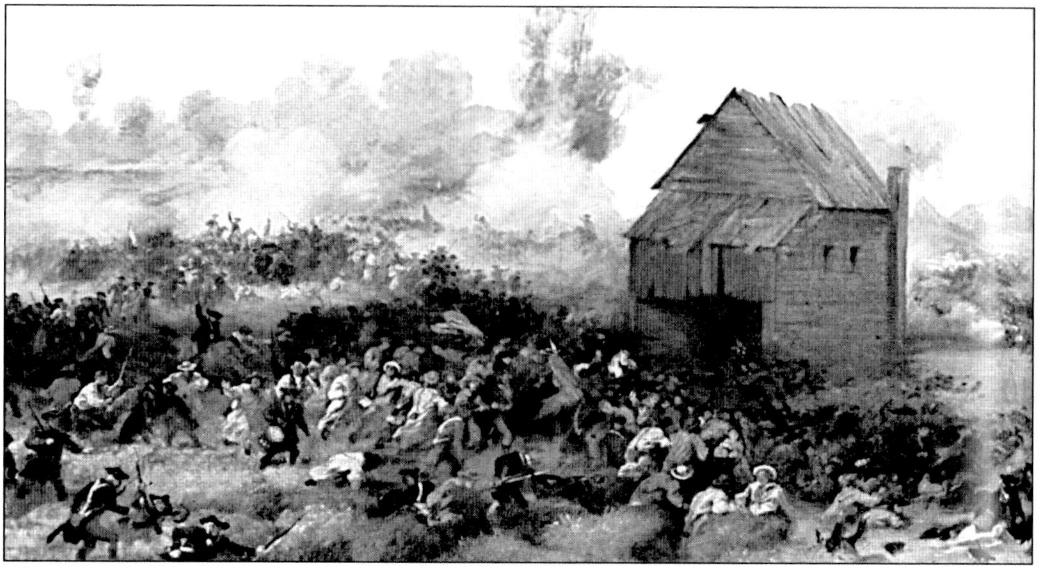

The Battle of Long Island was fought in Brooklyn on August 27–29, 1776. Some 15,000 British troops under Gen. William Howe landed at Gravesend. Opposing these forces was Gen. George Washington's army of almost 19,000 men. The British began to force back the American units. Washington soon found himself in an untenable position. Indeed, Howe said, "They are at our mercy and are ours tomorrow." Thus began one of the most famous retreats in the history of warfare. Under the cover of night, and aided by fog and calm winds, boats were sent over from Manhattan. (Courtesy Picture History.)

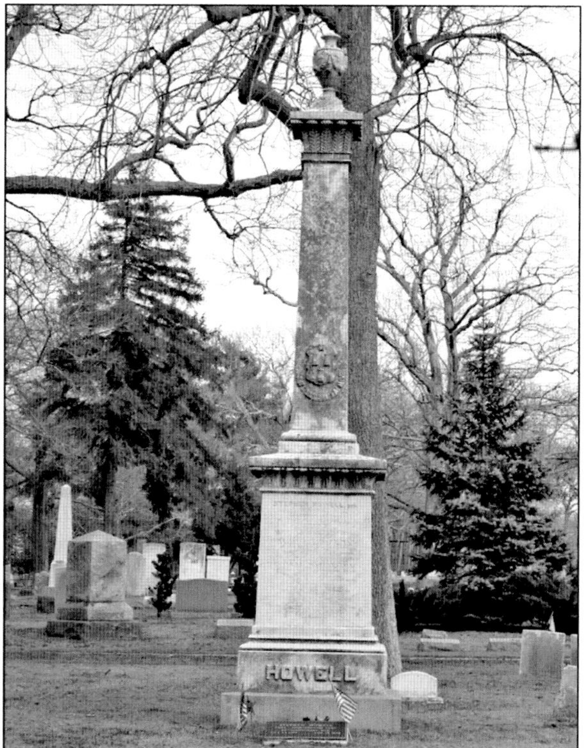

The evacuation had begun. By early morning, as the fog lifted, the British, expecting to deliver the coup de grâce, instead gazed upon a field devoid of a single patriot. The inscription reads, in part, as follows: "Stephen Howell, Sen., a native of Southampton, LI, an American Whig, . . . took an early and decided stand for his country at the commencement of the Revolutionary War. He entered the army as a soldier in the battle of Long Island, Aug. 26, 1776. He shared the sufferings and honor of that gloomy day."

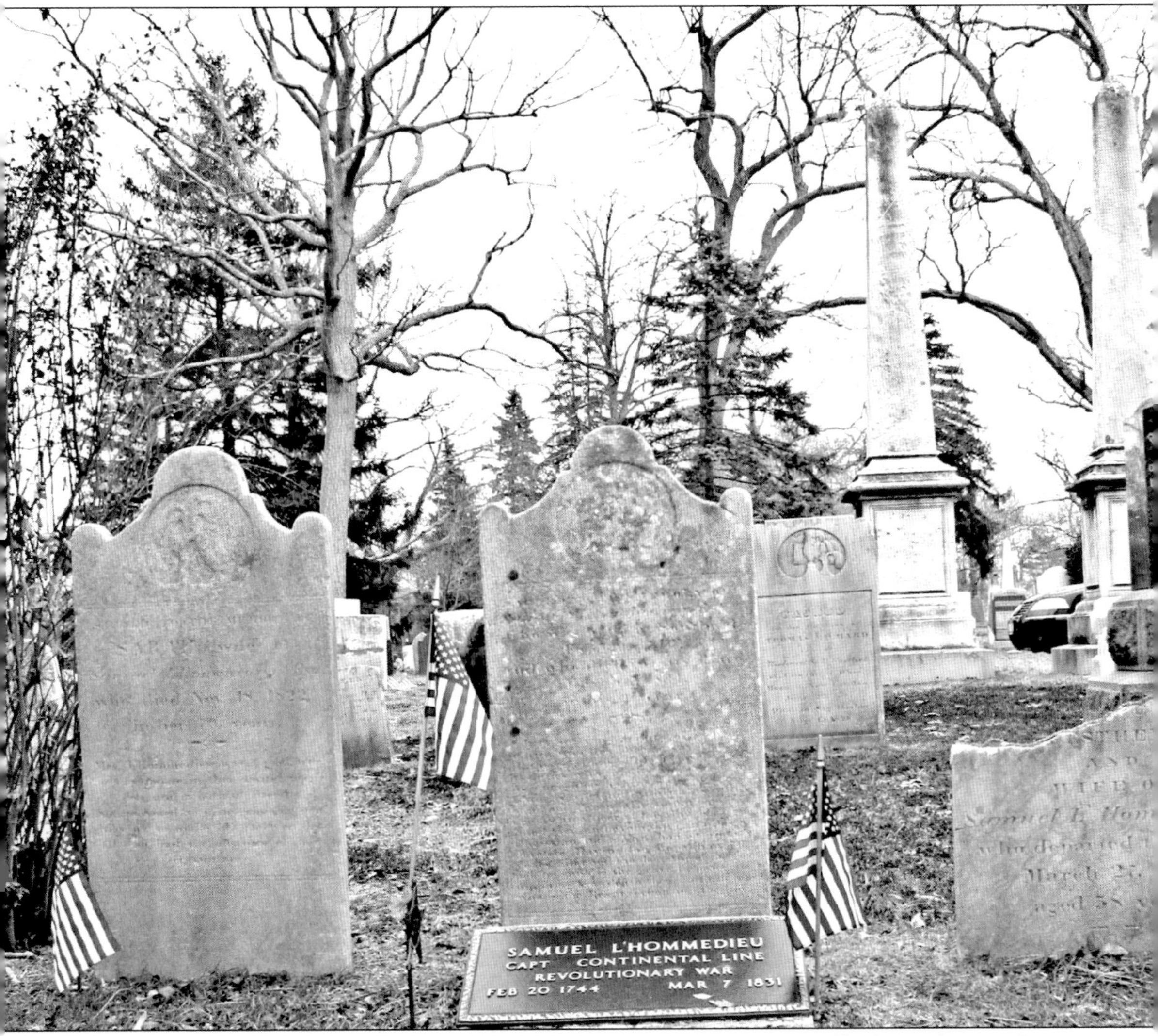

Methodism came late to Long Island. The early settlers were initially free of any religious establishments. Eventually, the Presbyterian and Congregational churches began to flourish. The latter two were predominant on the East End of Long island, whereas Methodism was more dominant to the west. It was not until 1764, when Rev. John Whitfield preached in the Hamptons, that the voice of a Methodist was heard on the East End. Whitfield was a colleague of John Wesley and an eloquent preacher. He visited the South Fork on his way to Boston. His message was well received by Samuel L'Hommedieu, who became a convert. L'Hommedieu was a captain in the Continental line during the Revolution. He died and was buried in Oakland Cemetery in Sag Harbor in 1831 at age 87.

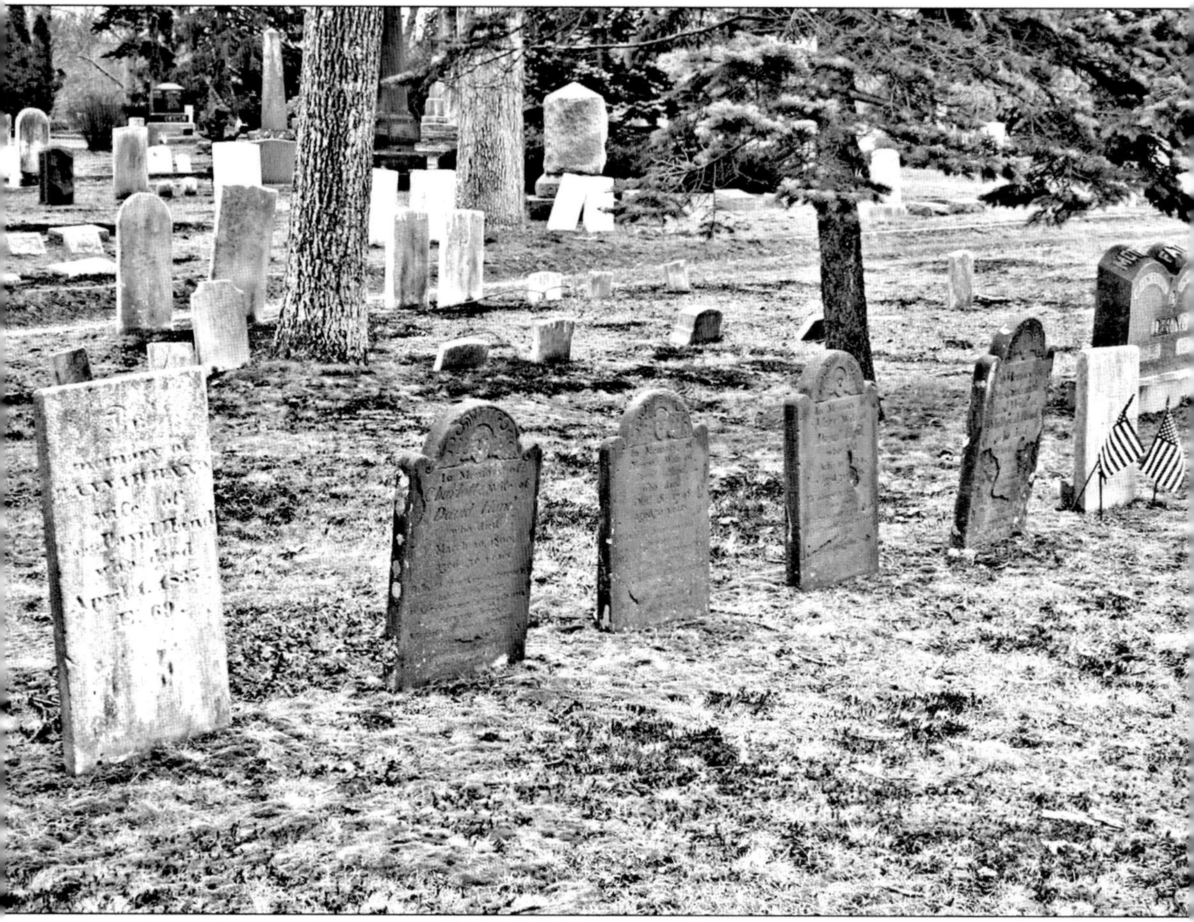

Capt. David Hand's adventures could fill a book—especially if the book included the lives of his wives, of which he had five. All of them are buried side by side in Oakland Cemetery. Hand was a sailor of both privateers and the fledgling patriot navy. He knew from personal experience the horrors of the prison ship *Jersey*. On one occasion, when captured while serving aboard a small frigate, he was brought aboard the British ship after being stripped of his clothing by the British crew. He approached the ship's commander and insisted his belongings be returned. When his demands were ignored by the captain, Hand hurled a challenge at the entire British crew: "All I ask now is to begin at your taffrail, and fight the whole ship's crew forward, and die like a man!" Fortunately for Hand's future wives, the commander dismissed the challenge and sent him to join the other prisoners. Hand's epitaph reads, "Behold ye living mortals passing by; / How thick the partners of one husband lie; / Swift and unsearchable the ways of God, / Just but severe his chast'ning rod."

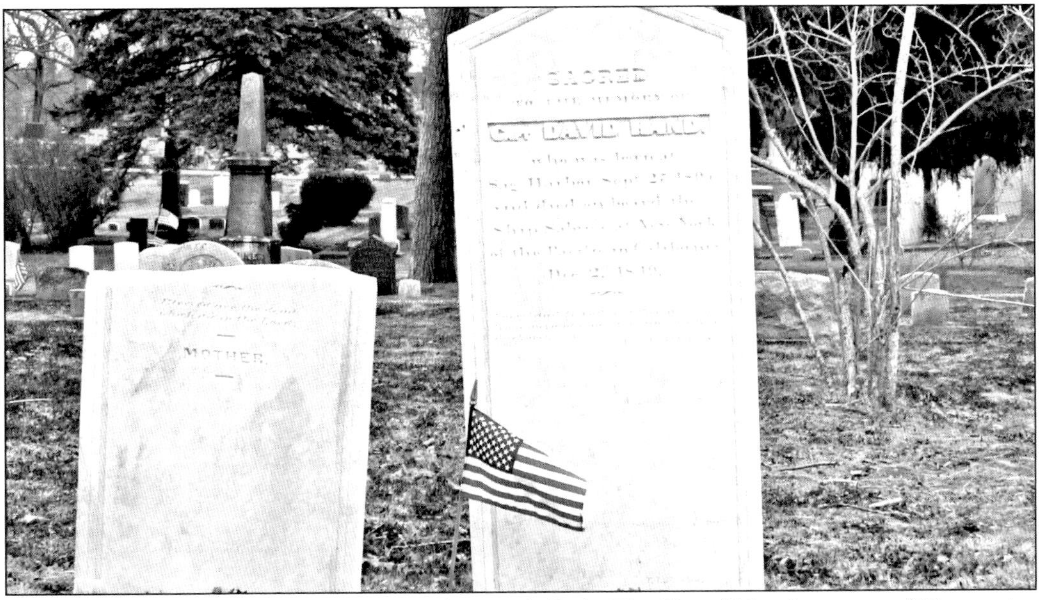

The name David Hand is ubiquitous on the South Fork. This David Hand was one of 19 captains who teamed up to resurrect to old whaling ship *Sabina* from rotting on the beach at Sag Harbor. The more obvious leaks were recaulked. Other repairs needed to be made after the bark had rounded Cape Horn. The year was 1849; the destination was California; the purpose was gold. Hand never had the chance to join his shipmates in the largely futile hunt. He died while still at sea, on December 2, 1849, at age 44.

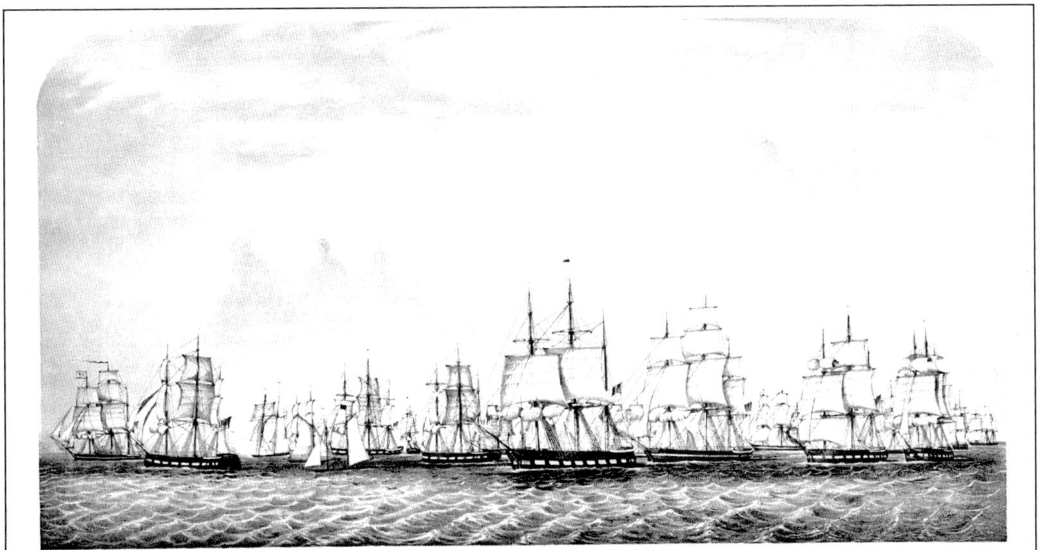

If the gold rush delivered a left that dropped whaling to its knees, then the Civil War delivered a right that was the knockout punch. At the outset of the Civil War, the whaling industry was in a marked decline. In 1862, the government purchased three Sag Harbor whaleboats, not to be used as transports nor merchant ships. Rather, they joined the "Stone Fleet." These slow, outdated whalers were brought to Charleston Bay, where they were filled with stone and scuttled in an unsuccessful attempt to disrupt the Confederate cause. (*The Stone Fleet*, Courtesy of the New Bedford Whaling Museum.)

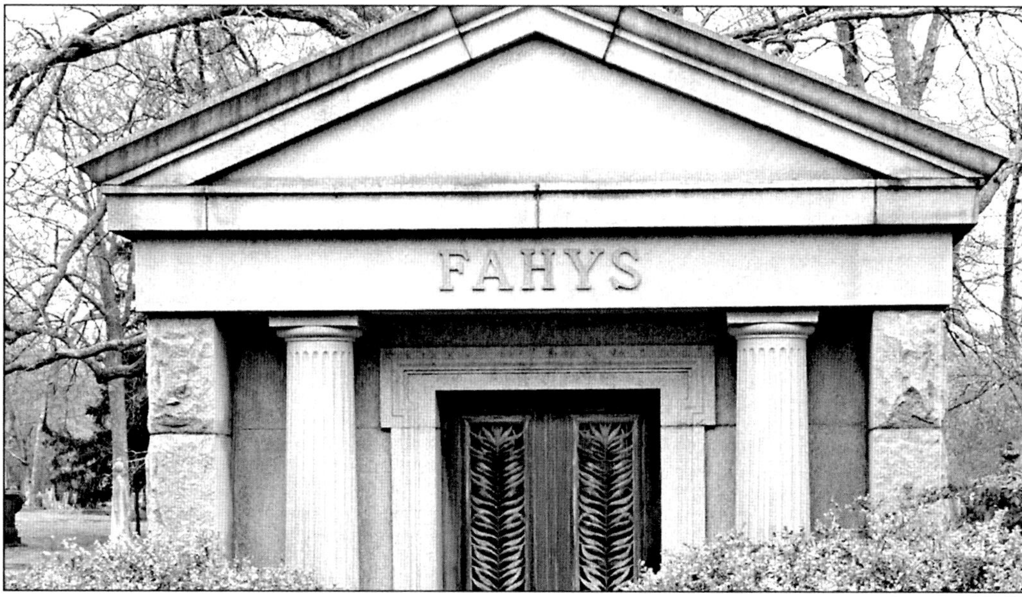

When the last whaling ship, the *Myrna*, sailed from port on April 25, 1871, the village was in great need to fill the void. Not only the main actors (captains and crew) but also the supporting cast (coopers, carpenters, and blacksmiths) were stranded in port. Other industries were needed to step in and fill the void. In came the textile industry, a pottery factory, a silver manufacturer, and a torpedo-testing station. In stepped Joseph Fahys, who began manufacturing watchcases. Sag Harbor was able to stay afloat.

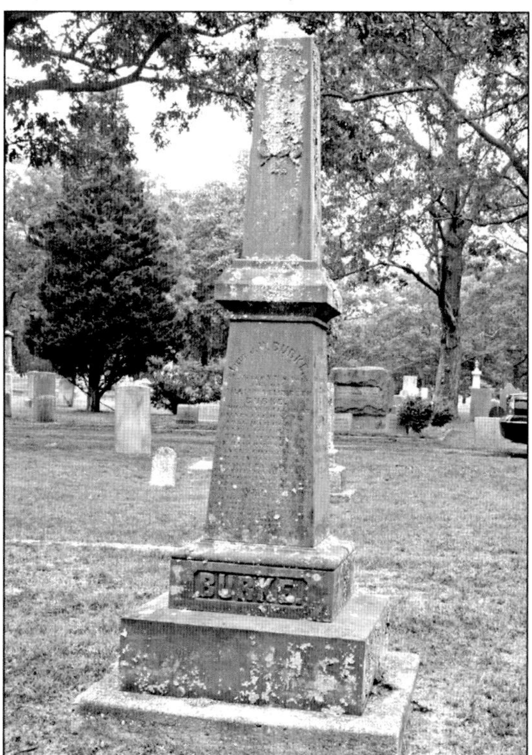

Lt. J. W. Burk was killed on June 2, 1864, at age 31 while serving in the 81st Regiment New York State Volunteers. His body was brought here from Gaines Ferry, near Cold Harbor, Virginia, where "while at the head of his company, gallantly cheering on his men, [he] was struck by a musket ball in the forehead, and fell to the ground dead."

A high infant mortality rate was a constant of the 18th and 19th centuries. Plagues were a frequent visitor. Death of the newborn and the young was high. This stone is a memorial to three children of Phinehas and Nancy Corey: William H. Corey, who died February 25, 1800, at age six years, six months, and six days; and twins, a son and a daughter, who died at birth on April 17, 1800. The triple stone is in the style of the Connecticut Valley craftsmen.

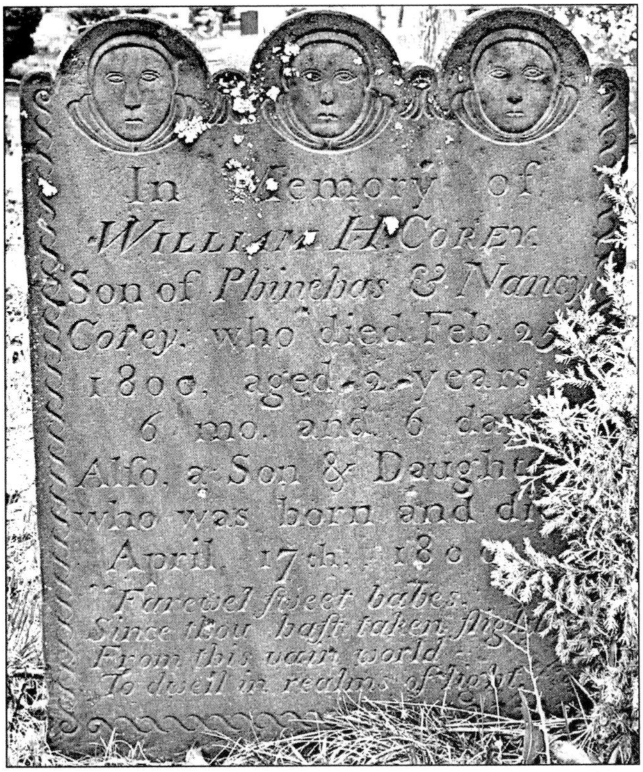

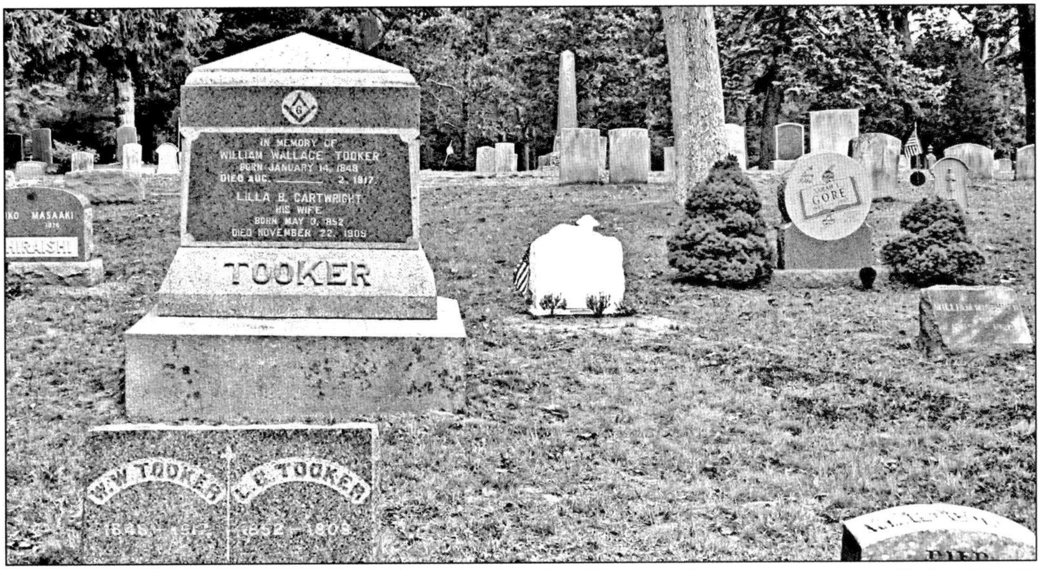

William Wallace Tooker (1848–1917) was born in Sag Harbor. His great-great-grandfather David Frothingham published the first newspaper on Long Island and printed it in Sag Harbor. Tooker was a pharmacist by trade, but his first love was the study of the local American Indian culture. He befriended the Montauk sachem "King" David Pharoah and members of the large Cuffee and Bunn families. In 1888, the *Brooklyn Eagle Almanac* began publishing "Tooker's Indian Place Names" in their annual editions. Eventually, the articles were collected into the definitive work *Indian Place Names on Long Island.*

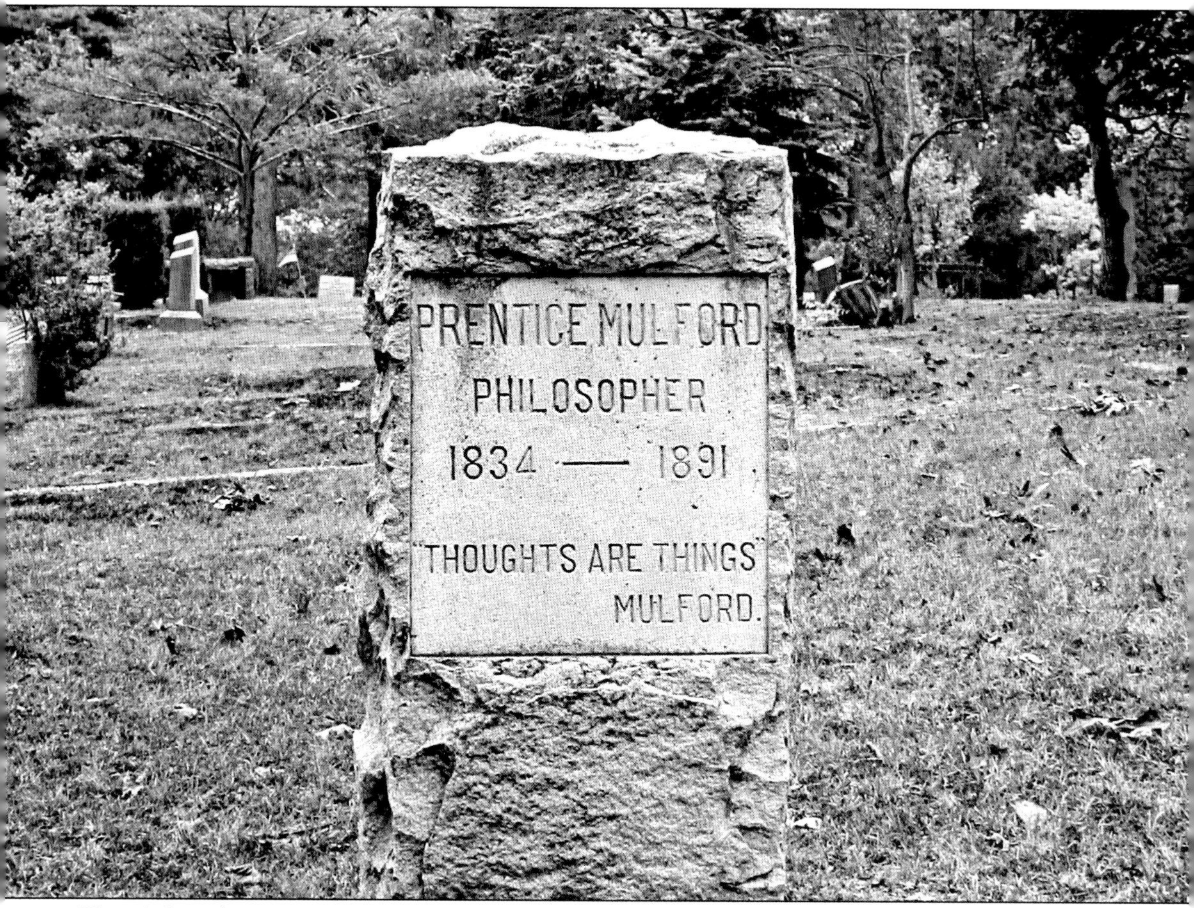

The philosopher Prentice Mulford (1834–1891) was born in Sag Harbor. As a young man, he joined in the rush of many Long Islanders to California in 1856. He was at times a cook, a schoolteacher, and a prospector. But his heart was not in it. For one thing, he cared little for money. While writing for the *Golden Era*, a San Francisco newspaper, he refused to place his money in banks, which he thought were immoral institutions. Shy in a crowd or with anyone he did not know, Mulford was nonetheless a favorite among his colleagues. He lived aboard an old whaling boat, which he anchored at some secluded spot in the bay. He believed thoughts were tangible: "If you keep any idea, good or ill, in your mind from month to month and year to year you make it a more enduring unseen reality, and as it so becomes stronger and stronger, it must at last take shape and appear in the seen and physical." When Mulford died he left behind a legacy of 36 volumes of his philosophy.

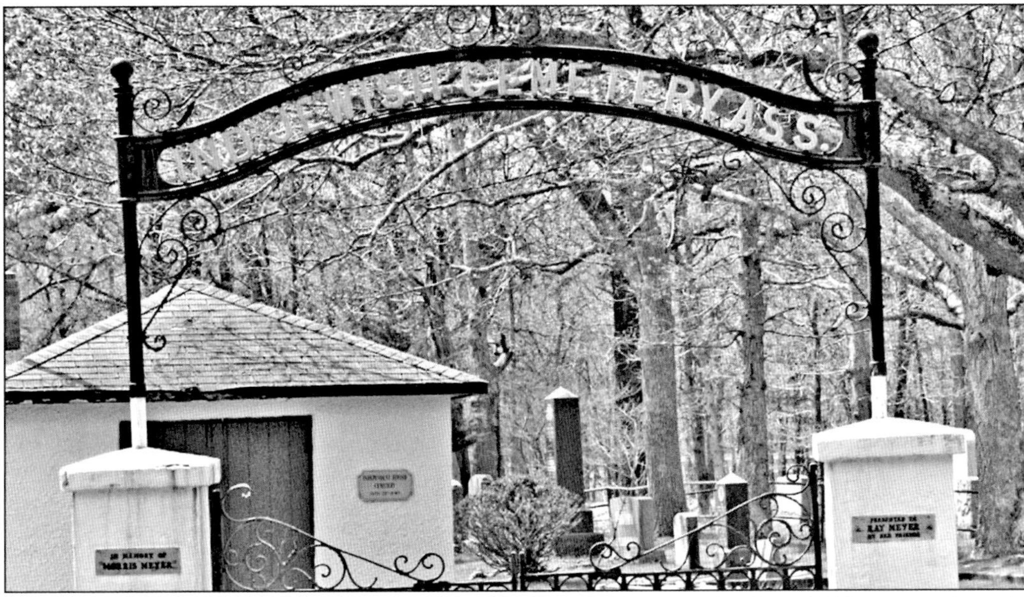

Joseph Fahys brought many European Jews to Sag Harbor in the late 1800s to work in his watchcase factory. Many were from Russia, Poland, and Hungary. A cemetery was opened in 1891, and the first burial was held for the infant child of Morris and Sarah Spodok in May of that year. The Hungarian section of the cemetery is separated from the adjacent burial ground for the Russian and Polish Jews by a simple iron rail fence. Pebbles, placed on and around the graves, are notable throughout the graveyards.

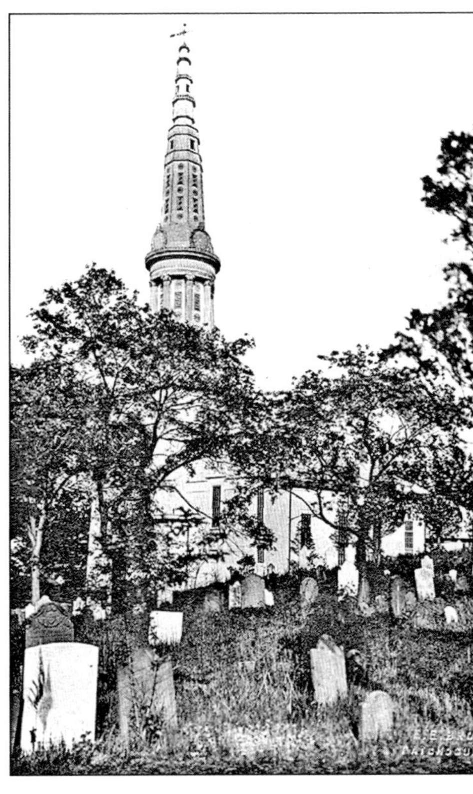

The Whaler's Church stands by the Old Burial Ground. Still an imposing structure, it is a mere shadow of its former self. The 150-foot steeple, reaching—along with its parishioners—to the heavens, is gone. The Hurricane of 1938 spared the lives of the villagers. But it took one of this village's landmarks away. For winters to come, in many a home in Sag Harbor, the fire that took the chill from bones of the locals was fueled by the wood from the spyglass-shaped steeple. (Courtesy Suffolk County Historical Society.)

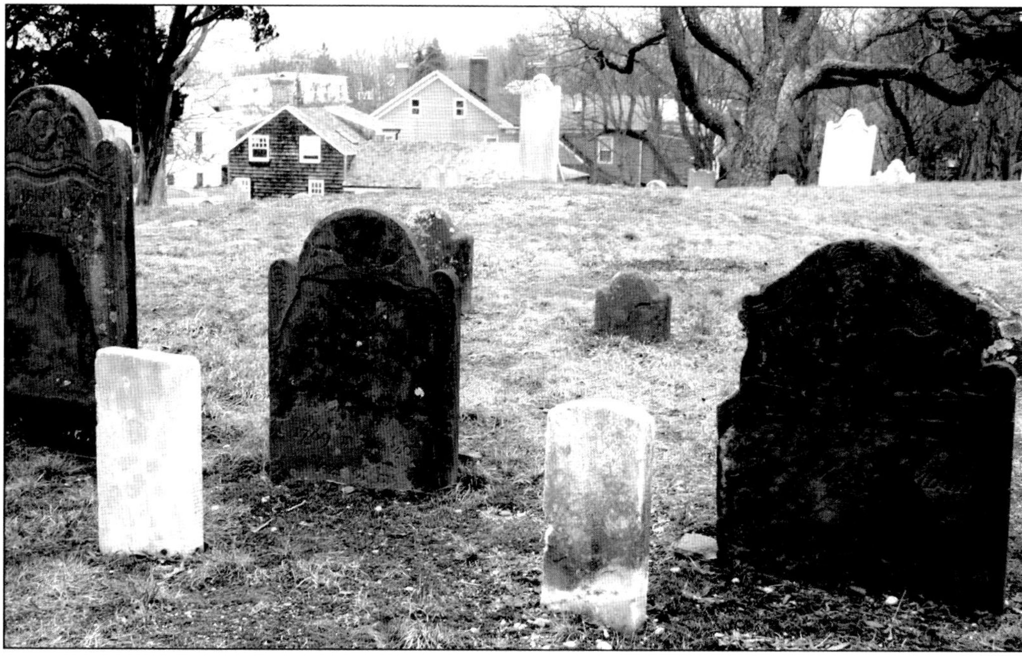

Nathan Fordham (1721–1805) was one of the first to settle at Sag Harbor. He lived near Otter Pond, where he farmed and fished. In the early years, the area was sometimes referred to as "Fordhamville." In 1772, Fordham and several others started a stagecoach route between Sag Harbor and Brooklyn.

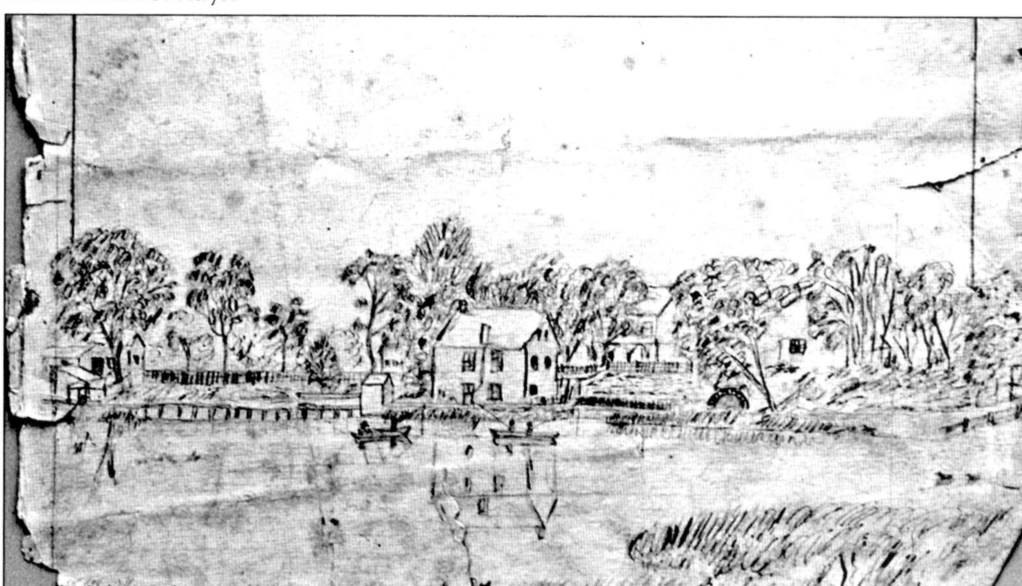

In 1782, Nathan Fordham received from the trustees of Southampton a grant to all the privileges of Otter Pond. The grant included the right to dig across the road, to have the pond "communicate with the salt water, in order to make a Fish Pond, together with the privileges of the brook that may run from said pond, so that the fish may not be hindered from coming in." The grant was in perpetuity to Fordham and his heirs, provided that they maintained a good and sufficient bridge across the brook. (Courtesy Suffolk County Historical Society.)

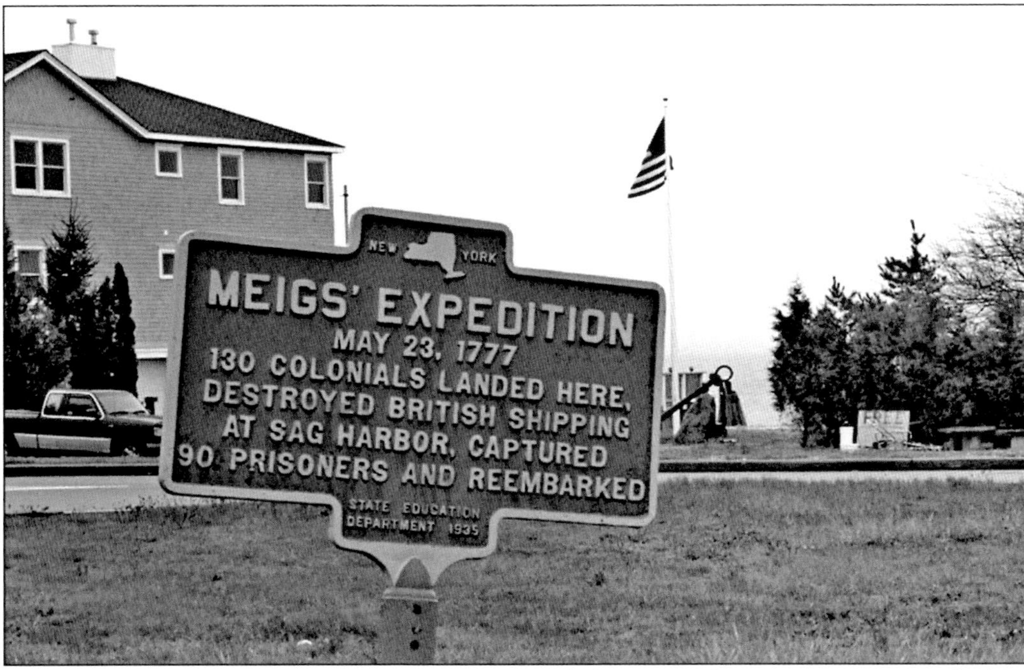

On May 23, 1777, Lt. Col. Jonathan Return Meigs led a party of 130 patriots on a raid of Sag Harbor. The men came in whaleboats across Long Island Sound and portaged at a narrow strip of land in Southold into Peconic Bay. Crossing under the cover of darkness, they landed at this beach in North Haven. The party relied on the element of surprise to attack a much larger British force, garrisoned in Sag Harbor.

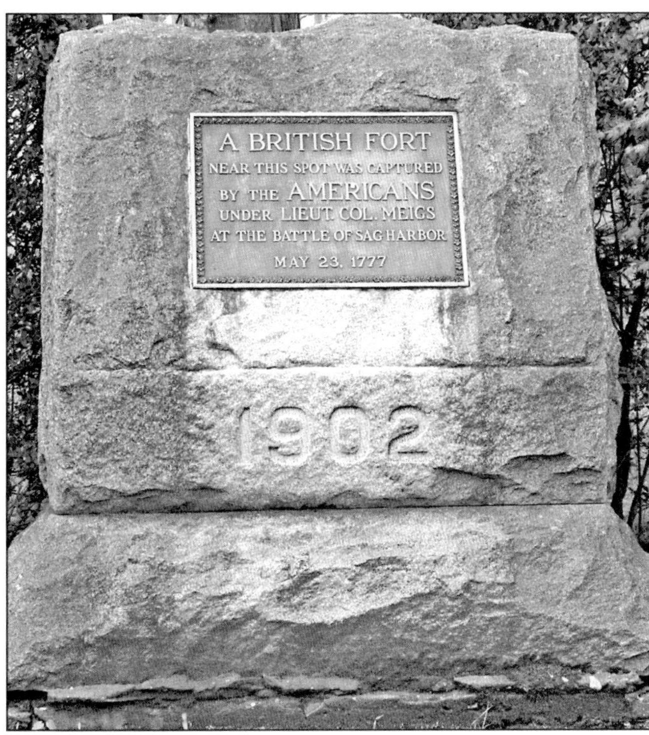

And surprise them they did. The English troops at the fort, which was situated near the Old Burial Ground, never knew what hit them. Within a few hours, the raiding party had destroyed several British ships and made off with a prize of 90 prisoners. Although of little strategic value, the raid was a tactical victory and gave a boost to the sagging moral of the Americans.

The American Navy was, at the start, no match for the royal fleet. Instead, the navy harassed the British fleet by hiring private, agile ships to prey on the vessels along the Northeast coastline. Unfortunately, some of the captains made no distinction between Tory and Whig, leading to additional hardship for many East Enders. In the Old Burying Ground, in Sag Harbor, lies the body of William Havens, captain of the privateers *Beaver*, *Jay*, and *Retaliation* during the Revolution.

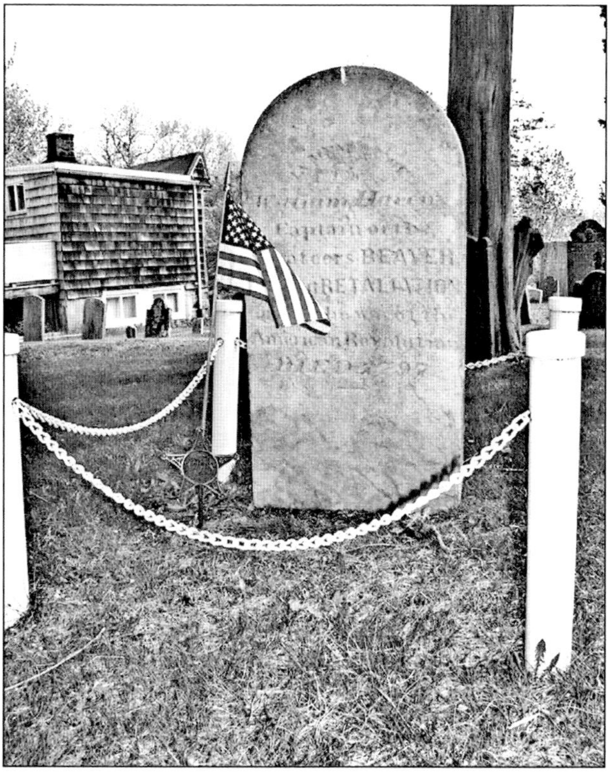

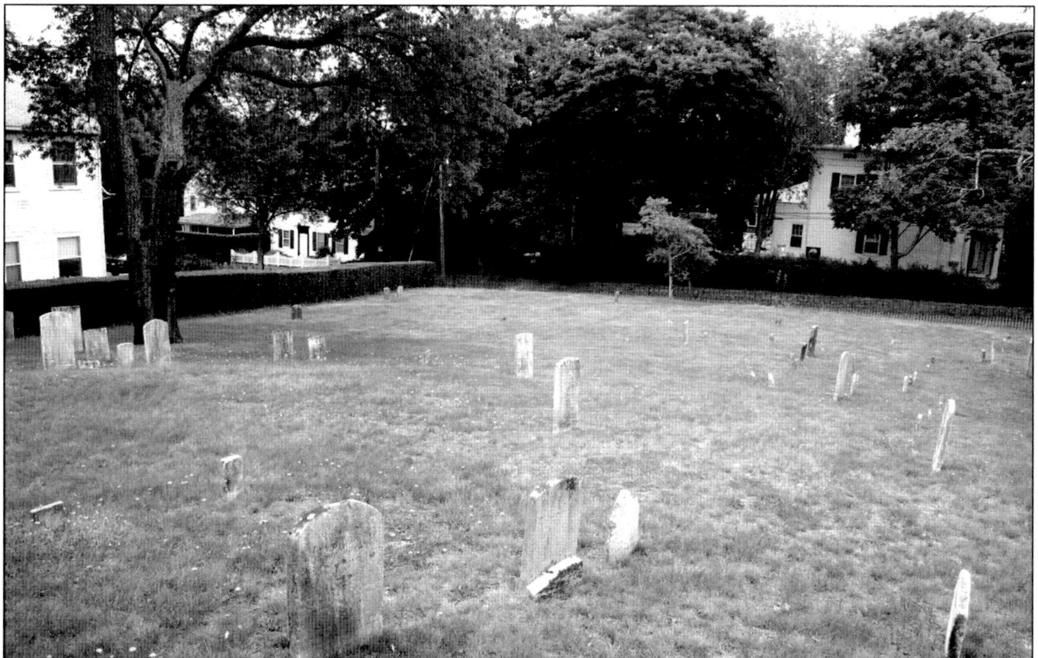

The back left corner of the cemetery is a segregated portion where both African Americans and Portuguese are buried. The latter were, for the most part, sailors. Indeed, one 19 year old had died in a fall from the foremast of the ship *Hannibal* in 1833.

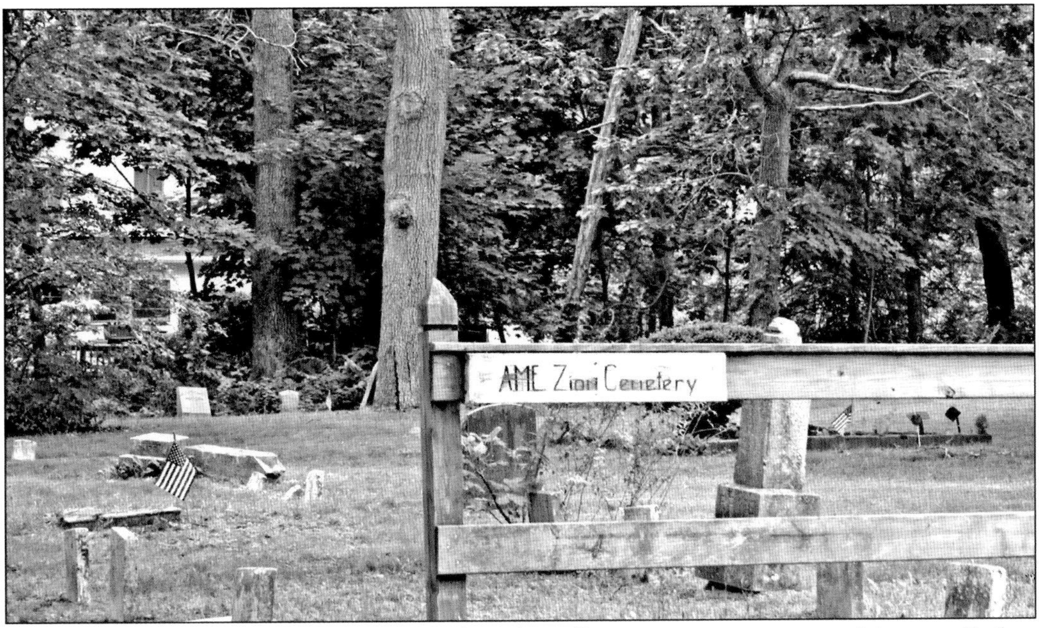

During the heyday of whaling in Sag Harbor, the village was, in a sense, a melting pot. Sailors from many countries and of many ethnicities made their living and their homes here. The area known as Eastville was a black community. As such, it had an African Methodist Episcopal church, founded in 1840, with a cemetery located just down the street. In 1858, the church was subjected to a power struggle between two groups seeking to control it.

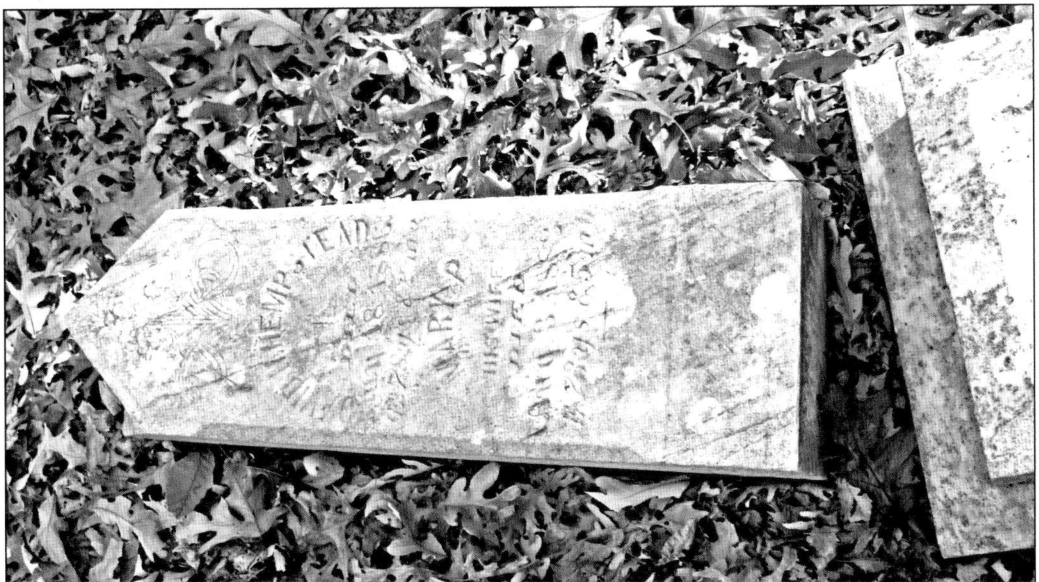

William David Hempstead came to the rescue. Hempstead won the highest praise from none other than Judge Henry P. Hedges as an outstanding member of the community. Through Hempstead's intervention, the African Methodist Episcopal Zion church retained control of the property. Several Civil War veterans are buried here. An interesting sidebar may be found on the Louisiana Civil War Web site. It states that "Louisiana's 24,000 Black troops distinguished themselves at the Battle of Port Hudson. And further, that they were the largest of any state contingent."

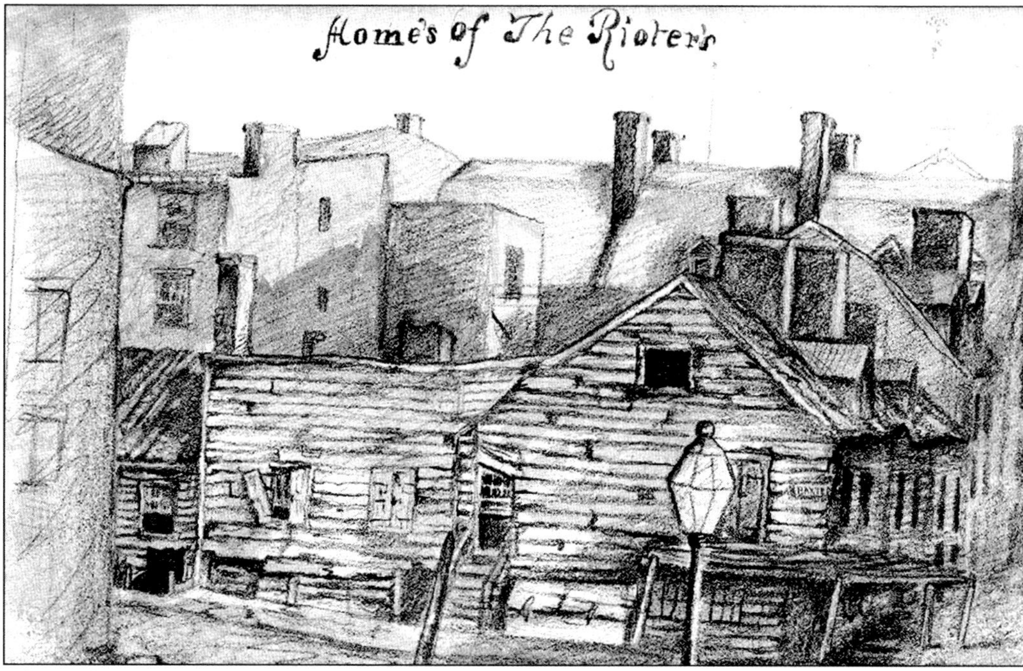

The enthusiasm for the War of the Rebellion gradually waned, and an all-volunteer army was not sustainable. On March 3, 1863, Congress passed the Enrollment Act of Conscription. The draft began in Suffolk County on Tuesday, September 1, 1863. A total of 1,120 men were called. Of those drafted, "some were at sea, some claim British exemption, some blind, and some have an eye on Canada, and others an eye on $300 with which to purchase a substitute," [Trustees]. In New York City, the act triggered protests that culminated in the Draft Riots of July 13–16. (*Homes of the Rioters*. Collection of the New York Historical Society.)

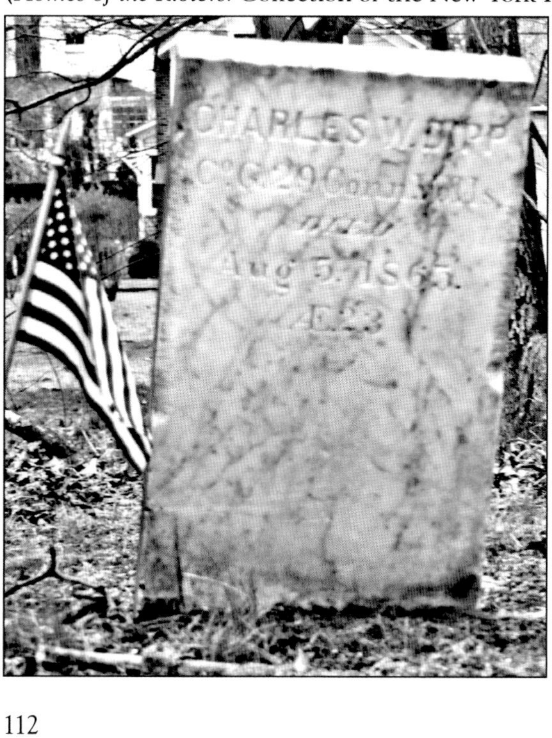

The rioters initially targeted draft offices and police stations, but soon, inexplicably, turned their wrath toward the African Americans. It took the 7th Regiment of New York State Militia to eventually quell the rioters, but not before 100 lives were lost and $1.5 million in property was damaged. When Eastville residents were threatened, white neighbors came to their assistance. Tensions abated, and no one was injured. Many African Americans of Sag Harbor served the Union cause. One was Charles W. Dipp of Company G 29th Connecticut Volunteers, who died on August 5, 1865, at age 23.

Eight

AMAGANSETT TO SPRINGS, FIREPLACE, AND MONTAUK

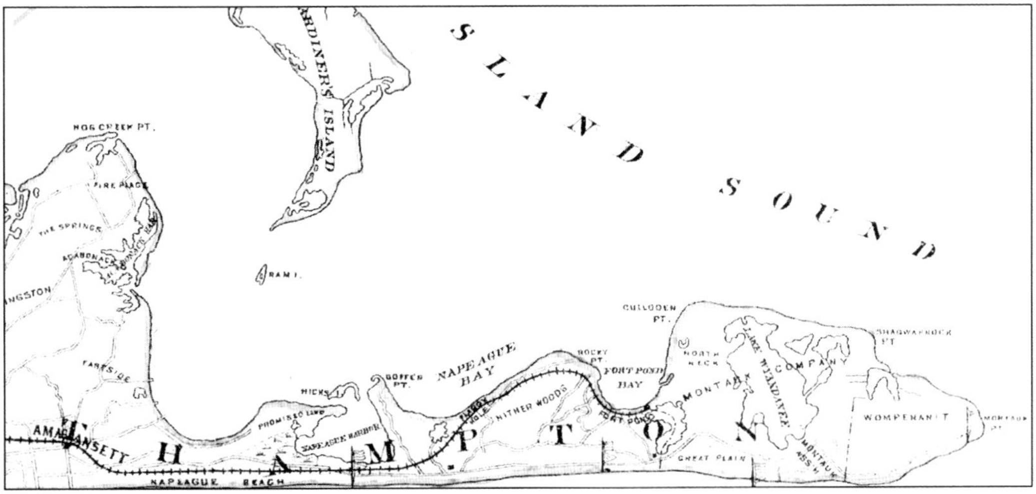

Montauk is the easternmost point on Long Island, with Montauk Light providing the exclamation point. Although the first visit to Montauk was Adrian Block in 1664, the Dutch made no attempt to establish a colony there. The English, on the other hand, wasted no time in staking their claim to this pristine land. They were aided by the fact that the Montauketts were on friendly terms with the English colonists. This relationship between the Native Americans and the English was solidified when Wyandanch, sachem of the Montauketts, and Lion Gardiner went through the right of blood brotherhood. In a deed of February 11, 1661, this goodwill was noted and the grant was made "in consideration of that love which we have and doe bear unto these our trusty and beloved friends of East Hampton." (Courtesy Stony Brook University, Special Map Collection.)

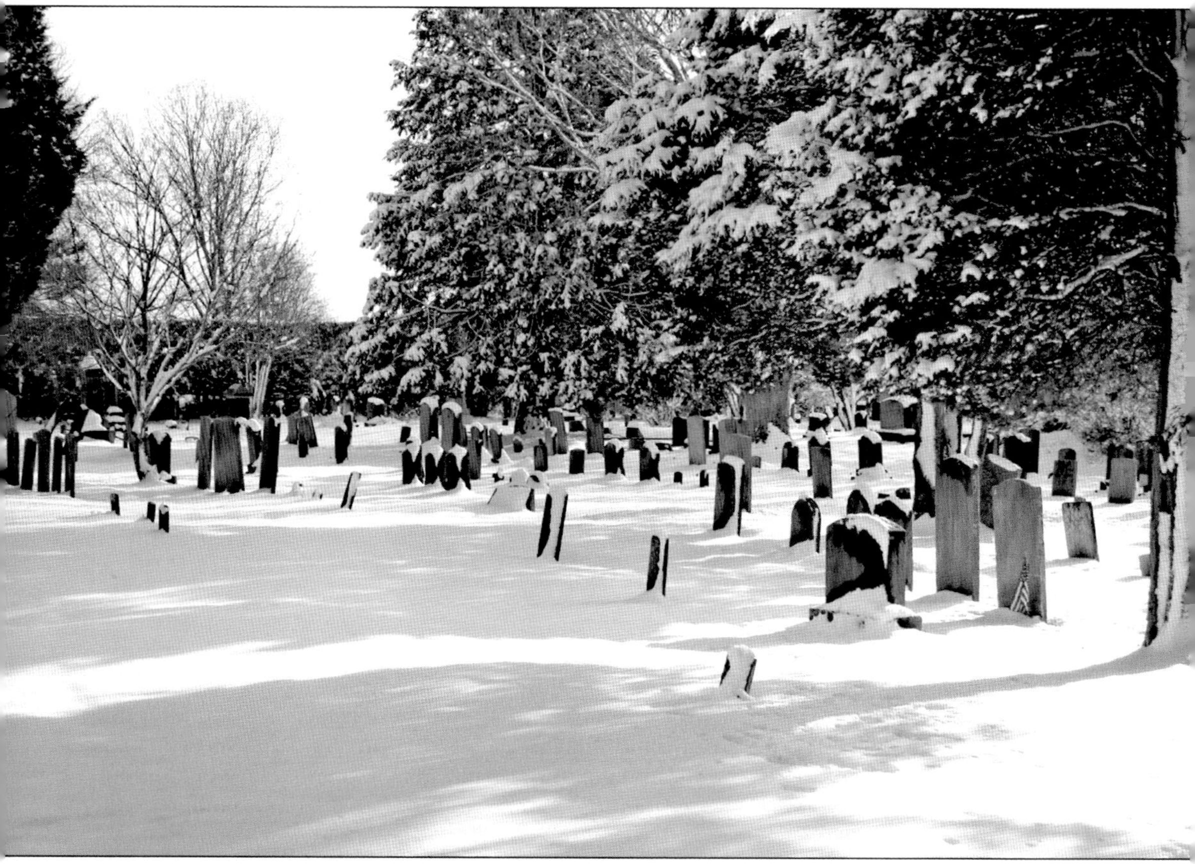

Springs lies on the shores of Gardiner's Bay. It was settled in 1649 around Accabonac Harbor. The railroad made the area accessible as a summer resort in the 1890s. Springs was first populated by craftsmen tending to the needs of the rich and famous. Later, artists were attracted to the bucolic surroundings and it became an artists' community. Amagansett is probably best known for the German spies who landed on the beach during World War II. On June 13, 1942, four men from a U-boat landed on the beach, intent on blowing up U.S. power and industrial sites. They were discovered by a Coast Guardsman who disbelieved their story that they were fishermen. The four men did get to New York City, but one of the men decided to alert the FBI. He also fingered another four-man team intent on sabotage. All eight men were quickly apprehended. All were convicted of spying, and six were electrocuted. The other two were imprisoned until the end of hostilities. Amagansett was founded by Jeremiah Conklin, who built his house here in 1695.

The first deed referring to Amagansett is dated 1683. By means of that document, the Reverend Thomas James sold to Abraham Schlellinger "52 acres of woods . . . by a highway commonly called Amagansett Way." The name Schlellinger is found on many of the tombstones in the ancient burial ground. The earliest families who settled in Amagansett were the Bakers, the Conklings, and the Mulfords. Alice Baker, who died on February 4, 1708/9, at age 88, was the wife of Thomas Baker, the first to settle the village.

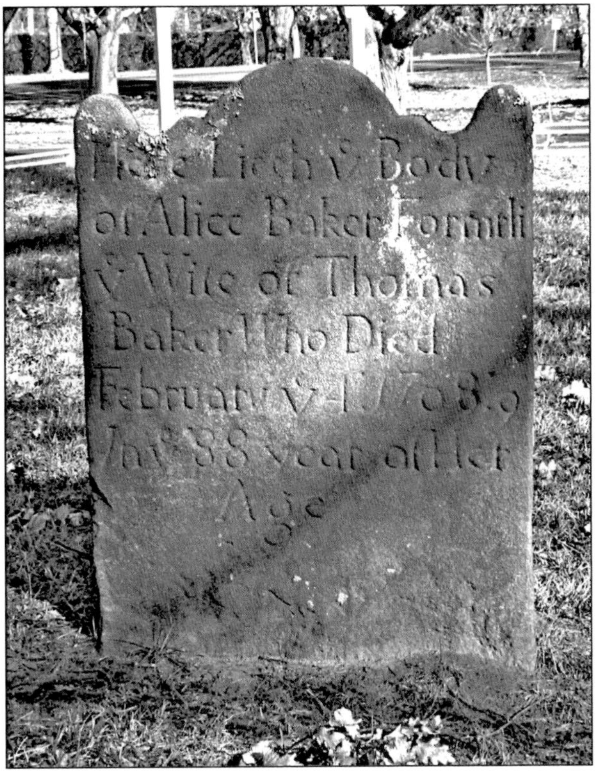

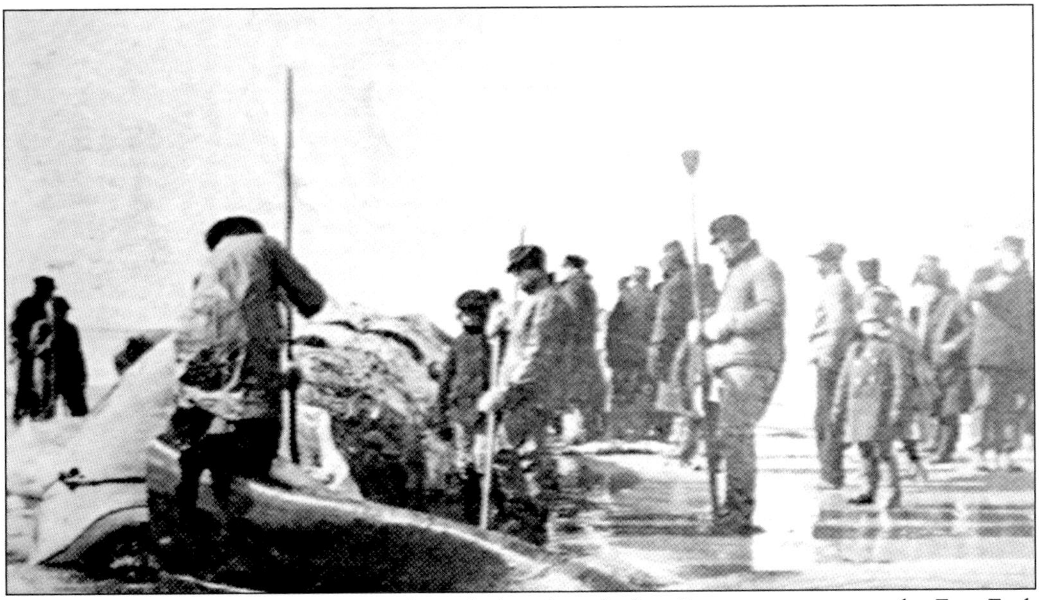

The local Native Americans engaged in whaling long before Europeans came to the East End. They simply waited for the whales to come to them. When the colonists arrived, they joined in and reached an agreement with the Native Americans for dividing up the bounty. The Native Americans were most interested in the fins and tail. The colonists took the rest. Shore whaling dropped off due to overfishing, but an occasional whale still washes up on the beach. (Courtesy Suffolk County Historical Society.)

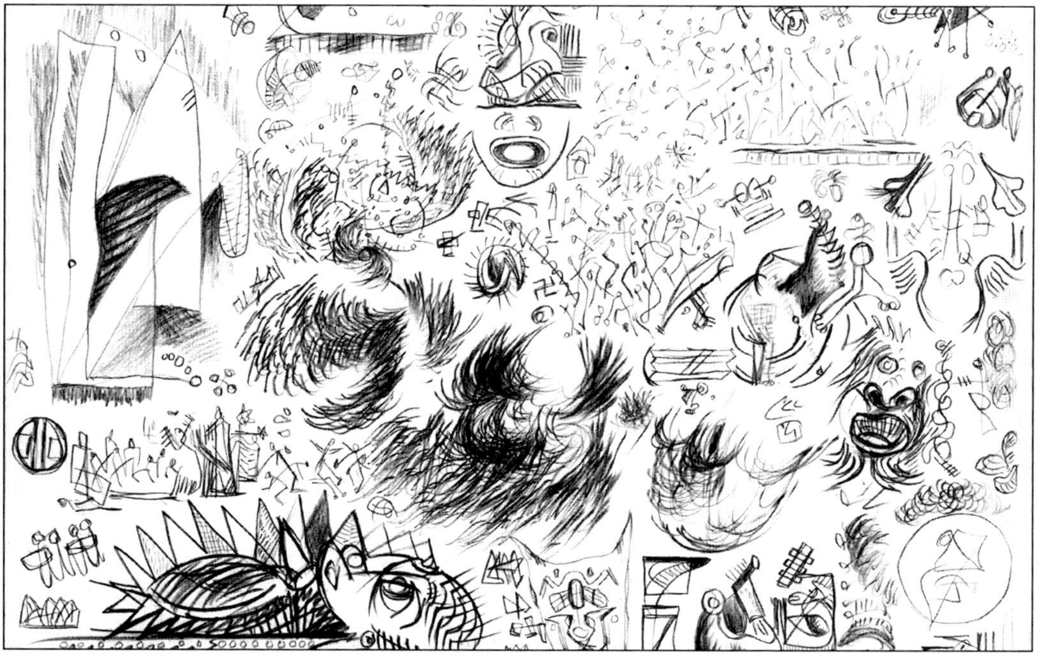

Paul Jackson Pollock (1912–1956) is credited with developing the abstract style of expressionism attributed to American painters. He studied under Thomas Benton at the Art Students League and traveled widely throughout the United States. He worked with house paint and large brushes, and his canvases were big enough to cover a wall. (Digital image copyright the Museum of Modern Art, licensed by SCALA/Art Resource, NY.)

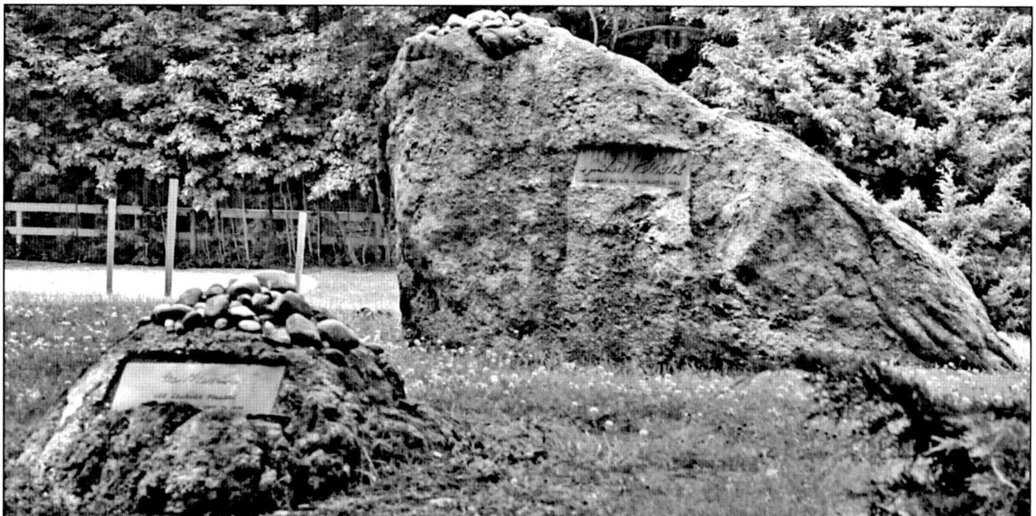

On August 11 or 12, 1956, a green Oldsmobile convertible, traveling at high speed, failed to negotiate a bend on Fireplace Road and overturned. The driver was hurled into a tree headfirst, and a woman passenger was also killed. Thus ended the life of artist Jackson Pollock, one of ten traffic fatalities that weekend in the Hamptons. Pollock's grave in the Green River Cemetery is the final resting place for many of East Hampton's notables, a large number of whom purchase plots well in advance of any impending need. To be buried in Green River is to demonstrate you have arrived (for a while), before you have left (for good).

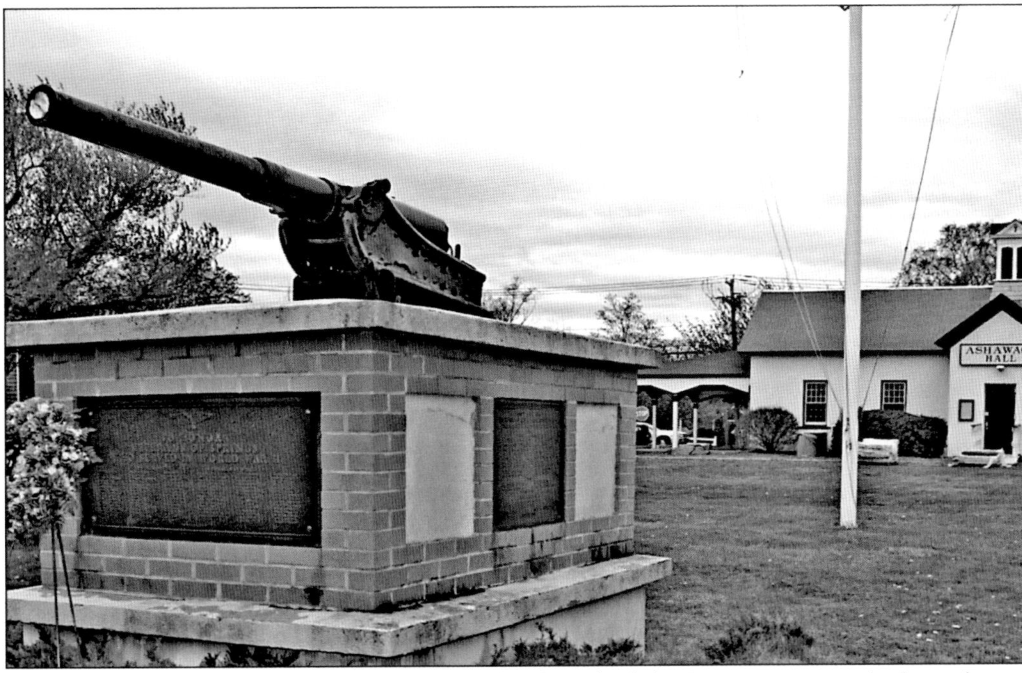

On his visit in 1873, historian Richard M. Bayles described the Springs as a neat little settlement of 60 houses. A recent Long Island Power Authority survey estimates the population at 5,356. The most prominent feature is Ashawagh Hall. Built in 1847, the "Little Red Schoolhouse" was sold in 1909. The price was $1, subject to the condition that it be used strictly as a public hall. The building stands at the head of a small commons, which also features a veterans memorial. A small cemetery lies across the road.

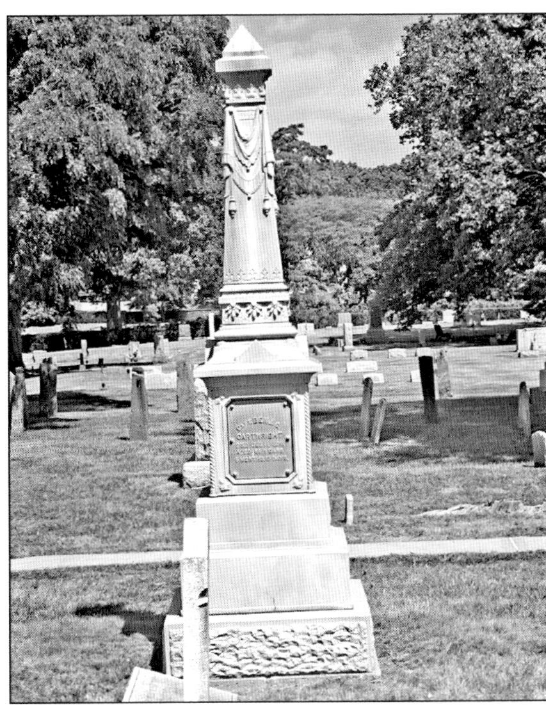

Ezra L'Hommedieu convinced local farmers of the efficacy of bunkers as fertilizer. As early as 1850, the fish oil business had sprung up to cash in on the growing demand for the product. Capt. Benjamin Cartwright owned a factory on Shelter Island for manufacturing meal and oil. It was a smelly business. In 1862, the factories were evicted by the Health Department and moved to Promised Land. With time, the menhaden schools—the source of the product—were virtually depleted and the industry disappeared along with them.

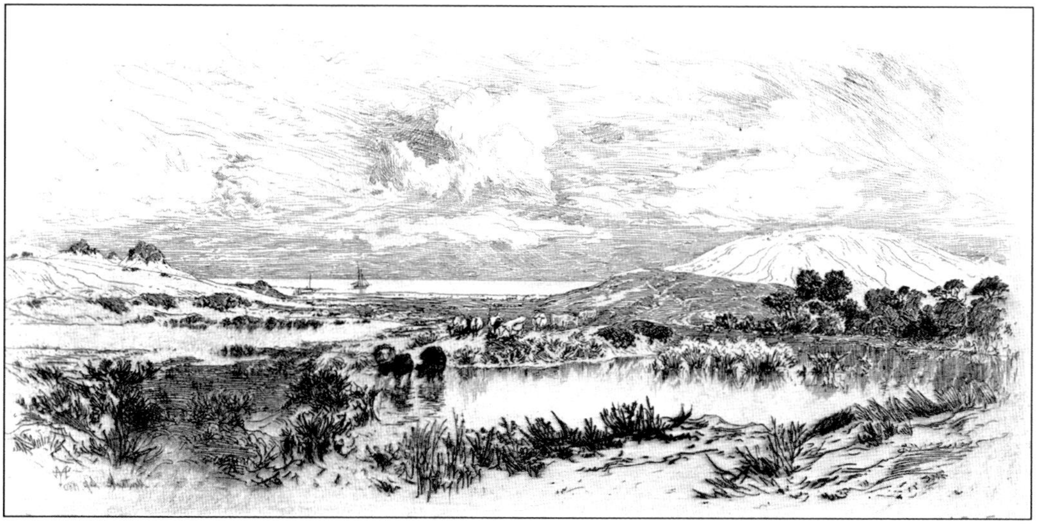

Thomas Moran captured the beauty of the region in 1850. When the settlers came to the East End, the American Indians greeted them without hostility. Indeed, their warm reception was largely the result the friendship between Lion Gardiner and the sachem Wyandanch. Gardiner went so far as to offer himself as a hostage to obtain the release of Wyandanch's daughter when she was abducted by the Pequots. (Smithsonian American Art Museum, Washington, DC / Art Resource, NY.)

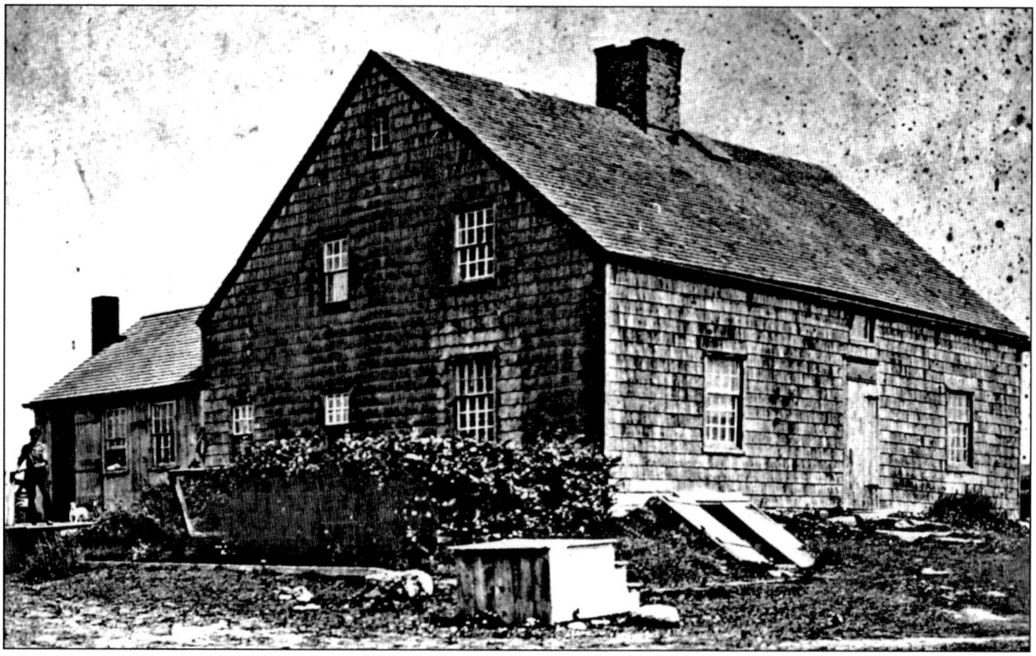

There were three houses built in the early days of Montauk. The first house was built in 1744. The other two followed, and together with the home of the lighthouse keeper, they were the only buildings to be found in Montauk in the 1700s. They were homes for the keepers of the cattle, sheep, and horses that grazed here each year. Indeed, the cattle drive was a major event for the settlers each fall, turning Montauk's 15,000 acres into a giant pasture. Cattle raising was an important part of the East End economy. (Courtesy Montauk Library.)

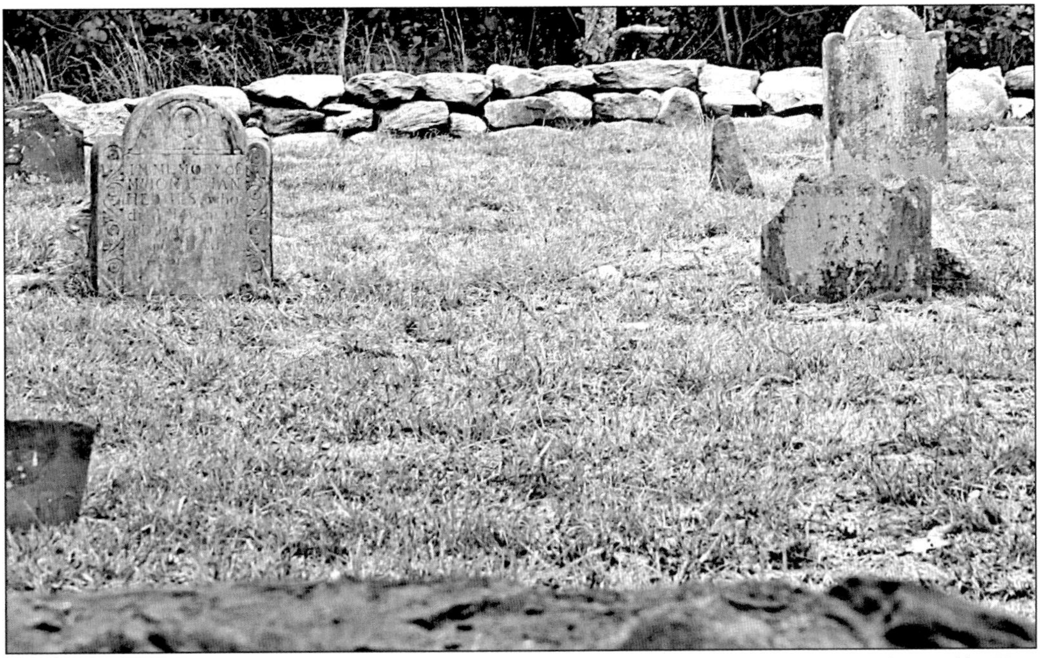

An old graveyard stands next to the site where the First House was located in Hither Hills. Two of the oldest stones are memorials to Jonathan Hedges (left), who died on January 16, 1763, at age 57, and to Mary Hedges, who died on August 3, 1787, at age 45. A small sign on Old Montauk Highway marks the road that leads to the burial ground.

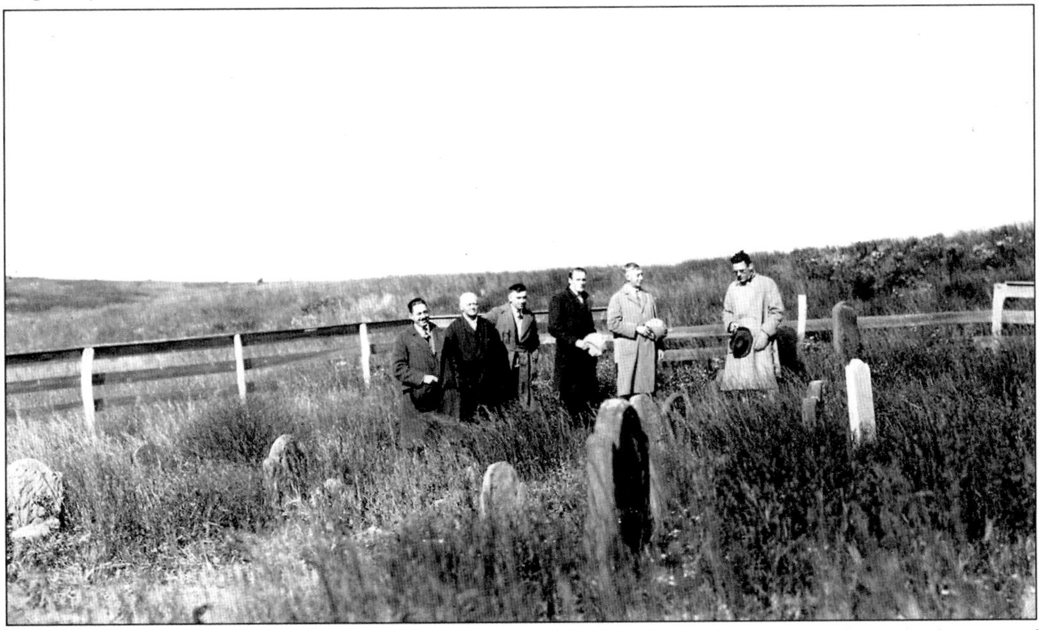

Carl Graham Fisher visited the East End in 1925. Fisher came to Montauk with dreams of Miami Beach North dancing in his head. Already given the moniker Mr. Miami Beach, he fully intended to add the title Mr. Montauk to his impressive list of credentials. Fisher was a self-made millionaire, who had built the Indianapolis Speedway and had created a sun lovers' paradise in Florida. (Courtesy Montauk Library.)

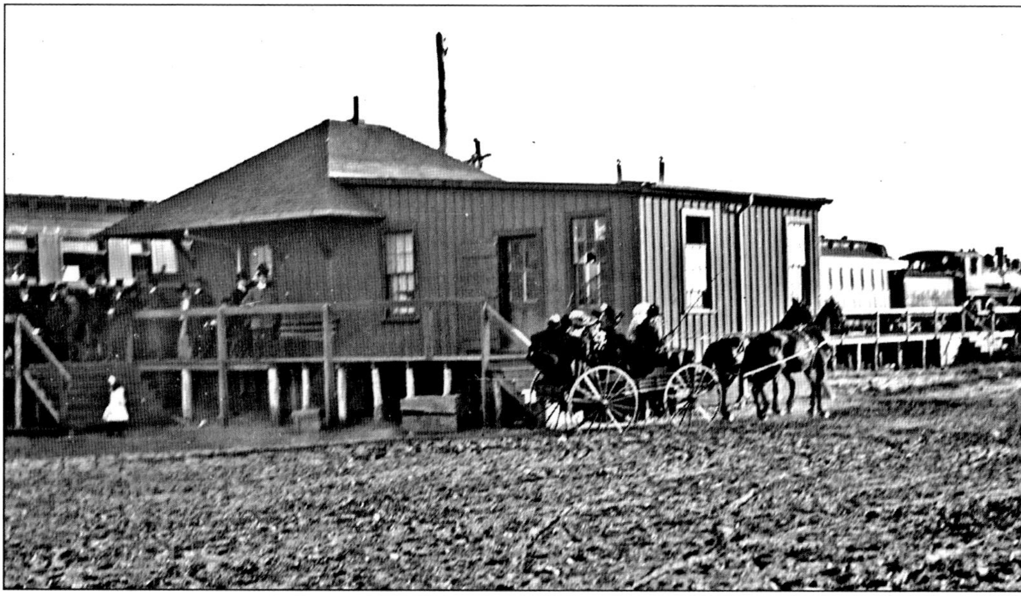

Once the railroad had been extended to Montauk in 1895, the last piece was in place to turn Carl Fisher's dream into reality. His plans included Montauk Manor (a 200-room hotel), a beach club, a half-mile-long boardwalk, and a racetrack. In just a few years, luxury hotels, golf courses, and swimming facilities had risen from the sand to create a playground for the rich and famous. Then, as he looked down on the freshwater pond called Lake Montauk, he saw a deepwater port. (Courtesy Suffolk County Historical Society.)

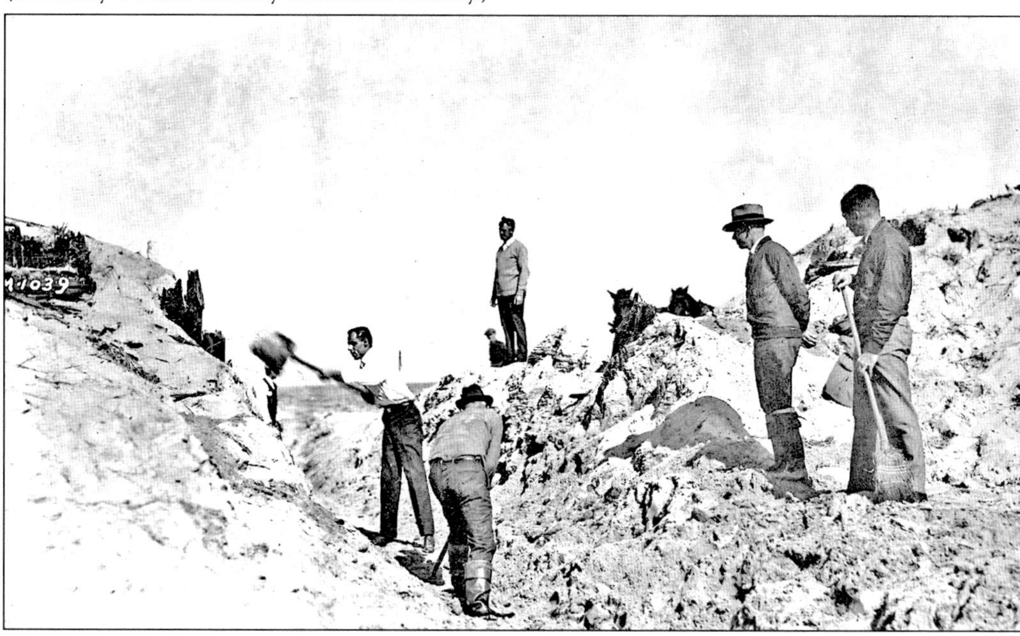

Carl Fisher saw a port that would rival New York City's. And so, the digging began. The one thing Fisher did not envision was the crash of 1929. His fortune, along with the vast wealth of so may other millionaires, evaporated almost overnight. Montauk Manor closed in 1932. Fisher returned to Miami Beach, where he soon died of cirrhosis of the liver. He was 63 years old. (Courtesy Montauk Library.)

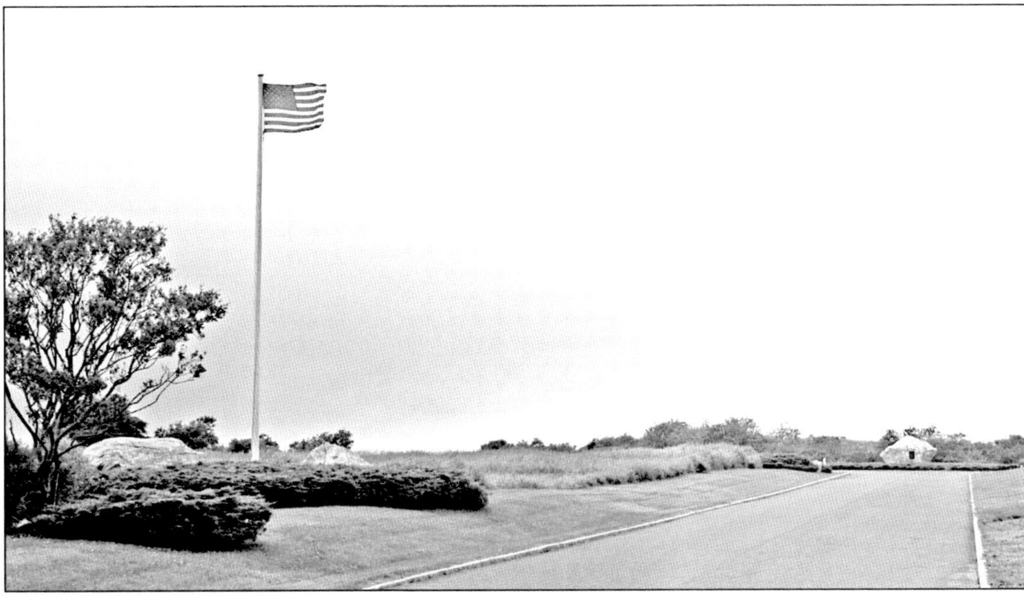

The American Indian name Montauk means fort country, and a fort was established here long before the settlers came to the South Fork. The Narragansetts, not the colonists, were the mortal enemy of the Montauks—a fact emphasized by Massacre Valley, next to Fort Hill Cemetery. In a surprise attack staged in 1653, the Narragansetts killed 30 Montauk braves and kidnapped Chief Wyandanch's daughter in the middle of her wedding. Lion Gardiner intervened on Wyandanch's part and rescued the daughter.

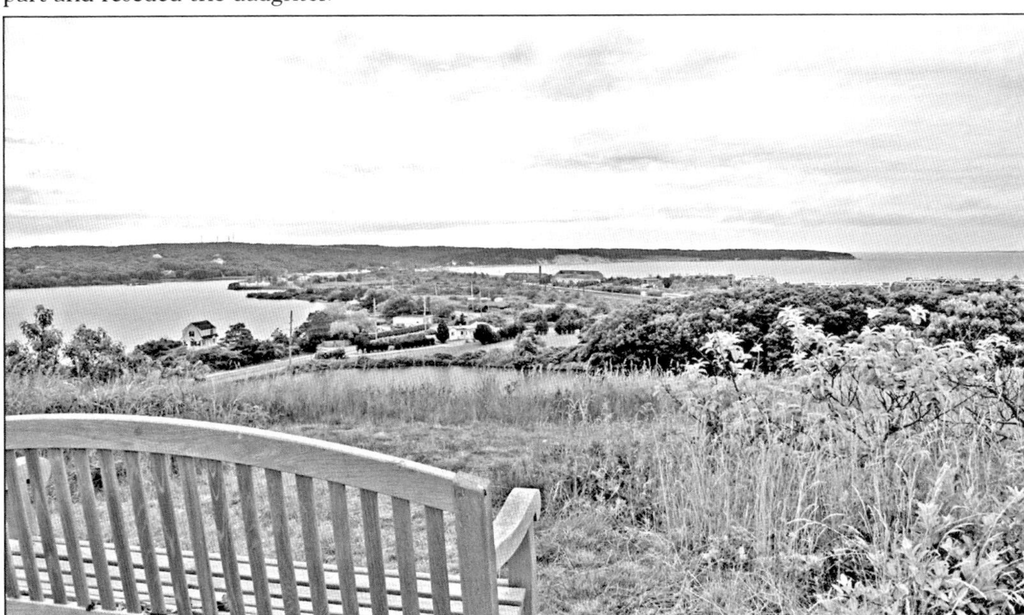

In 1985, the East Hampton Town Board purchased land on Fort Hill, 30 acres of which was set aside for a much-needed cemetery. Incorporated into the overall plan was a provision to preserve the battleground where the massacred braves fell. Up to 6,751 graves were to be accommodated, along with an area set aside for those choosing cremation. The design was along the lines of the memorial cemeteries that had been given their initial impetus in California.

There are few, if any, Montauketts left today. Already weakened through a protracted war with the Narragansetts, their number was more than halved by an epidemic in 1658. Others, who had converted to Christianity, followed their leader Occum to a new settlement in Upstate New York. After the death of Wyandanch, their numbers dwindled further. Stephen Talkhouse Pharoah (1819–1879) was a well-known full-blooded Montaukett. Often called King of the Montauks, he was said to be a lineal descendant of the sachem Wyandanch. (Courtesy Suffolk County Historical Society.)

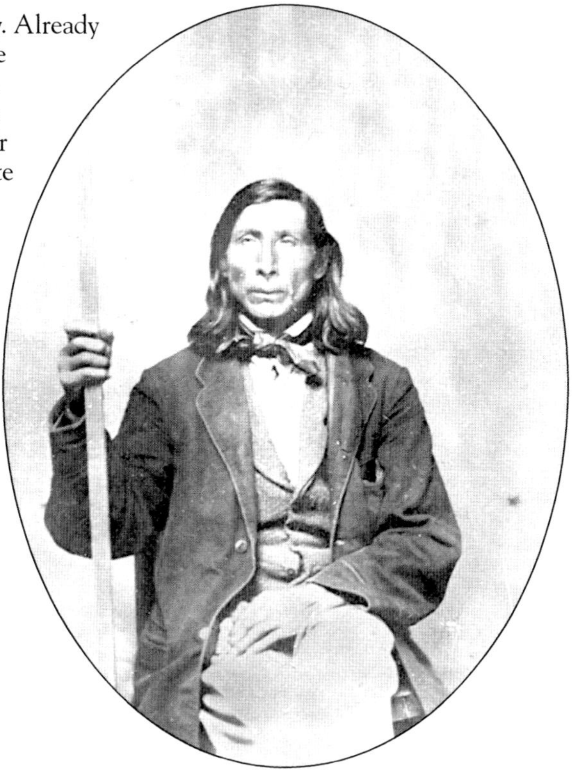

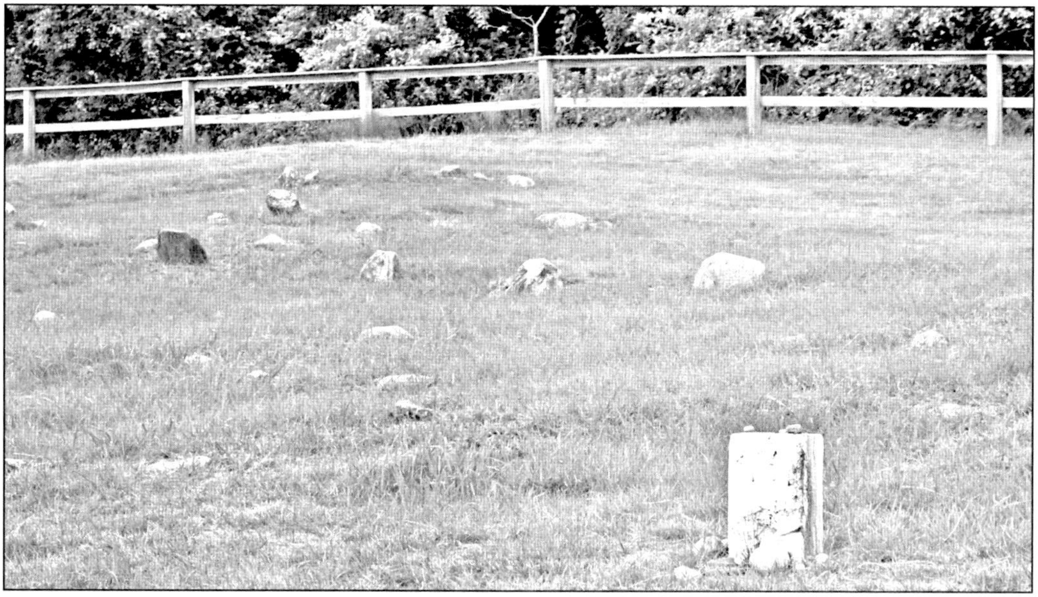

Pharoah was born in his mother's wigwam on Molly's Hill in Springs. A Civil War veteran, he is said to have walked the 30 miles from Montauk to East Hampton to work and returned the same day. On another occasion, he walked to Brooklyn in record time. His is the only marked grave in this Native American burial ground on East Lake Drive. According to an ancient custom, American Indians were buried in a sitting position, and samp and wampum were placed in the grave.

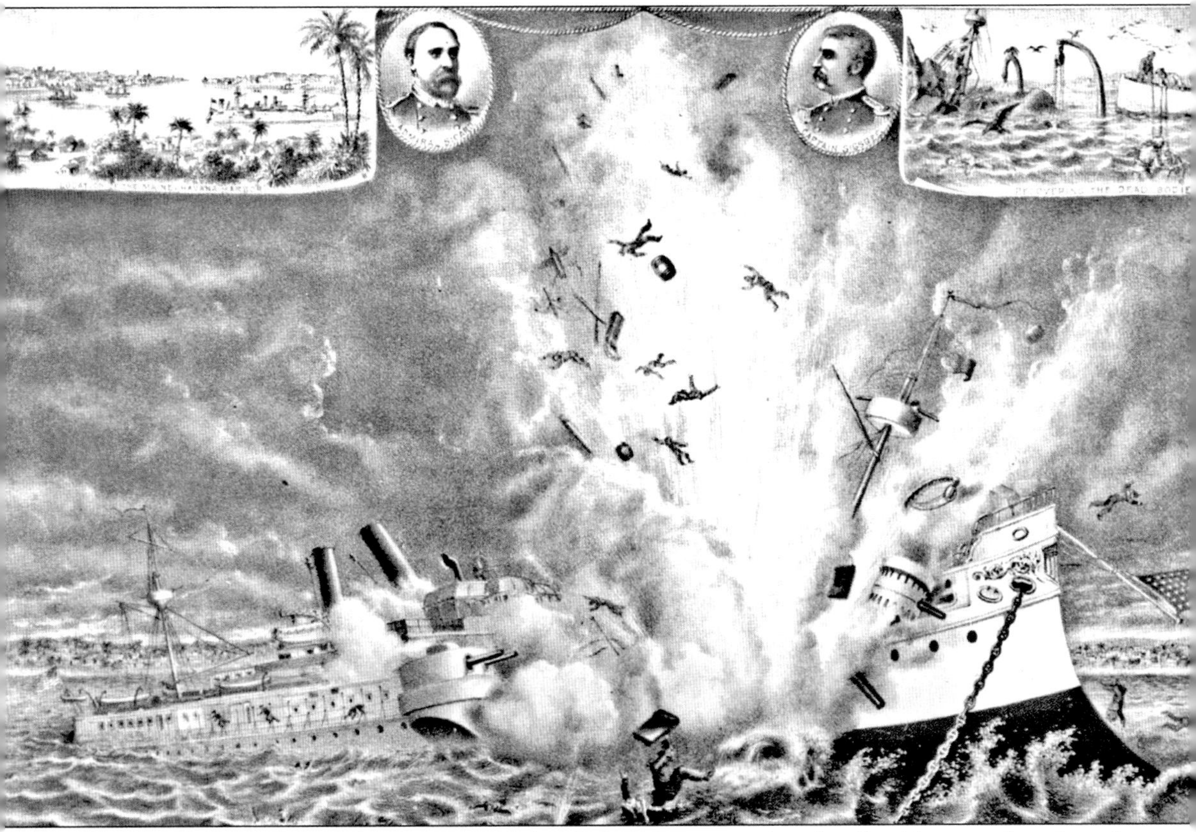

The USS *Maine* (ACR-1) was a 682-ton battleship. It operated in the Caribbean and anchored in Havana Harbor, Cuba, to protect American interests during a local insurrection. On the night of February 15, 1898, there was an explosion in the aft part of the ship. The vessel was quickly sent to the bottom, taking with it most of the crew. A total of 266 sailors out of a total of 374 lost their lives in the explosion. An investigation showed that more than five tons of power charges for the six-inch and ten-inch guns had ignited. Although not the cause, the sinking was certainly a tipping point in the charge to war that had been building up in the nation. "Remember the *Maine*" echoed throughout the land and was splashed across the front pages of the country's newspapers. Eventually, the wreck of the *Maine* was raised, towed out to sea, and resunk in the Gulf of Mexico. The cause was reexamined, and it was concluded that more likely than sabotage, a fire in the coal bunker had triggered the disaster. This was, however, long after the war was over. (Courtesy Picture History.)

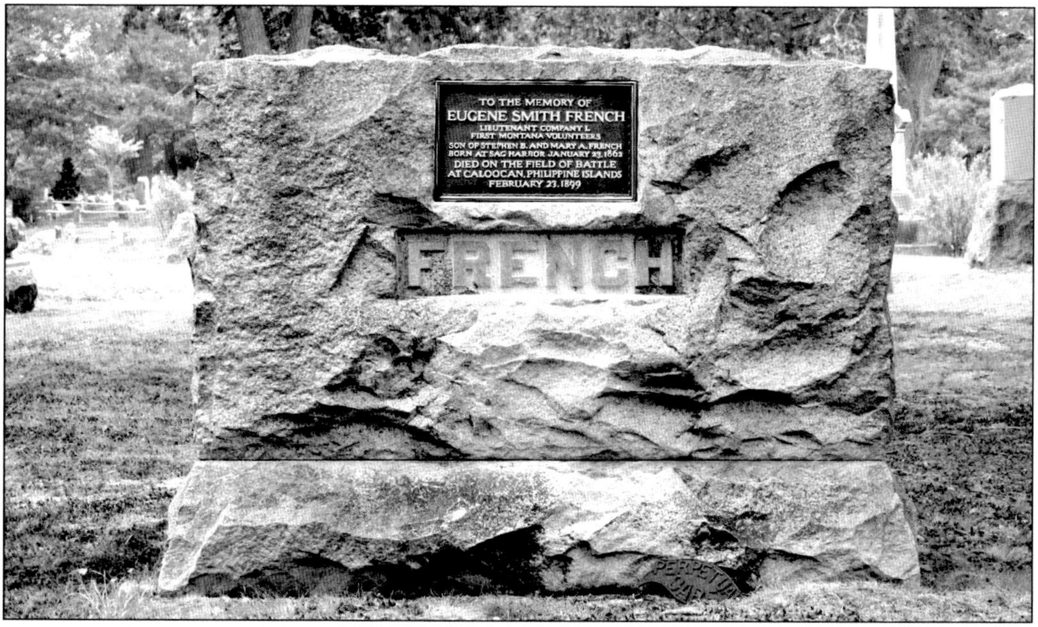

The Spanish-American War was short (April to August 1898) and relatively bloodless. In fact, the body count by the conclusion of hostilities was United States 2,664, Spain 5,500. The payoff was deemed worth it: the United States gained the Philippines, Guam, and Puerto Rico; the financial cost was a mere $20 million. Eugene Smith French died on February 23, 1899, in Caloocan, a city annexed by the United States during the war. He was 32 years old.

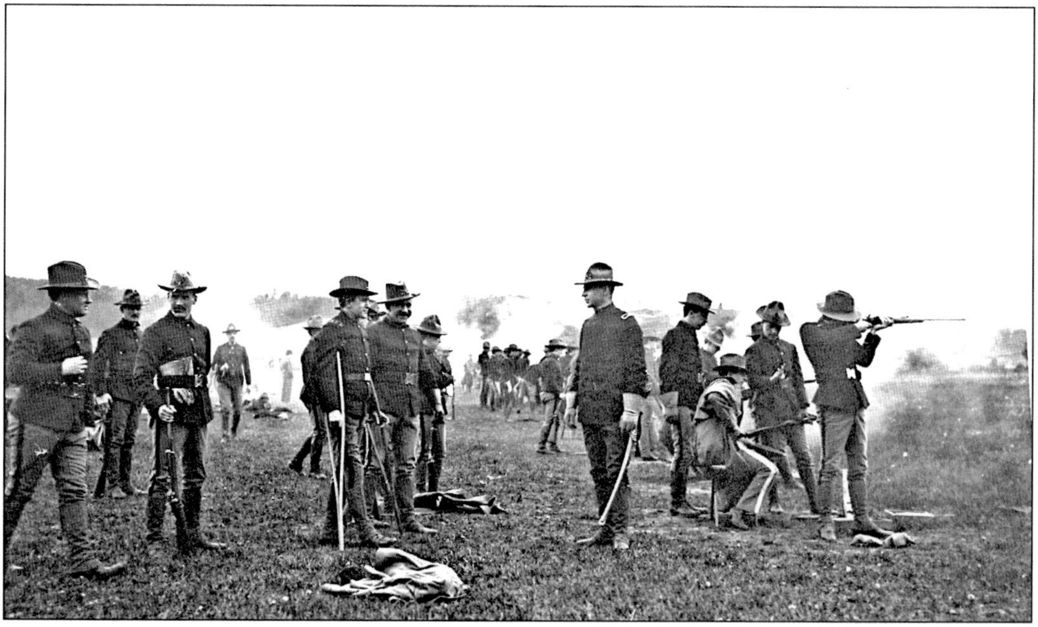

The real tragedy for the troops started after the war was over. It dawned on the government that the troops could not simply be discharged home. Diseases such as malaria and yellow fever would rapidly cause more casualties among the public than the military had taken in the war. Having soldiers die is an accepted consequence of war; civilians dying from an imported disease is a political disaster. (Courtesy Suffolk County Historical Society.)

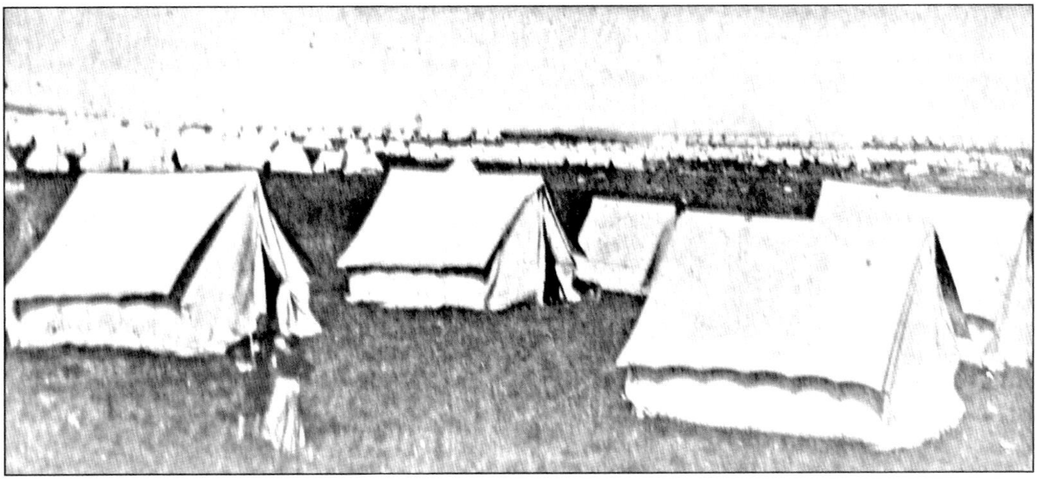

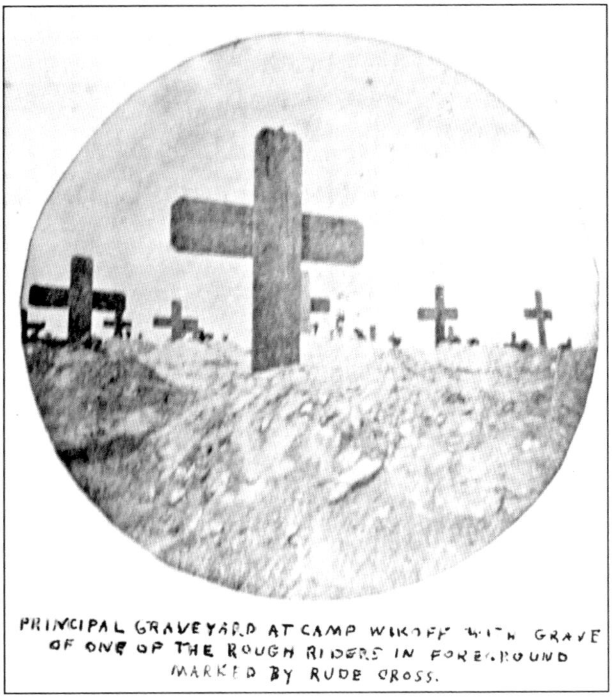

And so the government hastily established Camp Wykoff at Montauk, safely out of any highly populated area, where army troops could be quarantined until it was safe to send them home. However, there was simply not enough time to adequately set up an acceptable facility for 45,000 troops. And when word got out, the same journalism that had driven the country to war now skewered the army for its treatment of Johnny when he came home. Poor hygienic facilities, inadequate housing, and insufficient rations were a perfect storm to create intolerable living conditions. The constant drumbeat of the press led to redoubled efforts to improve conditions at the camp. But not before 126 soldiers had died by the time it closed later that same year. (Both, courtesy Suffolk County Historical Society.)

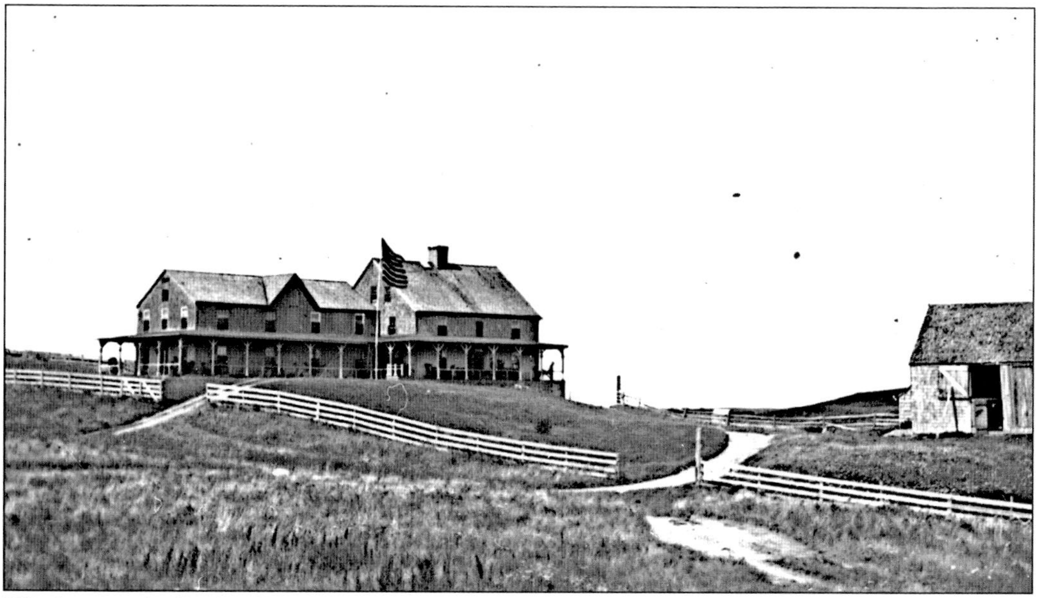

While at Wykoff, Third House was home to probably the biggest winner in the war: Theodore Roosevelt. Roosevelt led his Rough Riders up Kettle Hill during the battle at San Juan Hill. By nightfall, the American forces had taken Santiago but not without cost. The U.S. forces had suffered 1,600 casualties. Coming so soon after the Civil War, the conflict served as an opportunity for a rebonding of the North and South, and African American and white troops fought side by side in this battle. (Courtesy Suffolk County Historical Society.)

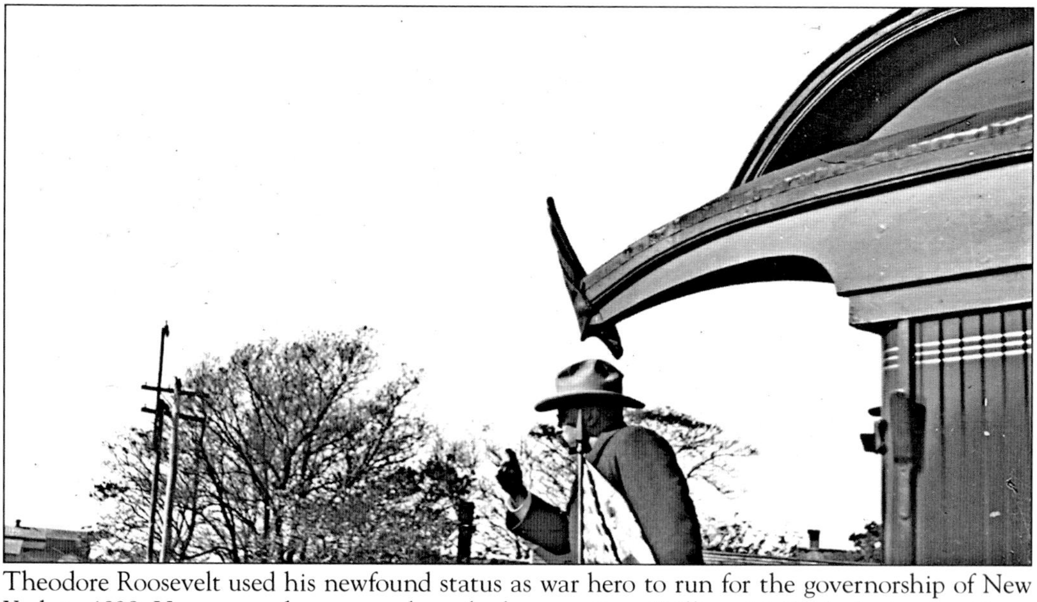

Theodore Roosevelt used his newfound status as war hero to run for the governorship of New York in 1898. He won, and two years later, he became Pres. William McKinley's vice president. When McKinley was assassinated in 1901, Roosevelt, aged 42, became president. He won the presidency outright in 1904, but refused to run for a second term. He was known for his support of labor and conservation and was the prime mover in the construction of the Panama Canal, thus, giving birth to the largest known palindrome: a man, a plan, a canal, Panama. (Courtesy Suffolk County Historical Society.)

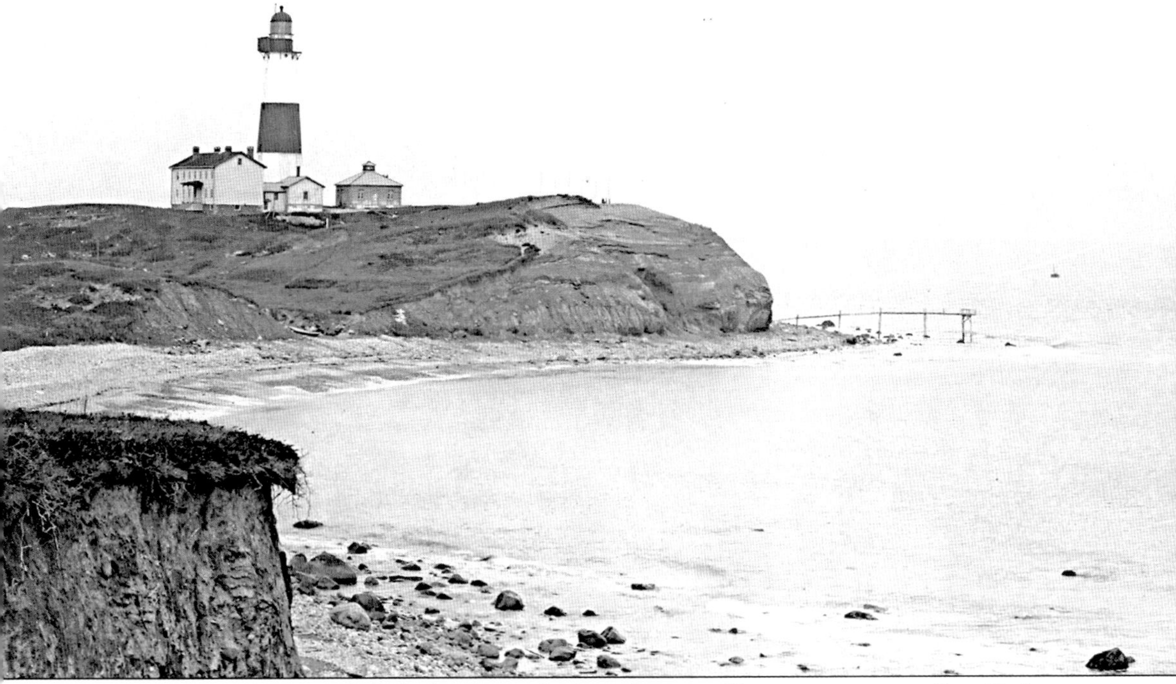

Since 1796, the Montauk light has been the last glimpse of home to many an East End mariner as his ship was outward bound. To many, it was to be forever the last glimpse of home. "I have listened upon the sands, as the surf was dashing and sparkling at our feet, to harrowing tales of bright hopes broken by this irrepressible thirst to tempt the deep. I heard a warm-hearted sister disclose, in faltering accents, the sad story of her younger brother, who would not be dissuaded from the peril . . . Recollect, a mariner's life is one of hardship, toil, and danger. Think of the anxious hearts you will leave among your friends. Even I shall think of my poor little cousin, rocked by Boreas in his hammock, dreaming of his native village, and mayhap to find his grave in its bosom. The poor lad, as his ship was sweeping before a gale, ran aloft to furl a sail. As the mast broke, he was heard to exclaim, 'God save me!' And he was seen no more." —*East Hampton Trustees Journal.* (Courtesy Montauk Library.)

BIBLIOGRAPHY

Adams, James Truslow. *History of the Township of Southampton*. Bridgehampton, New York: Hampton Press, 1916.

———. *Memorials of Old Bridgehampton*. Bridgehampton, New York: Privately printed, 1916.

Appel, Aneta, et al. *East Quogue Remembered*. Quogue, New York: East Quogue Civic Association, 1990.

Bayles, Richard M. *Historical and Descriptive Sketches of Suffolk County*. Port Jefferson, New York: Empire State Historical Society Publication XVII, Ira J. Friedman, 1873.

Calloway, Diana Stokes, ed., et al. *Quogue As We Remember It*. Quogue, New York: Quogue Historical Society, 1976.

Davis, Kenneth E. *East Hampton Trustees Journal*. East Hampton, New York: East Hampton Committee, 1925.

Epstein, Jason, and Elizabeth Barlow. *East Hampton: A History and Guide*. East Hampton, New York: Medway Press, 1976.

Gardiner, Jonathan T., et al. *Records of the Town of East Hampton*. Sag Harbor, New York: John H. Hunt, 1887.

Hazleton, Henry Isham. *The Boroughs of Brooklyn and Queens Counties of Nassau and Suffolk Long Island, New York, 1609–1924*. New York: Lewis Historical Publishing Company, 1925.

Hedges, Henry P., et al. *Book of Records of the Town of Southampton*. Sag Harbor, New York: John H. Hunt, 1874.

Huntington, Cornelia. *Odes and Poems and Fragmentary Verses*. A. Huntington, 1891.

Mather, Fredrick G. *The Refugees of 1776 from Long Island to Connecticut*. Albany: J. B. Lyon Company, 1913.

Muller, Barbara M. *Historic Profile of Hampton Bays Phase 1, Good Ground Montauk Highway Corridor and Canoe Place*. New York: Squires Press, 2005.

Onderdonk, Henry Jr. *Revolutionary Incidents of Suffolk and Kings Counties New York*. Leavitt & Company, 1849.

Seabury, Samuel. *Two Hundred and Seventy five Years of East Hampton, Long Island, New York, A Historical Sketch*. Privately printed, 1926.

Sleight, Harry D. *Sag Harbor in Earlier Days*. Sag Harbor, New York: 1930.

Tooker, William Wallace. *The Indian Place Names on Long Island and Islands Adjacent*. New York and London: G. P. Putnam's Sons, the Knickerbocker Press, 1911.

Weisberg, Henry, and Lisa Donneson. *Guide to Sag Harbor*. Sag Harbor, New York: John Street Press, 1975.

Welch, Richard. *Memento Mori: The Gravestones of Early Long Island, 1680-1810*. Syosset, New York: Friends for Long Island Heritage, 1983.

Wilcox, LeRoy. *1775–1975 History of Eastport Long Island, New York*.

Zaykowski, Dorothy Ingerso. *Sag—The Story of an American Beauty*. Sag Harbor, New York: Sag Harbor Historical Society.